AVID
READER
PRESS

TRADE IS NOT A FOUR-LETTER WORD

HOW SIX EVERYDAY PRODUCTS MAKE THE CASE FOR TRADE

     GOT

FRED P. HOCHBERG

Avid Reader Press

New York London Toronto Sydney New Delhi

Avid Reader Press
An Imprint of Simon & Schuster, Inc.
1230 Avenue of the Americas
New York, NY 10020

First Avid Reader Press hardcover edition January 2020

AVID READER PRESS and colophon are trademarks of Simon & Schuster, Inc.

For information about special discounts for bulk purchases, please contact Simon & Schuster Special Sales at 1-866-506-1949 or business@simonandschuster.com.

The Simon & Schuster Speakers Bureau can bring authors to your live event. For more information or to book an event, contact the Simon & Schuster Speakers Bureau at 1-866-248-3049 or visit our website at www.simonspeakers.com.

Manufactured in the United States of America

3 5 7 9 10 8 6 4 2

Library of Congress Cataloging-in-Publication Data is available.

ISBN 978-1-9821-2736-7
ISBN 978-1-9821-2738-1 (ebook)

In memory of my mother and father,
who instilled the curiosity and optimism
to keep looking further beyond.

And to Tom,
with whom I've exchanged
more than a few four-letter words—
mostly loving ones!

Contents

Introduction

My mother was ten years old when the specter of Adolf Hitler forced my grandparents to venture out beyond Europe to build a new life in America. After scouting out Palestine and Havana, my grandparents ultimately settled on New York. Though their visas were poised to expire during the long passage west, the American consular office in Amsterdam advised them to "just get on the next boat—I'm sure they'll let you get off." And so they did, coming safely through Ellis Island in 1937.

My grandfather had owned a small manufacturing and retail company in Leipzig, Germany, so after settling in America he decided to open a leather goods business making pocketbooks, wallets, and other accessories on Broadway and 31st Street in New York City. My mother, Lillian, scouted out product ideas and helped my grandfather by designing items that appealed to young women like herself. After marrying my father in 1949, she decided that she wanted to earn an extra $50 per week to make life a little better. She considered herself a "closet worker," since it wasn't appropriate among many of her friends to go to work—back then, it signaled that your husband wasn't a good enough provider. With a reliable leather goods supplier in the family, she decided to start designing and selling handbags and belts of her own, personalized with customers' initials. She wasn't thinking

September 1951, back when the company that would become known as Lillian Vernon went by the name of Vernon Specialties.

about global trade when, at twenty-four, she placed her first ad in *Seventeen* magazine—she was just thinking about how to build a better life and livelihood for herself and her family.

It didn't take long for my mother to realize that she had tapped into something that had been missing from American life. There had been strict quotas and restrictions on leather goods during the war, and the market was hungry for the products she wanted to sell. Women were entering the workforce in record numbers, and had less time to shop in stores—ordering innovative products from around the world right from the comfort of their own homes proved pretty appealing. The retail and catalog business she started at our kitchen table would go on to become the first company founded by a woman to be publicly traded on the American Stock Exchange; today, that kitchen table, with many of my early scratch marks, can now be found in the collection of the Smithsonian in Washington, D.C., along with her portrait.

After finishing college and business school, I joined that company, Lillian Vernon, and my mother and I worked side by side for almost twenty years. Her vision and nose for products had laid an extraordinary foundation—one that I had the opportunity to then channel into a modern, efficient company that served millions of customers every year. The experience gave me the chance not only to rapidly grow a business virtually from scratch, but to travel the world and better understand Americans' desire to connect with it. As the company grew, we were always on the lookout for products that offered something different from what you would find at your local department store—and that led us to cross oceans in search of unique, innovative, affordable merchandise that hadn't yet made it to our shores. In the process, we developed a real understanding of the desires of American consumers.

My mother didn't think that we were running a global business, but, looking back on it, that's exactly what we were doing. When Richard Nixon took his famous trip to China in 1972, the Lillian Vernon Corporation was hot on his tracks. We sourced our products from around the world, and I traveled a number of times over the years to the Canton Fair to scope out the latest Chinese products that weren't yet available to U.S. consumers. I recall vividly my first trip in 1981, flying in from Hong Kong to the metropolis now known as Guangzhou was a memorable experience: the city was larger even then than Los Angeles is today, yet it was pitch black on arrival—there was very little electricity to go around. Our boarding passes were on paper as thin as tissue. The closer you got to the back of the plane, the more you noticed the rows start to inch closer and closer together; they hadn't been properly measured

Catalog request advertisement that appeared in the early 1980s and showcases Lillian's knack for finding innovative products in every corner of the world.

out. The runway would abruptly light up just before we touched down, and no sooner would we land than it would go dark again.

Once on the ground, however, we found creative people and innovative products—everything from covered celadon soup bowls that I still use today to pendants made from broken Ming vases (we referred to them as *rescued* Ming vase pendants). We met Michael Tam, an entrepreneur from Hong Kong who operated our quality assurance workshop to ensure our products met our standards of quality and were properly marked with "Made in China." We worked with our partners in China to grow our business and theirs, teaming up to produce designs that catered to our customers' tastes and importing and exporting to get the most out of our global connection. China would open itself up to the world in the years that followed, and it is the most incredible experience to go back today—just a few decades after my earliest visits—and see just how dramatically the country has changed. In my first visit, the streets were filled with bicycles, then scooters, and ultimately clogged with cars. It's a reminder of everything that stands to be gained when we connect ourselves with the rest of the globe—and of what stands to be lost, as well. It's a reminder of what the seemingly simple universe of imports and exports can really mean in the lives of people and the life of a country. And, most of all, it reminds me of a story I came across years ago, when I was serving as the chairman and president of the Export-Import Bank of the United States. It's a story I used to tell small business entrepreneurs who were thinking about expanding their reach beyond America's borders—and it's one that I'd like to share with you.

In ancient times, dating back to the earliest myths of Hercules, legend held that on each side of the Strait of Gibraltar stood a monolithic pillar, inscribed with a warning for any sailor who might harbor dreams of venturing west: *Nec Plus Ultra.* Translated from Latin, the warning meant "Nothing Further Beyond"—for the passage marked the end of the known world.

For centuries, most Europeans believed that there was indeed nothing out there beyond the water's edge. It wasn't until Christopher Columbus reached the Americas that this sentiment began to change. Not long after word got back to Spain about the discovery of the New World, King Charles V decreed that the historic adage—*Nec Plus Ultra*—would be shortened to simply *Plus Ultra*: "further beyond." The phrase endured as the national motto of

Spain—and it can still be found on the Spanish flag today, etched onto a banner entwined between the Pillars of Hercules.

As it happens, a leading theory among historians is that those pillars (and the banner of *Plus Ultra* snaked around them) would go on to become one of the world's best-recognized and most meaningful symbols—a symbol that serves to remind us, even today, that opportunity and prosperity have never been confined within our own immediate borders. Perhaps you recognize it?

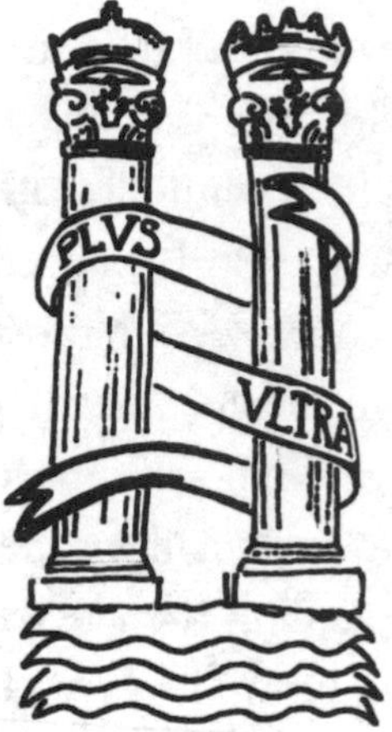

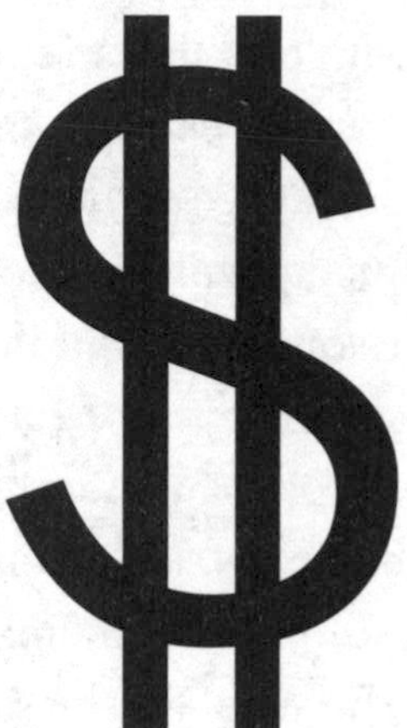

Pillars of Hercules.

The dollar sign carries endless connotations, but at its best it stands for opportunity. For countries, the symbol (and its international counterparts) means stability and security. It represents the opportunity to thrive, save, and innovate—to invest in education, culture, science, and the welfare of the people. For American families today, the dollar sign means groceries in the pantry and new tires on the car; peace of mind when you need medical care; tuition to further your daughter's education; a little savings for retirement; the breathing room you need to start a business, take a risk, or chase a dream. For better or worse, our fortunes are often wrapped around those pillars just as immovably as the *Plus Ultra* banner.

The good news is that while nearly everything about our lives has changed since the era of Columbus, including his reputation, the truth of the Spanish motto has not. The prosperity of our nation—and the opportunities available to every single person who comprises it—can still be magnified, broadened, and enriched so long as we are willing to venture out *Plus Ultra*: further beyond.

Before we go any "further beyond" this page, however, let me be clear that what follows is not a book about Hercules, Columbus, Spanish heraldry, or anything else of the sort. This book is about something much more exciting by far: trade. At its most basic definition, trade is the exchange of goods and services between people for mutual benefit—put another way, it's the opportunity we net for ourselves and for others when we travel further beyond our borders. And yet somehow, for far too long, we have allowed trade to become twisted into so much more than that: an easy excuse for struggling economies, a scapegoat for our failures to adapt to a changing world, a bogeyman for xenophobes and nationalists, and—for many Americans on both the right and the left—nothing short of a four-letter word. Let's remember it was only a short 700 years ago that Marco Polo trekked valiantly across the Silk Road; explorers from every continent braved the gleaming seas to look further beyond. So how on earth did we allow trade to become so controversial?

I wrote this book to let you in on a little known secret: it isn't. Trade can be a little complex; it may not mold itself easily along partisan lines or lend itself to bite-sized talking points, and it may not be a popular topic at dinner with all your friends. It may seem hopelessly convoluted and far removed from your day-to-day concerns. But the truth is, no matter who you are, where you stand, or what you care about, trade absolutely touches your life. Not only does it shape the price of almost everything we buy—from the grocery store to the app store; from the pharmacy to the car dealership—but it also shapes the culture around us in profound ways. It helps determine how many of those dollar signs end up in your pocketbook, in your neighborhood, and in our national treasury—and how many end up fueling opportunities somewhere else. Trade carries an enormous impact on all of our fortunes, both personal and shared. It is a powerful instrument of war and of peace between nations. It is singularly responsible for so many of the things we take for granted in our lives, from our laptops to our cell phones to our avocado toast.

I know what trade really means in people's lives because I spent eight years as America's top official responsible for the financing of exports. In my time as the chairman of the Export-Import Bank of the United States, I was responsible for helping equip U.S. businesses of all stripes—from Bassetts, a fifth-generation family-owned ice cream business in Philadelphia, to giants like Boeing and Caterpillar whose long supply chains keep Americans working in towns across the country—to venture further beyond and seize opportunities overseas. I visited factory floors and design labs from Maine to California, and spoke with thousands of workers and entrepreneurs who owed their livelihoods to the spirit of *Plus Ultra*. In Chippewa Falls, Wisconsin, I saw how a town of 14,000 could be rejuvenated by trade; there, a hundred-year-old fire truck manufacturer called Darley found new life—and 100 new jobs for its community—by securing the sale of thirty-two American-made fire trucks to the city of Lagos, Nigeria. In Nashua, New Hampshire, I visited a small business called Boyle Energy that had created a new technology to clean and test power plants in ways that drastically cut down on both costs and carbon emissions—a groundbreaking idea that had everything going for it, except U.S. customers. New trade opportunities freed that company up to take on over 400 projects across almost thirty countries, doubling their revenue twice over and enabling them to grow from a team of twelve to a team of more than fifty. In Mesquite, Texas, a family-owned small business called Fritz-Pak that once produced concrete admixtures for U.S. sports stadiums had to lay off workers when their domestic opportunities ran dry. But when the doors of global trade opened up to them, they got back to work making parts for soccer complexes in Brazil—and hired back every one of their employees in Texas whose job had been lost.

Those jobs mean everything to the families and neighborhoods they touch—they represent so much more than just a paycheck. I've met thousands of people who work on factory floors and in design labs; those jobs bring a strong sense of dignity, purpose, and identity, while strengthening the broader community as well. But you don't have to work at a manufacturing plant or on a family farm to have your life improved by trade. If you've ever eaten an apple, downed a glass of scotch (or Chianti . . . or a Heineken), or sat down to watch an episode or six of *Game of Thrones*, you've reaped just a few of trade's endless litany of benefits. Even your copy of this book was very likely assembled using products and processes procured from as many as a half dozen countries—and if you're reading or listening to this on a device of some sort, that number is even higher.

Does trade have its downsides? Of course it does. Just like every other policy issue you could name, actions we take on trade have consequences—there are winners and losers, but *inaction* also creates winners and losers. A deal that brings relatively inexpensive denim to the U.S. market could result in dozens of job losses at a fabric mill in Louisiana—a devastating blow to the families and towns involved—while at the same time lowering the price of blue jeans in clothing stores throughout the country, making life a little bit easier for millions of families on a budget. Naturally, there are moments when these sorts of calculations aren't entirely clear-cut in advance. Predicting the impact of trade on prices, jobs, and the health of industries is a bit like predicting the weather: however strong and data-driven your estimates are, you can never be certain that the elements won't take a sudden turn. Trade policy is all about projecting and negotiating these trade-offs as best as we can to ensure that the deals we make deliver an overall benefit to the American people—while acknowledging that there will always be winners and losers. Or at least that's what it's supposed to be all about.

As it turns out, though, trade policy is crafted in Washington, D.C., which also happens to be the home of its infinitely louder cousin: trade politics. The politics of trade skew the basic math of trade policy by introducing powerful interest groups, favored and disfavored industries, and electoral concerns into the equation. Sectors with strong lobbying power (see: oil and gas; pharmaceuticals), regional voting clout (see: Midwestern manufacturers and farmers), or good old-fashioned American nostalgia (see: coal mining) all have cards to play as trade policies take shape. As a result, the decisions we make on trade are often colored more by the prospect of good or bad headlines than by what makes the most sense for our country.

Take the recent real-life case of President Donald Trump's tariffs on foreign steel and aluminum. Tariffs, for the uninitiated, essentially act as the opposite of free trade agreements: rather than opening doors between nations to encourage mutually beneficial exchanges, they close them shut in the hopes of preserving what's already inside. Instead of importing less expensive foreign denim to lower clothing prices, for example, a tariff places a tax on U.S. consumers who *purchase* foreign denim—with the result being that the American manufacturer doesn't have to go up against what otherwise would have been a competitor offering better prices. The theory is that, while inflating the price of goods we buy, these taxes preserve U.S. jobs by eliminating competition. In practice, however, tariffs mostly just serve to shutter us from the world and let the global marketplace march on without us, leaving us on the sidelines. And while they can temporarily (and artificially) keep American industries afloat, the protection they offer also prevents those same industries from adapting, evolving, and growing healthy enough to compete on the world stage—think of an animal raised in captivity that will never learn the skills it needs to survive in its natural habitat. They're also hard to undo—once industries get used to protection, they tend to fight like hell to keep it in place. At the same time, of course, our tariffs invite retaliatory tariffs from the countries whose goods we tax. This hamstrings American businesses from selling to the 95 percent of potential customers who happen to live beyond our borders, driving down sales of American-made goods and crippling U.S. job growth on the back end. This is what's known as an all-around bad idea.

That didn't stop President Trump from declaring his intention to impose hefty steel and aluminum tariffs on a range of countries in the spring of 2018. This action, which was apparently meant to be a strike against China (our tenth-biggest source of imported steel), also managed to catch countries like Canada (our first-biggest) in the crossfire. While the legal rationale used by the administration for these tariffs was "national security"—a curious justification for an act targeting a number of traditional allies such as the European Union and Mexico—the president had previously pledged during the 2016 campaign to levy tariffs as a way to "discourage companies from laying off their workers." Of course, it's good politics to make a show of going to bat for heartland steelworkers; indeed, the president's announcement even drew a rare show of support from Midwestern progressives like Ohio senator Sherrod Brown. But in the ensuing months, Americans have seen the fallout of what can happen when trade politics consumes trade policy whole.

We have no way of knowing how many U.S. steel and aluminum jobs will be momentarily salvaged by the Trump tariffs—but we *can* anticipate a number of other consequences. The price of every razor blade, frying pan, refrigerator, and car will rise across the board, while major American industries that rely heavily on these metals—including everything from agriculture to aerospace to energy to construction—will be hit by cost increases that could ripple out and result in untold job losses in these critical fields, while making the export of their goods less competitive! Already, representatives of one industry that is vitally important to many Americans—the U.S. beer sector—are projecting that these tariffs will increase the price tag of American beer production by nearly $350 million per year. Smaller brewers have raised concerns that exploding costs will drive them out of business, while industry giants like MillerCoors have taken to the airwaves to alert beer lovers that the experience of drinking a cold one will soon become a pricier proposition. Further complicating matters is the fact that our capacity to produce aluminum and steel here at home is relatively limited—even if the intent of the tariffs is to force U.S. industries to "buy American," in many cases America can't come close to meeting its own demand. In the wake of President Trump's announcement, for example, a trade group representing U.S. oil pipeline owners and operators warned that American steelmakers only produce about 3 percent of the steel necessary to build and maintain American pipelines. For many companies, tariffs aren't creating an incentive to reward domestic industries—they're just jacking up the prices of foreign imports and the domestic versions of those products we need.

The purpose of this illustration—and, in fact, the purpose of this book—is to demystify, debunk, elucidate, and enliven one of the most consequential global issues of our lives. When we allow ourselves to dismiss trade as too difficult to understand, we open the door for it to be manipulated against our interests by ideologues and profiteers. In well-intentioned hands, there is no more powerful a tool for lifting people out of poverty at home and abroad, for reanimating stagnant communities, for stoking innovation, and for fortifying our economy for the future. But as long as trade remains poorly understood by the American people, it will also be a powerful weapon for confusing us, dividing us, and holding us back from the opportunities that lie beyond our shores.

Fortunately, the story of trade is not horribly complex—and you don't need an advanced degree to understand it. In these pages, we'll puncture the myths, unpack the arguments, and connect all the dots so that you can see the full picture of what trade really is and the many ways that it impacts your day-to-day existence. You'll learn how NAFTA became a populist punching bag on both sides of the aisle. You'll learn how Americans can avoid the grim specter of the $10 banana. And you'll finally discover the truth about whether or not, as President Trump once famously tweeted, "Trade wars are good and easy to win" (spoiler alert—they aren't).

Finally, we'll unravel the mysteries of trade by pulling back the curtain on six everyday products, each with a surprising story to tell: the taco salad, the Honda Odyssey, the banana, the iPhone, the college degree, and, of course, the smash hit HBO series *Game of Thrones*. Behind these six items are meaningful stories that help explain not only how trade has shaped our lives so far, but also how we can use trade to build a better future for our own families, for America, and for the world. The solutions aren't beyond our reach—for the most part, all they require is that we as a nation dispense with a few popular misconceptions and start being honest with ourselves about the trade-offs of trade. Do that, and we can multiply opportunity for farmers, factory workers, and entrepreneurs. We can bring greater peace of mind to blue-collar families, white-collar families, and no-collar families in every corner of the country. We can parse the sea of inscrutable acronyms, sail past the disorienting jargon of Most Favored Nation and the Doha Round, and arrive at a new world of understanding.

A stronger, more durable economy awaits us. A smarter strain of politics awaits us, too. Of course, like the explorers of old, we'll only reach it if we're willing to journey further beyond together. Shall we?

Glossary of Baffling Trade Jargon

One of the most frustrating things about trade is the terminology involved; it's a world of obscure words and acronyms that can seem almost intentionally designed to be inaccessible to the public. I remember having to confront trade jargon for the first time—and I certainly wished that there was a cheat sheet or an app to help me. That's why I put together the following handy guide to some of the terms you might hear in the world of trade; please feel free to make liberal use of it to impress your family members, coworkers, or dinner party companions as needed.

AD/CVD

Not to be confused with the Australian rock band AC/DC, AD/CVD is short for "antidumping and countervailing duties." These are extra fees that a country can impose on imported products to discourage customers from buying them. They can be imposed if we suspect that the products are being sold at unfairly low prices (antidumping) or that their home governments are unfairly subsidizing them (countervailing).

BRICS

Not to be confused with the clay building material, BRICS is an acronym used to refer to five emerging economies that have become loosely affiliated with one another: Brazil, Russia, India, China, and South Africa. Together, they represent more than 40 percent of the global population, and carry major influence over world economic affairs.

CFIUS

No, not Sisyphus—but close. The Committee on Foreign Investment in the United States is a group made up of leaders from a range of government agencies; it serves as a sort of watchdog, looking out for potential national security issues that arise when U.S. companies engage with the global marketplace (for example, they may speak up if a Chinese firm wants to acquire a U.S. business that happens to be next door to, say, an American naval base).

COMPARATIVE ADVANTAGE

The principle upon which all trade is founded! A country's "comparative advantage" is the edge it has over another country when it comes to some sort of economic activity. Saudi Arabia's geology has given it a comparative advantage in oil, for example, but not in growing rice, so it makes economic sense for it to export the former and rely on imports for the latter.

THE DOHA ROUND

A series of negotiations between countries that began in 2001 with the goal of lowering trade barriers worldwide—the talks broke down seven years later. Often the parties can't decide what a meeting is about . . . so to keep it simple, they name it after the city where they meet.

EXIM

The Export-Import Bank of the United States, a government agency that equips private U.S. companies with financing to win export sales. I ran it for eight years beginning in 2009.

FREE TRADE AGREEMENT

A deal between two or more countries to encourage trade—how controversial could that be? The word "free" refers to the fact that these agreements reduce or eliminate taxes on imports (like the "duty free" shops you find in airports).

G7

The Group of Seven—that is to say, the seven major advanced economies—which gathers annually to discuss global economics and other issues. The G7 first met in the 1970s to respond to an Arab oil embargo, and is made up of the U.S., the U.K., Germany, Japan, France, Canada, and Italy. It used to be the G8, but Russia was expelled in 2014 after its invasion of Ukraine; a larger group called the G20 periodically convenes as well.

GATT

The General Agreement on Tariffs and Trade, a pleasant-sounding 1947 agreement designed to lower trade barriers and increase global economic cooperation after World War II. It no longer exists, as it was succeeded by the World Trade Organization in 1995.

IMF

The International Monetary Fund, another post–World War II abbreviated organization created to promote economic stability and growth among its 189 member countries—unlike the World Bank, its focus is on overall economic and budgetary health rather than poverty reduction and infrastructure investment.

INTELLECTUAL PROPERTY

The latest big frontier of global commerce, "IP" or "IPR" (the "R" is for "rights") is intangible material that, when traded, is considered a "service" rather than a good. It includes things like copyrights, trademarks, patents, franchises, and technological designs—all the fruits of creative thinking.

MOST FAVORED NATION

Sometimes called "MFN" or "PNTR" ("Permanent Normal Trade Relations"). This is a status granted by one country to another—often as a result of a free trade agreement—that gives them the best trade terms offered to anyone else. For the U.S., this is no longer an exclusive club; every country except for Cuba and North Korea is a "Most Favored Nation." It sounds more special than it is.

NAFTA

The North American Free Trade Agreement was created to bring the U.S., Mexico, and Canada together as seamless trade partners and a formidable economic bloc. Dreamt up by Ronald Reagan, negotiated by George H.W. Bush, and signed by Bill Clinton, it came into effect on January 1, 1994—and forever changed the way we talk about, feel about, and campaign about trade.

OECD

The Organisation for Economic Co-operation and Development, yet another economic and trade-boosting coalition created in the wake of World War II to spark economic progress. Its thirty-six member countries meet regularly to coordinate on policy and set trade standards. Some sharp-tongued academics refer to it as the Organization for Endless Conversation and Dialogue.

ROO

Short for "rules of origin," these are the criteria used to figure out what country a product comes from—that can get complicated sometimes!

ROW

No, it has nothing to do with crossing the Delaware. ROW is Washington insider speak for "Rest of (the) World." That is to say, everybody other than U.S.—the United States.

SMOOT-HAWLEY

An ill-fated 1930 tariff passed by the U.S. Congress that raised taxes on thousands of products imported from American allies. Those countries retaliated with their own tariffs targeting U.S. goods, grinding American trade to a halt . . . just in time to exacerbate the effects of a crashing stock market and precipitate the Great Depression.

TAA

Trade Adjustment Assistance, a much maligned federal program first laid out by President John F. Kennedy. Its purpose is to compensate Americans hurt by free trade policies, either by paying them or by providing them with job training or other opportunities.

TARIFF

A tax! A consumption tax. A sales tax. No matter how you slice it, it's a tax. More specifically, it's a tax placed by a country on its own businesses and citizens when they purchase imported goods. Tariffs can be used to raise revenue or to protect domestic industries from having to compete with foreign rivals—in either case, they raise prices on domestic consumers.

TRQ

A tariff-rate quota is a trade barrier that sets a quota on a category of imported products—until the quota is met, tariffs on that product are very low, but once the quota is reached, tariffs go sky-high on any further imports of that product. We use these for dairy products in order to let in fancy French cheeses while keeping out foreign milk.

TPA

Short for "trade promotion authority" (and also known as "fast-track authority"), this is a power that Congress can hand over to the president as trade deals are being negotiated. It is seen as necessary in order to get other countries to negotiate a trade deal in good faith, knowing it will only be subject to an up-or-down vote by Congress without amendments. Congress generally doesn't like to grant this authority.

TPP

The Trans-Pacific Partnership—a proposed free trade agreement between the United States and eleven Pacific nations representing 40 percent of the world economy. Because free trade agreements had gotten such a bad rap, our leaders decided to ditch the word "free" and come up with a new name. On his first weekday in office, President Donald Trump pulled America out of the deal.

T-TIP

The Transatlantic Trade and Investment Partnership—a proposed free trade agreement (again, without the word "free") between the United States and the European Union that, if ratified, would unite the world's two largest economies. As with the TPP, negotiations were halted by President Donald Trump.

USMCA

The U.S.-Mexico-Canada Agreement is a trade agreement designed to supersede NAFTA—as of 2019, it has been signed by each country, but not yet ratified by our Congress. The agreement tinkers with the terms of NAFTA, modernizing a number of provisions while strengthening some of the labor protections of the original deal.

USTR

The U.S. Trade Representative, a government agency charged with shaping American trade policy. The head of the agency, whose title shares a name with the office itself, traditionally serves as the lead U.S. negotiator when trade agreements are forged. The Trade Representative also has the title of Ambassador.

WAYS AND MEANS

The committee within the U.S. House of Representatives responsible for handling trade issues, including tariffs and the passage of free trade agreements. Its counterpart in the Senate is the Finance Committee.

WORLD BANK

Yet another post–World War II institution, its mission is to reduce global poverty by financing infrastructure projects and supporting the development of countries' economies.

WTO

The World Trade Organization, which replaced the General Agreement on Tariffs and Trade in 1995. With 164 member countries, its mission is to set the rules and regulations of global trade and resolve trade disputes that arise between nations.

ZERO-SUM GAME

Any situation in which a victory for one party necessarily means an equivalent loss for someone else—if I win a poker hand, I've gained the exact same amount that one or more other players lost. Trade has winners and losers, but it is not a zero-sum game!

PART ONE

CLEARING THE AIR

CHAPTER 1

The Rockies, the *Rockys*, and 300 Years of American Trade

Trade does not exist in a vacuum, despite the fact that American companies export more than $7 billion worth of vacuum parts each year[1]—so in order to understand it, we have to first understand the historical and political atmosphere swirling all around it. That might be easier if it operated along the simpler lines that we associate with other types of trading, such as the deals that happen between sports teams. If the Rockies need a pitcher and the White Sox have a surplus, they might work out a deal that creates a benefit for both squads—drawing from each other's stronger resources to shore up weaker sectors. But global trade is complicated by both domestic politics and geopolitics; the North American Free Trade Agreement, for example, was as much about immigration, regional security, and stopping the flow of illegal drugs as it was about swapping imports and exports. If the Yankees were hell-bent on stopping the influence of the Reds from spreading—or if the Royals were required by law to send their shortstops to as many markets as possible—trading in baseball would be a much trickier affair. As it turns out, however, the simple trades of baseball have little in common with global economic trade, apart from the occasional historic relevance of Pirates.

Before we can tackle the most important trade issue of this century (China) we need to wrap our minds around what exactly trade *is*. To do that, we should begin by recognizing that trade is a tool—and, like any tool, we can't fully appreciate it unless we know what it's being used to accomplish. Naturally, it can be employed to meet domestic demand for particular goods like oil, milk, and steel; in fact, this most basic rationale for trade remains among its most vital uses. Adam Smith, known as the "Father of Economics," articulated the underpinnings of this idea back in 1776: "If a foreign country can supply us with a commodity cheaper than we ourselves can make it, better buy it of them with some part of the produce of our own industry, employed in a way in which we have some advantage." This was pretty novel thinking back in Smith's day! Thanks to David Ricardo, a British economist who later fleshed out the concept, Smith's idea would come to be known as "the principle of comparative advantage." The concept of comparative advantage is the basis for why modern economists—as one of them, MIT's David Autor, expressed it to me—have "almost a religious belief that trade is good." We've learned as a society that trade *is* good in the aggregate—but that isn't always the case in every individual community.

Nearly as often today, though, trade is wielded as a tool not only of economics, but of security, politics, and diplomacy. It can be used to exert leadership in a strategically important part of the world, manage relationships between regions, keep the peace with precarious regimes, and spread (or halt the spread of) ideologies. While politicians like to insist to folks back home that free trade agreements are all about creating good-paying jobs and saving industries, the reality is that these effects are often secondary concerns for the governments involved—some of the time, all that truly matters to them is which nations signed the agreement, and who got left out.

To wrap our minds around why and how we use trade in the United States today, we need to understand the larger forces that have shaped American trade policy over the course of the last three centuries. If that sounds daunting, fear not! It's actually remarkably simple, and you'll be done in just a couple dozen pages. In fact, it only requires us to appreciate two factors—the two factors that explain virtually everything about U.S. trade policy.

The first factor is so achingly simple that you'll kick yourself for not thinking of it by the end of this sentence (time's up). It's geography—and, more specifically, the unique location and environmental circumstances of the North American continent. Throughout modern history, the world powers of Europe have had to conduct diplomacy and trade beset by close neighbors—often powers in their own right—and without the full breadth of natural resources necessary to sustain a thriving society. Isolation isn't an option if there are mountains where you were planning to plant your wheat fields, and handling your international relationships requires a bit more finesse when a spurned nation could show up at your front door (with less than friendly intentions) at any moment. So while Europe learned to trade in a world of interdependency and close quarters, America did so in a world of self-reliance and humongous oceans.

At times, our pride in that self-reliance has been a fiction—much of our early economic growth in the South, for example, was only possible because of the violent, involuntary importation of human beings we then forced into slave labor. But it's a story we've held on to nonetheless, instilling an isolationist bent into our thinking. From our colonial days to westward expansion and onward through the generations, relying on ourselves and on our own land has been central to the American ethos. And while the attack on Pearl Harbor may have snapped us out of our isolationism for the seventy years that followed, it remains to be seen whether World War II truly altered our national DNA—or whether the impact was merely temporary. Our capacity for self-reliance is indeed immense, at least in theory; if all worldwide trade were to cease this very moment, the United States would arguably be the only country on earth with the diversity of innate resources needed to survive and succeed for the long haul. As we'll see, these geographic quirks of remoteness and abundance have meant that—for better or worse—America has always had the option of withdrawing from the world when it comes to trade. And while we *could* do better than anyone else if we were to isolate ourselves, that freedom could also be seen as a curse: as we'll explore throughout our story, it probably wouldn't lead to a strong economy or a very fulfilling existence.

The second factor that explains U.S. trade policy takes slightly longer to explain—but once you make it to the end of the chapter, you'll be a bona fide expert on the whole history of American foreign trade. For this one, we'll trade out the Rockies for the *Rocky*s. The element that earned Sylvester Stallone's celebrated boxing franchise nearly $2 billion and made it an enduring part of the culture is the same element that helps explain why America has approached trade in the way that we have ever since the days of fur trappers, armadas, and Plymouth Rock, straight through to the days of Donald Trump. That element? Having an enemy—a long string of compelling arch-nemeses.

While it's true that, in every period of our history, America has proactively pursued trade policies to advance specific goals of our own, it's also true that those goals were largely born as reactions to the specter of some rival power. Rocky Balboa's entire story was that of a great champion for whom every career move—to fight, to retire, to emerge from retirement, to develop others, and so on—was triggered by the behavior of his opponents. Like America's early relationship with Great Britain, Rocky's first great nemesis, Apollo Creed, would go on to become a close ally. Like Rocky, America was compelled to reenter the international arena as the Soviet threat gained steam. Every step of the way, the actions of both Rocky and America were motivated by a series of external threats—and, at times, a little inner turmoil, too.

By taking a closer look at the rivalries that scared and spurred America through the years, we can better understand the central role that trade has come to play in our politics. More importantly, we can learn something crucial about the role trade can—and should—play in the century ahead. Before we do that, though, an important disclaimer: this is the short version of the story. Three centuries is a long time, and history has many mothers and fathers whom we won't be meeting in this chapter. So yes, in the interest of your interest, we're going to be jumping around a bit from one critical moment to the next—leaving out a little nuance and a lot of detail, but preserving the big picture. Fear not! There are plenty of great books out there that dig deeply into American economic history. For now, though, let's just cover the episodes we need to know.

Arch-Nemesis #1: Great Britain

Borrowing one last time from *Rocky*, our story begins in '75 in downtown Philadelphia. That would be 1775, more precisely, at a time when the Second Continental Congress was grappling with the question of what to do about escalating tensions between the thirteen American colonies and their ruling government in London. In the dozen years that had passed since Britain's coffers were depleted by the Seven Years' War, the British Crown had attempted to raise revenue by imposing increasingly severe taxes on its subjects across the Atlantic—a tactic that riled the colonists, who had no representatives in Parliament to stand up for their interests. These taxes lit a fuse that led to protests in the streets of American cities, inspired Samuel Adams and his compatriots to form the Sons of Liberty, and incited the Boston Massacre. As King George III used his trade policy to siphon money away from America, angry groups of colonists retaliated through a series of public actions; the most notable of these was the famous Boston Tea Party, when 342 chests of tea were liberated from ships of the East India Company and unceremoniously dumped into the harbor.

You know the rest. The Battle of Lexington and Concord is waged in 1775, and the Congress in Philadelphia drafts up its Declaration of Independence, laying out the reasons for their desired separation—including, among a litany of grievances, "For cutting off our Trade with all parts of the world" even before the first mention of taxation without representation. And so it was that America was born: the child of a bloody, righteous revolution, conceived in bitter anger, embroiled by the sexiest and hottest-button of all issues known to humankind: import duties!

It isn't hyperbole to say that trade was on the mind of America from the moment of its birth. In fact, once the Constitution was ratified, the very first major act of the U.S. Congress was to put a tariff in place to help pay off war debts and protect fledgling American manufacturers against cheaper British imports—the brainchild of Alexander Hamilton, years before his Broadway hip-hop career took flight (as a reminder for those who shamefully skipped the introduction, tariffs are taxes a country places on its own citizens for purchasing designated foreign goods; in essence, they hike up the prices of imported products in order to encourage people to buy domestic products instead). The Tariff of 1789 set off a debate that would play an enormous role in

shaping American politics for the next 125 y[illegible]
Hamilton, who wanted to use tariffs strategic[illegible]
industries, against those like Thomas Jefferson, [illegible]
tariffs should be kept low and only used to rais[illegible]
the government (remember, there was no incom[illegible]

As debates go, it would be fair to look at this [illegible]nsider it more than a little wonky. But at the heart of the disagreement was a fundamental rift that has echoed throughout our history, right through until today. By pushing policies that insulated U.S. manufacturers from competition, Hamilton was representing the interests of cities in the North. But an estimated 90 percent of the economy came from agriculture—by fighting to limit tariffs, Jefferson was speaking for the rice, tobacco, and cotton farmers of the South, who exported a healthy share of their crop to feed the appetites and addictions of Europe. This dynamic, and the question of whether our trade policy should primarily serve the interests of urban or rural Americans, has persisted even as our agricultural economy has given way first to industrialization and, more recently, to the age of digital services.

But we're getting ahead of ourselves. After Hamilton wins the argument, the country enters an era of high tariffs designed to keep otherwise low-cost British imports from snuffing out American-made goods (for enforcement, they create a roving tariff collection force in 1790 that would come to be known as the United States Coast Guard). Even Jefferson ultimately comes around to the idea that the U.S. must produce more than just crops to survive, and for a time protectionism (along with the Atlantic Ocean) gives young industries like textiles and iron a chance to get on their feet. With our cities thriving and our federal government well-funded by sky-high import duties, we never anticipated—just as you haven't here—that our story would be abruptly interrupted by Napoleon.

es, Napoleon! When the French emperor decides that he wants to conquer Europe, America's chief rival, Britain, gets thrust into yet another costly war. Starved for resources, the British begin seizing cargo from American ships—they even seize the sailors, and impress them into service on behalf of their former king. Jefferson, now the president, faces enormous pressure to respond either militarily or economically, and opts for the latter, signing an embargo in 1807 to block the importation of British goods. The hope is that depriving the Brits of their American customers will cause King George to change his ways—but one of the benefits of being an empire is that you're never beholden to any one market. The Crown upped its exports to South America to make up for the lost cash, and without imports to tax, it was the United States that found itself in dire financial straits. With economic warfare having backfired spectacularly, America decides to go back to original-recipe warfare by taking up arms against Britain in the aptly named War of 1812.

Three years later, our country had little to show for that choice but an empty Treasury and an extra-crispy White House. Britain, too, was gaining nothing from the hostilities, and the two sides stood down in the hopes of restoring their relationship. The period of isolation exacerbated by the war had caused the American economy to move in two different directions: with imports limited, the North had the chance to escalate its manufacturing output and nurture its industries—while the South floundered without overseas markets in which to sell its crops. With the U.S. short on funds and still reliant on tariffs for about 90 percent of its revenue, new import duties were put in place in the wake of the war to restock the national purse. With the British threat having subsided, a new period of relative national unity known as the "Era of Good Feelings" took root. Spoiler alert: it wouldn't last.

Arch-Nemesis #2: Ourselves

As Hamlet, Dr. Freud, or Dr. Jekyll could tell you, not every great conflict requires a second actor. And so it was that having thawed our relations with Europe after the War of 1812, our next defining rivalry came from within. The high tariffs instituted to raise money after the war continued to perk up northern factories while hamstringing southern plantations, adding fuel to the fire as the nation began to fracture over the issue of slavery. Industrial interests weren't just gaining capacity and cash—they were gaining ever more political power, too. Each additional tariff further widened the gulf between the economies of the South and the North, the latter of which ingeniously used the money collected from tariffs to build infrastructure in every new western state that joined the Union, cementing their allegiance.

The situation came to a head in the election year of 1828, when President John Quincy Adams signed what would come to be dubbed by its detractors, a bit histrionically, as the "Tariff of Abominations." This new law placed a flat tax of 38 percent on nearly every imported good, a burden so onerous that America's new best friend, Britain, retaliated by scaling back on its own importing of American cotton—a further blow against the South. By the time the tariffs went into effect, the voters had already swept a new president into office: a charismatic southern populist riding a wave of anti-northern (and anti-tariff) sentiment to victory in the South and West.

On paper, Andrew Jackson should have been just what the doctor ordered for southern farmers. But when South Carolina took the unprecedented step of threatening to actively ignore the recent tariffs—even going so far as to openly contemplate seceding from the union—Jackson turned his back on his region and its native ardor for states' rights to stand up for the federal Constitution. The Nullification Crisis, as it would soon be known, saw the president come a hairsbreadth from sending American troops to Charleston, and resulted in the dramatic resignation of Jackson's South Carolinian vice president, John C. Calhoun. A compromise was ultimately reached that would roll back tariff levels over the course of the following decade, but the damage to relations between the North and South was done—if there were any "good feelings" remaining between the regions, they were extinguished by the collision of northern trade policy and southern furor.

Trade didn't cause the Civil War to break out thirty years later—the South's refusal to abandon its abhorrent dependence on slavery is squarely to blame. But there is no question that seven decades of near-constant disagreement over tariffs had

An 1846 Edward Williams Clay cartoon depicts prominent Democrats preparing to bury free trade.

fanned the flames of resentment and driven a wedge through the center of the nation in its formative years. We still see echoes of that tension today, even as the battleground has shifted from how northern states versus southern states view global connection to how urban centers versus rural areas do. Until slavery surpassed it, trade policy was the single most heated, most talked about, and most consequential issue in America—and it is entirely likely that the North's near-constant success in passing tariffs caused the South to cling ever more tightly to slave labor as their export opportunities waned. If southern farmers hoped that secession would deliver them to a world of unfettered trade, however, those hopes were quickly dashed. Tariffs represented more than just a philosophical stance—they represented cold, hard cash, too. The price of a prolonged war was astronomically high, and before long both the Union and, ironically, the Confederacy were forced to impose steep tariffs to fund the fight.

By the time the war had ended, there was no longer any question about whether American trade policy would be deployed to serve the interests of the rural South or the industrial North. A new, pro-tariff party called the Republicans was ascendant, backed by the powerful northern iron and steel industries (which still counted on limiting cheap foreign imports in order to grow). During the half century that followed Abraham Lincoln's election, they would enjoy lopsided majorities in the Senate for forty-four out of fifty years while winning six presidential contests in a row. The House of Representatives was not much kinder to advocates of low tariffs, though Democrats did manage to eke out control of the body for eighteen years during that half century stretch. This was the heart of the Industrial Revolution—an age of smokestacks and tenements, and a time when a booming, rapidly expanding population made it possible for the country to isolate itself from the world while still growing its economy. Waves

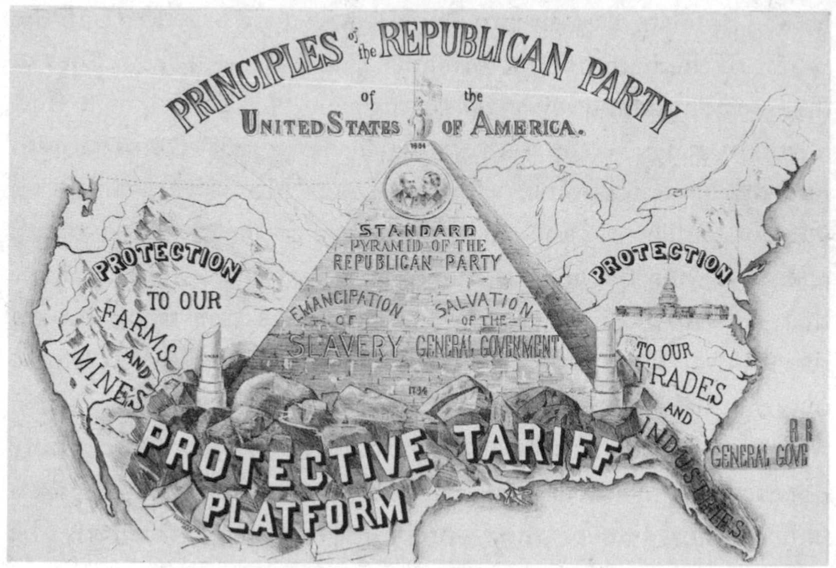

This 1880 party poster leaves little doubt about which issue was foremost on the minds of Republicans in the first decades of their existence.

of immigrants arrived to fuel the swell of northern production. The Wild West was tamed by the telegraph and the transcontinental railroad. And as the American economy evolved, distinct new concerns materialized that would prove enormously consequential: those of the laborer, and those of the consumer.

It was a Democrat, Grover Cleveland, who first popularized the argument that high tariffs lead to high consumer prices in the 1880s—the side of the trade equation that touches everybody's lives. America's working class was exploding in numbers, and as pay stagnated and urban conditions worsened, the interests of those who toiled in the factories began to diverge from the interests of the wealthy men who owned them. Before long, the virtue of keeping U.S. industries in a protective bubble seemed less appealing to many Americans than the virtue of paying less for clothes, toys, and tools. We weren't some upstart nation anymore—our manufacturers were no longer infants that needed to be coddled and sheltered from outside competition.

The debate over protectionism would splinter the once solid Republican Party into progressive and traditional camps, threatening the supremacy of the tariff that had defined American trade policy for its first 124 years. That supremacy would be mortally wounded after a Democratic Party breakthrough in 1913, when lawmakers acknowledged that the extraordinary growth of the country—and the roads, utilities, and defenses that came with it—required the creation of an income tax. The Sixteenth Amendment was a seismic shift that flipped the primary source of federal revenue from import duties to an income tax, eliminating the only rationale for tariffs that everyone in America had always agreed on. Twenty-nine days after its adoption, Democrat Woodrow Wilson enters the White House on a platform of slashing tariffs now deemed unnecessary for raising revenue—but all trade policies are rendered moot when the First World War breaks out, grinding global trade to a sudden halt.

America's first major entrée into twentieth-century international affairs left a terrible taste in our mouths, and no sooner had Republicans been dispatched to the wilderness than they were swept back into office once again. But the dimensions of trade had changed in their absence—American manufacturing had begun to outgrow its limited base of U.S. customers, while new advancements in communications and transportation had further integrated the European economies as they picked up the pieces of their shattered continent. Republicans missed the memo, and sought to raise tariffs aggressively in an effort to return to the glory days of the industrial boom (there is a reason that this twelve-year run of protectionist GOP leadership did not score Warren Harding, Calvin Coolidge, or Herbert Hoover a place on Mount Rushmore). The most notorious of these acts—the name of which you might recall from the slowest day of your high school history class—was the Smoot-Hawley Tariff, which hiked up duties on tens of thousands of imported products, including everything from perfume to light bulbs to macaroni.[2]

For our friends in Europe and Canada, Smoot-Hawley was the breaking point. America's allies passed retaliatory measures that effectively halted U.S. trade in both directions—causing both U.S. imports and exports to wither at the worst possible time. Without a trade economy to speak of, the country became exceptionally vulnerable to swings in the domestic market. And so in large part due to Smoot-Hawley, when the stock market crashed, it didn't provoke a mild downturn—it unleashed the Great Depression.

Arch-Nemesis #3: The Soviet Union

Trade was once the most important issue in American politics, but the relentless middle years of the twentieth century saw it recede from the spotlight at last. The fallout of the Depression, the promise of the New Deal, and the looming specter of European fascism each took their well-deserved places at center stage of the national conversation. At the same time, the old dividing lines between the northern and southern economies began to be blurred by modernization. Like every war before it, World War II incurred enormous costs—but it also triggered monumental changes in what America is and how America works. Mass wartime production shocked the economy out of its doldrums, wages rose to record heights, and with the boys occupied overseas, women entered the labor market in vast numbers, changing the face—and expanding the potential—of the U.S. workforce.

Less tangibly, but no less critically, the defeat of the Axis forces compelled America to rethink its role in the world. Just a few years earlier, the U.S. had denied asylum to 907 Jewish refugees who had arrived off the coast of Florida aboard the MS *St. Louis*; upon returning to Europe, hundreds of these same passengers would perish in the Holocaust. The visceral nature of the horrors of this era entered American homes like never before—for some it was only one degree away, and therefore became impossible to ignore. In our family, we were always conscious of the fact that my mother had been about the same age as Anne Frank, and each had moved from Germany to Amsterdam in 1933 to evade the Nazis. After the war, the world came together to prevent these events from ever happening again—and Americans of all backgrounds came to understand that oceans could no longer protect them from global affairs, be they military conflicts or ideological collisions. We had become a superpower, and, having seen firsthand the harrowing consequences of indifference, we understood that our newfound strength brought with it newfound responsibilities.

In his 1801 inaugural address, Thomas Jefferson famously paraphrased the doctrine left behind by George Washington as he departed from national life: "Peace, commerce, and honest friendship with all nations; entangling alliances with none." But Washington and Jefferson had not dreamed of airplanes, of Auschwitz, or of atomic weapons—they could not foresee the economic prosperity or the existential security that might come from a deeply entwined, American-led system of global commerce. As badly as the world needed American leadership in the aftermath of World War II, America needed to engage with the world as well if it hoped to continue growing its economy and sustaining the aspirations of its people. When the United States finally let go of protectionism and ventured out further beyond its borders, the world opened its arms—and its markets. We didn't know it at the time, but we also opened a dark door here at home to those who eyed the outside world with skepticism and fear.

With its eyes at long last on the rest of the globe, America went to work on the world stage for the first time as something more than just a military power. Our new focus on the international rebuilding effort wasn't just about diplomacy or charity, of course—it was also about creating a market for American goods. When I became the chairman of the Export-Import Bank of the United States, I discovered that the bank had once helped finance major infrastructure projects abroad that fueled American job growth and integrated ourselves into foreign economies. The 1930s saw U.S. companies financed by the EXIM Bank help construct the Pan-American Highway (which would ultimately stretch from Buenos Aires to Alaska) and the Burma Road—we financed the Chryslers, Fords, and Chevy trucks and equipment required to construct it.

Europe, still smoldering, cried out for international order—and a bevy of transatlantic institutions were born. As the Marshall Plan set American dollars to work rebuilding Europe—again financed by the EXIM Bank—the finishing touches were put in place on the International Monetary Fund, the World Bank, and the General Agreement on Tariffs and Trade. Though all three would play different roles, each was created to serve a singular strategic purpose: to bring the economies—and therefore the interests—of the world's free nations into closer cooperation with one another. This was a system that benefited America enormously, allowing us to become the world's top exporter for the rest of the century—and the largest economy to this day.

It was against this backdrop of postwar unity that a new threat rose in the East. America, Europe, and the Soviet Union had shared a common enemy during the conflict, but as the western powers came together to resurrect the global economy and liberalize trade in the Atlantic, the Soviets chose not to engage in the new era of integration. Their preference, as it turned out, was a more literal form of integration—insofar as they took the opportunity to actually absorb the countries that would form the Eastern Bloc. Using lucrative trade deals as a carrot and threats of force as a stick, Joseph Stalin brought Poland, Czechoslovakia, Hungary, Romania, Bulgaria, Albania, and East Germany under his control by way of a defense treaty called the Warsaw Pact and an economic collective called Comecon (later to be joined by Cuba and other Communist nations). These institutions were created to mirror the North Atlantic Treaty Organization, or NATO, the military alliance that in 1949 had formally united the West.

More explicitly and comprehensively than at any other time in human history, the world was effectively split in half. Within the span of only a few years, the economic playing field had flipped from hundreds of individual countries cooperating regionally and doing sporadic business with one another to the simpler landscape of two giant world markets—each unusually open to its own members, and spectacularly closed to the other side. In the so-called "First World," the developed western nations prospered on people's newfound hunger for consumer goods like televisions, refrigerators, and family cars. In the "Second World," trade was conducted behind an Iron Curtain and heavily controlled by the Soviet Union. The "Third World" of developing economies was up for grabs—it would become a critical battleground for the ideological tug-of-war ahead.

In the decades that ensued, the near-constant threat of military and economic opposition terrified and inspired nations on each side of the global partition. For Americans, the Soviets were a bogeyman far more enduring and mysterious than any prior threat; their mere existence drove schoolchildren—including me—under their desks during air-raid drills, provoked military engagements in Korea and Vietnam, and motivated critical U.S. industries to reach new heights (including those of the lunar variety). Like Rocky Balboa leaving the safety of his own country to square off against a cold, determined, machinelike rival in Ivan Drago, America entered arenas all over the world to face down the Soviet threat. For the U.S., it was a new, more open stance—and trade became our most effective jab.

Free trade was a term in use since the earliest days of the Republic; initially, the word "free" referred specifically to absence of any import tax on goods entering the country. But by 1962, the phrase was beginning to take on a new connotation as open markets became a signifying feature of life in the "free"—that is to say, non-Communist—world. That year, President John F. Kennedy delivered a State of the Union address to Congress advocating for free trade on very different grounds than his predecessors in the Democratic Party—who since the days of Grover Cleveland had been focused on trade primarily as a means of lowering consumer prices—ever had. So critical to the president was this message that he reserved it for the grand finale of his well-publicized address:

> We need a new law—a wholly new approach—a bold new instrument of American trade policy. Our decision could well affect the unity of the West, the course of the Cold War, and the economic growth of our nation for a generation to come. . . . For together we face a common challenge: to enlarge the prosperity of free men everywhere—to build in partnership a new trading community in which all free nations may gain from the productive energy of free competitive effort. . . . This is our guide for the present and our vision for the future—a free community of nations, independent but interdependent, uniting north and south, east and west, in one great family of man, outgrowing and transcending the hates and fears that rend our

> age. . . . There is no comfort or security for us in evasion, solution in abdication, no relief in irresponsibility.

For Kennedy, free trade was a way to keep the world itself free. No longer merely a tool for raising revenue or lowering the price of milk, trade had been reborn as a tool of peace, order, and moral leadership on a global scale—and a thread to weave together the fates of like-minded nations the world over.

Arch-Nemesis #4: Japan

While the Soviet Union cut an impressive figure as a twentieth-century supervillain, the truth is that the Red Scare was less of an economic threat and always more of an existential one. As the

Archival footage of the precise moment that the Cold War ended.

of low trade barriers—and the new universe that came with them—to prosper steadily in s, the Soviet preference for central planning over s led to inefficiencies and shortages across the Eastern ut while the U.S. remained singularly focused on stopping e spread of Communism and avoiding the prospect of nuclear annihilation, we failed to anticipate a different type of threat to our success. That threat, namely, was the possibility that someone else would come along who made products that were better than ours.

Enter Japan. Its super power? Quality. Somewhat ironically, the rapid rise of the Japanese economy can be traced back to the paranoia of the Cold War's early days; a beneficiary of the Marshall Plan, Japan had received significant financial and development assistance from the United States that enabled the country to jump-start its postwar boom. America was gambling on the idea that a prosperous, self-sufficient Japan would be less likely to succumb to the Soviets—but what they hadn't bet on was just how serious a competitor Japan could eventually become.

In Tokyo, they call it 経済的奇跡. In New York, it's better known as the "Japanese economic miracle." Whatever you choose to call it, the facts are astounding: in less than four decades, Japan blossomed from a small, stagnant presence, defeated in war and devastated by nuclear bombardment, to become the second-largest economy in the world. By 1960, Japanese industrial output had reached 350 percent of its prewar levels, sparking GDP growth that topped 10 percent an astonishing six times during the next decade. Theirs was a rise fueled by smart government policies, an ethos that encouraged productivity, and a wise, rapid transition from protectionism to aggressive exporting. The model wasn't completely capitalist—the government directed a good deal of the national economic traffic. By actively supporting some strategically important private firms—a concept, alien to American thinking, known as "national champions … government gave special power to companies that generated ou… profits, which in turn led to higher wages and thus some politic… economic stability. With that said, however, their economy wa… tightly controlled by the state, either. Most crucially of all, Japan w… the first nation to crack the code on the technologies and advanc… manufacturing techniques that would redefine the most popular consumer products of the late twentieth century.

Few forces on earth could have frightened the United States into backsliding toward protectionism in the thick of the Cold War, but the Japanese found one: they called it Toyota. The twelve-year-old automaker had flirted with bankruptcy in the wake of World War II; in 1950, it had produced a grand total of 300 cars. But when a recovering Japan began to open its doors to trade with the West, Toyota seized the opportunity to build a facility in California in 1957. Between the 1950s and the 1960s, Japanese car exports jumped by a factor of nearly 200, as first Nissan—and later Honda, Subaru, Mitsubishi, and others—joined Toyota in American auto lots. The secret to their success wasn't much of a secret at all: despite being lighter and offering less horsepower, their cars simply ran better, lasted longer, and proved more reliable than anything Detroit had to offer.

Before long, Japanese cars became synonymous with quality; Toyota leapfrogged Volkswagen to become the number one importer in the United States, and later cruised past GM to claim the title of the world's biggest automaker. Outclassed by their new rivals, the first reaction of American automakers was to fall back on the oldest of American traditions: using tariffs to keep cheaper, better-performing foreign goods out of the marketplace (hey, it worked for George Washington back when British textiles were the hot new thing). In 1964, President Lyndon Johnson slapped a 25 percent tariff on light trucks in a deal that, decades later, was revealed to have be[...]e at least in part in exchange for the support of the U[...] Auto Workers for Johnson's civil rights agenda. Beli[...]r not, that tariff still exists today. In the years to come, [...]oit would take full advantage of its political power in th[...]dwest to press for big new taxes on imported vehicles.

[...]his return to protectionism may have boosted the prospects of American pickup trucks, but it soon became clear that tariffs had lost a good deal of their power over the previous two centuries. While France couldn't evade tariffs in the 1850s by simply sailing over and opening up their own ironworks in Pennsylvania, the Japanese could do exactly that in the far more open world of the twentieth century. By 1988, Honda, Nissan, Mazda, and Toyota had constructed manufacturing plants in Marysville, Ohio; Smyrna, Tennessee; Flat Rock, Michigan; and Georgetown, Kentucky, respectively. The fact that many Japanese cars were being assembled by American autoworkers helped erase some of the stigma that had built up around buying "foreign" vehicles; Americans fell head over heels for Japanese cars, and, more than three decades later, we are still in love.

What made the threat posed by Japan so revolutionary was that—unlike the great arch-nemeses of the past like the British and the Soviets—it came from an ally. Japan wasn't a colossal empire or a Communist scourge; they were a free society with a mixed economic model, a liberal stance on trade, and membership in cooperative institutions like the International Monetary Fund, the General Agreement on Tariffs and Trade, and the Organisation for Economic Co-operation and Development (or OECD). Trade and technology were converging; the only true way to defeat our competition was to improve. So Detroit set to work doing just that, harnessing new technology and advanced manufacturing techniques introduced by the Japanese in order to raise the quality of American cars. The result was good for U.S.

consumers, who enjoyed a wider range of higher quality choices than ever before. The techniques were not as well-received by the labor community, however, as they introduced more robotics and fewer flesh-and-blood workers.

By the early 1990s, the Japanese economy began to slide into a recession—but not before Japan had used their automotive blueprint to corner the American market on household electronics, toys, and other major sectors, making "Made in Japan" a beacon of quality here at home—a far cry from earlier opinions of Japanese manufacturing. U.S. manufacturing jobs began a slide from their all-time high of nearly 20 million in 1979 that would continue more or less unabated until our recovery from the Great Recession of 2008, when they fell to only about 11.5 million (though it's worth noting that even as jobs were shed, American manufacturing *output* actually climbed steadily throughout that stretch—evidence of how technology, for better or worse, has enabled us to produce more with fewer workers).

In an effort to compete with Japan, America had learned to mimic its rival's embrace of technology, inadvertently setting off an entirely new era of trade politics. For the first time, the most significant fault line on U.S. trade policy wasn't simply between political parties or geographic regions: it was between labor (which valued jobs and wages) and business (which valued production and profits)—two metrics that had previously risen and fallen in lockstep before technology and quality changed the equation. Beginning in the mid-1970s, workers' hourly pay no longer tracked a company's success; as AFL-CIO president Richard Trumka put it to me, this was the moment when the bond—the idea that we were all in this together—was broken.* As these

* Between 1948 and 1973, for example, productivity rose by 96 percent while incomes rose by 91 percent—since 1974, however, productivity has gone up by 77 percent, while workers' hourly pay has risen by a mere 12 percent.

battle lines were redrawn, most Republicans—long supporters of the business community—joined forces with most Democrats—who, despite their affiliation with organized labor, had been consistently in favor of low trade barriers since the end of the Civil War—and by the middle of the 1980s, just about everybody was a free trader. It was against this new landscape that President Ronald Reagan would propose, President George H. W. Bush would negotiate, and President Bill Clinton would later enact a free trade agreement that would integrate America with its closest neighbors—a deal called NAFTA.

Arch-Nemesis #5: China

We'll soon explore the story of NAFTA in more detail, but, suffice it to say, the deal fundamentally flipped the entire American trade conversation on its head just in time for a new world power to rise up. America had managed to grow out of its precarious youth, survive the rupture of its southern half, the threats of rival ideologies, and the challenge of a well-oiled competitor in Japan. As ever, however, the next great battle lay in store. China had been conspicuously quiet on the world stage for much of the twentieth century, but a series of sweeping economic reforms set the stage for a comprehensive boom. In 1978, Chinese leader Deng Xiaoping set in motion large-scale changes to the national economy in order to adapt the ostensibly Communist state to becoming more globally competitive. Deng neither embraced western capitalism nor clung to the ideologies of China's past—he famously summed up his philosophy on China's economy by saying that "it doesn't matter whether the cat is black or white, as long as it catches mice." With state-backed industries across every major sector and a population north of a billion, all of the ingredients were in place for China to become a dominant global player once it decided to emerge from its long period of isolation. But what America—and Richard Nixon after his famous visit to China in 1972—may not have fully anticipated was the extent to which their latest challenger sought more than mere economic success. As it turned out, China wanted to exert a broader influence over the world, too.

As the golden age of consumer products gave way to the digital era, the production of physical goods began to lose some of its economic importance—ceding that ground to a rising tide of services and intellectual property. In that regard, America, too, was well-positioned for global leadership, having adapted to become the largest exporter of services in the entire world. And while the U.S. was evolving its export focus from traditional, job-rich manufacturing to digital, profit-rich industries like entertainment and financial services, China was moving up the food chain as well. As the twenty-first century got under way, they began to qui-

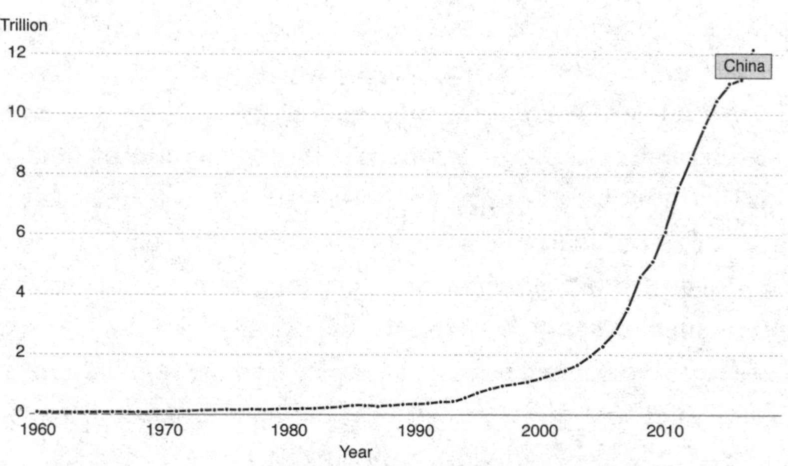

This artwork, titled "Uh Oh," depicts China's GDP growth from 1960 to 2015.

etly shed the image of inexpensive "Made in China" clothes, toys, and other basic products (with which every American is familiar) to become a producer of strategically critical goods like energy-efficient vehicles, medical devices, IT products, and airplanes. Not only that—they were prospering under a planned economy and five-year plans in a way that the Soviet Union never managed to do. The sheer size and capacity of China, along with their stated desire to move from prioritizing export quantity to prioritizing export quality, leaves little doubt as to who the next great American rival would be.

As the world fought to recover from the global financial crisis of 2008, the United States sought a way to counter China's ascendancy before it could surpass us to corner the market on the most critical sectors of the twenty-first century. Once again, the answer was trade. President Barack Obama led the charge to orchestrate a major free trade agreement in the Pacific that would expand America's influence in the region—while leaving China out, at least initially. The Trans-Pacific Partnership, or TPP, included twelve nations representing 40 percent of the global economy; it was a chance to simultaneously decrease the reliance of China's own neighbors on Chinese goods, services, and markets while strengthening their economic bonds with the U.S. Harkening back to President Kennedy's vision of trade as a tool of moral leadership, TPP was also meant to ensure that America—not China—was writing the rules of global commerce with regard to human rights, labor rights, gender equality, and environmental standards (and China would have to abide by those rules if it wanted to be a major player in the region). For the American economy, for global working conditions, and for the future of U.S. leadership in the world, the TPP was critical.

Heading into the 2016 presidential race, TPP enjoyed modest—but not enthusiastic—support from both parties. But even after more than two decades, the wounds of NAFTA hadn't fully healed. The difficult political work of being truthful with the American people about globalization, automation, and how the economy had changed—and how it would continue to change—hadn't been done. Protectionists on the wings of each party launched insurgent campaigns for the White House, decrying TPP and promoting American isolationism as a path to protecting U.S. jobs. On the left, Senator Bernie Sanders disparaged free trade agreements as tools that corporate interests use to consolidate power and subjugate workers; though he was defeated in the Democratic primary, the surprising groundswell of support his campaign generated was enough to drive the nominee, former secretary of state (and former TPP supporter) Hillary Clinton, to turn against the agreement. On the right, Donald Trump bucked his party to lash out aggressively against TPP as a "bad deal" that would (somehow) allow nonmembers China and India to "take advantage of the United States." He went further at a June 2016 campaign rally in St. Clairsville, Ohio, declaring that "the Trans-Pacific Partnership is another disaster done and pushed by special interests who want to rape our country—just a continuing rape of our country. . . . That's what it is, too. It's a harsh word. It's a rape of our country." Six weeks later, Trump became the Republican nominee for president.

On January 23, 2017, in one of his first acts in office, President Trump issues an executive order directing the United States Trade Representative to withdraw from TPP. The agreement progresses without us, and America's sudden withdrawal from the region opens the door for China to push forward on new development and infrastructure tools, as well as a new free trade agreement—called the Regional Comprehensive Economic Partnership, or RCEP—that includes original TPP members Japan, Australia, Vietnam, Singapore, New Zealand, Malaysia, and Brunei, along with India and other Asian states. The dream of an American-led Pacific economic bloc to frustrate China's supremacy is replaced by a Chinese-led bloc that excludes the United States—the first of several steps toward a renewal of U.S. isolationism. While China continues making moves to impart its values and economic preferences on Asia and the developing world—at the expense of U.S. interests, I might add—we proceed to dramatically diminish our influence as a global leader. We begin by proposing steep new tariffs on steel, aluminum, and other goods, which sparks trade wars with Europe, China, and Canada. Meanwhile, we publicly undermine NATO and the western alliance under the credo of "America First"—forgetting that those arrangements had largely benefited us, and others along the way, fueling peace, security, and growth since the end of the Second World War. Having emerged from the postwar period as the largest economic and military power the world had ever seen, we now face a new type of competitor in China—a force with whom we are deeply entangled, and one that we'll need to both cooperate with and, at times, confront.

CHAPTER 2

The Giant Sucking Sound

On October 15, 1992, 70 million Americans turned their eyes to the University of Richmond to watch three candidates go head-to-head-to-head in the second presidential debate—a town hall meeting with an audience made up of 209 undecided voters. It was no surprise to anyone paying attention that the first question of the evening was on trade; after all, President George H. W. Bush was on the verge of signing a major new pact with Canada and Mexico that would create the largest free trade area in the world. First proposed to the American people thirteen years earlier by then-candidate Ronald Reagan, the notion of a free trade agreement linking the North American continent was something of a political enigma. Poorly understood by everyday citizens—and even more poorly explained by politicians—it had scrambled the dynamics within both parties as negotiations ramped up at the end of the 1980s.

NAFTA, as it would come to be known, was initially dreamed up to solve a problem across the Atlantic. As the existential threat of the Cold War began to peter out, it was becoming clear to U.S. politicians of all stripes that the biggest danger to America was the commercial success of its friends—our experience getting pummeled by Japan on cars and electronics had given us a taste of what that looked like. Europe had recovered and grown stronger in the long, peaceful stretch that followed World War II, and once the Berlin Wall came down there would be little standing in the way of true economic unity across the continent. Even years before it formally fell, the writing was already on the wall: the future of Europe was an integrated European Union. Officially established by the signing of the Maastricht Treaty in February 1992, the new EU—nearly 500 million strong—was poised to become an economic competitor the likes of which America had never seen before.

The United States couldn't build a union of its own—we had already played that card 216 years earlier. But we *did* have friendly neighbors. In 1984, as the idea of a unified Europe had already begun to gain traction, Congress voted to give President Reagan "fast-track authority" to negotiate separate trade agreements with Canada and Israel. A quick note on fast-track authority: when a president has this power—which has more recently been rebranded as "trade promotion authority," or TPA—it means that members of Congress can't tinker with, filibuster, or object to specific provisions in proposed trade agreements . . . all they can do is vote yes or no on the final deal that the administration has negotiated. This is an important draw for nations we sign agreements with, as they would be loath to negotiate and grant concessions only to have our lawmakers later fiddle with the terms. Normally, members of Congress hate voting yes or no without an opportunity to object to or amend parts of a proposal they aren't happy with. But they do it for trade deals sometimes, because it speeds up the process and dramatically increases the chances of passage—and when other nations know that our Congress can't tinker with the terms, it induces them to negotiate and make concessions, knowing they will stick. But with both parties largely in favor of free trade by the mid-1980s, hastening these deals was smooth sailing: the House approved fast-track authority for Reagan by a vote of 368–43, while the Senate clocked in at 96–0.[1] By contrast, a 2015 vote on fast-track authority was far less lopsided than it was in the 1980s—the consensus has mostly disappeared.

In 1988, the U.S. and Canada signed a deal known by the phlegm-inducing acronym CUSFTA—the Canada–United States Free Trade Agreement—which accelerated trade, essentially eliminated already low tariffs, and unleashed cross-border competition and investment between the two nations. Not wanting to be left behind in the region, Mexico soon began lobbying for a free trade agreement of its own. The Canadians grew concerned that a U.S.-Mexico deal would undercut the terms of their brand-new agreement with America, and so it was decided that all three countries would negotiate a triangular deal to replace CUSFTA. By the final stretch of the 1992 presidential election, NAFTA had been all but signed—but factions on the wings of each party had already begun to raise concerns.

The campaign had been a strange one, and not only because Americans were unaccustomed to the presence of a serious third-party candidate. With an astronomically high approval rating of 89 percent following the end of the Gulf War in March of 1991, President Bush had looked like a safe bet to cruise to reelection twenty months later. But a sputtering economy, racial unrest set in motion by the high-profile beating of Rodney King by Los Angeles police officers, and the persuasive messaging of the youthful, charismatic Democratic nominee—dark horse Arkansas governor Bill Clinton—quickly decimated Bush's popularity. By the summer of 1992, his approval rating had cratered from the highest number ever recorded by Gallup to one of the lowest: 29 percent.[2]

The wild card, however, was a five-foot-five Texas billionaire named H. Ross Perot. As candidates go, he was one of a kind; a former computer salesman who became the founder of a wildly successful IT and data processing company called EDS (Electronic Data Systems), Perot had no political experience whatsoever when he decided to seek the presidency in 1992. An eccentric libertarian whose platform was largely centered on reducing the federal deficit, Perot was also pro-choice, supported LGBT civil rights, and openly suggested expanding Medicare to cover all Americans decades before the idea would take root even among progressive Democrats. Riding a wave of anti-establishment enthusiasm—and offering something for everyone from his medley of positions—Perot led the race over Bush and Clinton in a June Gallup poll, 39–31–25.[3] A month later, he abruptly halted his campaign, later explaining in a *60 Minutes* interview that he had done so in order to foil a plot by Bush to disrupt his daughter's wedding using computer-altered photographs.[4]

Perot would reenter the race on October 1 after it became clear that he had qualified for the ballot in every state (and after his daughter Carolyn had wed without incident). Though his support had dipped in his absence, he remained an electoral X factor when he took the stage in Richmond alongside Bush and Clinton two weeks later. The debate's first question was directed to Perot; a member of the audience asked him what he planned to do "to open foreign markets to fair competition from American business, and to stop unfair competition here at home from foreign countries so that we can bring jobs back to the United States." In their follow-up answers, the Republican and Democratic candidates would sound somewhat the same—Bush touted NAFTA as a springboard of export-backed U.S. jobs and defended "free and fair trade" as "the thing that saved us," while Clinton spoke of the need to expand America's export base in order to ensure that trade agreements create more new jobs than they drive overseas. Yet it was Perot's response, bucking the orthodoxies of both parties and their candidates, that would garner the most attention:

To those of you in the audience who are business people: pretty simple. If you're paying $12, $13, $14 an hour for a factory worker, and you can move your factory south of the border, pay $1 an hour for labor, hire a young—let's assume you've been in business for a long time. You've got a mature workforce. Pay $1 an hour for your labor, have no health care—that's the most expensive single element in making the car. Have no environmental controls, no pollution controls, and no retirement. And you don't care about anything but making money. There will be a giant sucking sound going south.

Perot went on to capture nearly 19 percent of the vote in the election three weeks later, but the specter of the "giant sucking sound"

"I don't know what the hell happened - One minute I'm at work in Flint, Michigan, then there's a giant sucking sound and suddenly here I am in Mexico."

The debate quip that sucked in a nation.

would echo on long after his departure from the national stage. Despite the support of elected officials in both parties, NAFTA never became the popular darling that first Bush—and later his successor, Clinton—might have hoped. Polling that fall from NBC and *The Wall Street Journal* put support for NAFTA at only 27 percent, versus 34 percent of the public who were opposed. Trumping both sides was "unsure" at 40 percent—a remarkably high number given how prominent NAFTA was as a campaign issue, and a testament to the lack of clear messaging offered by politicians and the media.[5] These camps would level out a year later, after a well-publicized TV debate on the issue between Perot and new vice president Al Gore went poorly for the Texas tycoon.

While George Bush had overseen negotiations and signed the agreement on his way out of office, it was left to Bill Clinton to steer NAFTA through Congress before it could take effect. Hoping to mollify trade skeptics in his own party, the first-year president held off on ratifying the agreement until he could secure a series of side deals with the Mexican government to alleviate environmental and labor concerns. By August of 1993, he had done just that—but the new agreements were derided by environmental groups and labor leaders for not going far enough. Political support for NAFTA was eroding by the day as members of Congress began to increasingly fixate on how it would be perceived purely from a jobs perspective (the "giant sucking sound" phenomenon), despite the fact that the agreement, as we'll explore shortly, was never supposed to be about job creation or protection at all.

In the end, the deal would make it through Congress with margins that were solid, but not entirely comfortable. NAFTA passed the House on November 17, 1993, by a vote of 234–200; with most Democrats voting against it, it was left to the Republican minority to carry it through.[6] The story would repeat itself three days later in the Senate, as the president's party rejected NAFTA

President George H. W. Bush (who bears little resemblance to Bill Clinton no matter how hard you squint) presides over the NAFTA ceremonial signing in San Antonio, Texas, on October 7, 1992. Mexican President Carlos Salinas stands left, and Canadian Prime Minister Brian Mulroney stands right. Seated are Canadian Ambassador Derek Burney, U.S. Trade Representative Carla Hills, and Mexican Ambassador Gustavo Petricioli.

by a single vote, only for the Republicans to vote in favor by a margin of more than three to one.[7] NAFTA would become the law of the land on New Year's Day 1994—and forever after, in the eyes of the American public, its legacy would fall squarely on the shoulders of a president who, though ultimately supportive of the deal, had neither proposed it, negotiated it, nor signed it, and whose party had rejected it in both houses of Congress.

Why NAFTA?

For all of the ink spilled, fists clenched, and campaigns waged around NAFTA, one important question never seems to get addressed: what was the point of it? We know that NAFTA's proponents weren't thinking about jobs when they envisioned a continental free trade zone; we also know that the daunting prospect of an economically powerful European Union loomed large in their imaginations. For what it's worth, the agreement itself lists six specific purposes for its own existence:

- ☑ To eliminate trade barriers and facilitate trade between the three countries;
- ☑ To promote fair competition in the region;
- ☑ To open the door for cross-border investment opportunities;
- ☑ To ramp up protection and enforcement around intellectual property;
- ☑ To establish a process for dispute resolution; and
- ☑ To create "a framework for further trilateral . . . cooperation to expand and enhance the benefits" of the deal.[8]

These objectives are all well and good—and the agreement has inarguably furthered each of them. But the true goals of NAFTA were more complicated than that, likely having just as much to do with regional unrest as they did economics.

The decade leading up to NAFTA's passage had not been the easiest time for Latin America. A boom in the 1960s and '70s had prompted rapidly developing countries like Mexico, Argentina, and Brazil to invest heavily in infrastructure and industry; to finance those investments, each country took out large loans from foreign commercial banks. A global recession in the mid-1970s prevented countries from repaying those loans. When oil prices plummeted, the peso collapsed in turn, leaving the petroleum-reliant Mexican economy in shambles. High taxes on the revenues of Pemex have provided about a third of all the tax revenues collected by the Mexican government; in short order, things had gone sour for them by the middle of the 1980s.

As so often happens when neighboring countries see their fortunes move in opposite directions, the Mexican debt crisis provoked new tensions along America's southern border. The "illegal" immigration of Mexicans—a concept that had literally not even existed twenty years earlier, before the first laws were put in place limiting entry from the south[9]—made its way into the national discourse for the first time in U.S. history. It becomes a minor campaign issue in 1984,[10] and, like clockwork, no sooner does it penetrate the political atmosphere than the American people begin to increasingly and unfairly associate their southern neighbors with drugs and crime. Though the collapse of the Mexican economy did exacerbate both concerns (just as every economic downturn does in every country), it is a safe bet that America's isolationist streak and suspicion of foreigners had a lot to do with the shift in our perspective of Mexico in the 1980s and '90s.

Fairly or not, fears about drug smuggling and a steep climb in the U.S. violent crime rate beginning in the early 1980s were certainly on the minds of many politicians as they considered their position on America's relationship with Mexico. And, putting aside any impact it might have on the home front, a free trade agreement was likely to do wonders for the Mexican economy—gaining access to U.S. markets would help them boost GDP and lift themselves out of their debt crisis, while integration with the American and Canadian economies would be a stabilizing force for the long haul. By increasing Mexico's prosperity, the U.S. could help neuter drug trafficking at its root and stem the flow of migrants crossing the southern border in search of opportunity; as Mexican president Carlos Salinas de Gortari memorably put it, in NAFTA, Americans faced a "choice between getting Mexican tomatoes or tomato pickers."[11] Of course, a stronger partnership between Washington and Mexico City would further ease tensions along our 2,000-mile border, and elevate Mexico as an American ally on the world stage. The U.S., in essence, was like a homeowner seeking to increase her own property value by offering tools to help her neighbor make home improvements—a bit of a paternalistic stance, to be sure, but an effective strategy nonetheless.

In the wide variety of issues it was created to address—curbing migration, containing illegal drugs, stabilizing Mexico, gaining access to more customers for American farmers, uniting the continent to compete with Europe on exports—NAFTA perfectly demonstrated the impressive versatility of trade as a tool for achieving our national goals. But just as all roads lead to Rome, it turns out that all political issues lead to jobs. No matter how successful the agreement may have been in delivering on both its stated and unstated objectives, that one metric—the number of jobs it created and destroyed, which was never supposed to be part of the official NAFTA calculus—would soon become the sole arbiter of whether the deal would be considered an American triumph or a toxic stain on our history.

So How Did It Go?

As you've probably gathered by now, determining the success of NAFTA depends entirely on what it is that you're measuring for. If we're to take the agreement at its word and focus simply on the six objectives it sets out for itself, the only conclusion we can reasonably draw is that NAFTA came through on its goals with flying colors. The United States, Canada, and Mexico now represent the largest free trade area in the world in terms of GDP, and each country has become substantially more competitive in the global economy since the agreement was signed. Relations among the trio have grown stronger over time (until recently, of course . . . but more on that later), while trade flows freely and frequently throughout the region, with Canada and Mexico remaining among America's top import and export partners—and vice versa—consistently over the last twenty-five years. In fact, the first decade of NAFTA's existence saw total trade between the three nations more than double, from $306 billion to $621 billion, growing everybody's economy and lowering U.S. consumer prices due to the influx of new imports.[12] This has been an especially welcome development among American farmers (a constituency that has been supportive of NAFTA and other trade deals), who now export globally more than 20 percent of what they harvest.[13]

In the context of global leadership, it's equally difficult to make the case that NAFTA has fallen short of its unspoken aims. The U.S. has warded off threats from the EU and China to remain the world's largest economy, and all three of the NAFTA countries have thrived as exporting heavyweights in the years following its passage. Canada and Mexico would eventually join the U.S. as top ten worldwide exporters—and those export-backed economies would be instrumental in helping each nation recover from the global financial crisis of 2008. Globally, the strength and stability of the region helped cement America's position as an economic superpower, enabling the U.S. to spread its influence to new parts of the world. Between 1994 and 2012, we would sign separate trade agreements with five Central American nations plus the Dominican Republic (CAFTA-DR), as well as with South Korea, Australia, Chile, Morocco, Colombia, Peru, Panama, Jordan, Oman, Bahrain, and Singapore—agreements that have delivered millions of new customers to U.S. businesses and farmers, and that gave us the chance to transmit our values by raising labor, environmental, and human rights standards on four continents. When we signed

NAFTA, we were ahead of the curve: there were fewer than a dozen free trade agreements in force around the world. Today, we are arguably behind it—though we have agreements in place with twenty countries, there are now more than *400* agreements in effect globally. Putting our relative idleness on free trade agreements aside, the point still stands: without NAFTA and the wave of free trade it precipitated, America would absolutely not have been positioned to keep pace with China and Europe as players of consequence in the global arena in recent years.

It goes without saying that immigration and drug trafficking have lingered as political issues in the United States after NAFTA. But while U.S. politicians have made a habit of blaming Mexican migrants for all manner of problems—both real and imagined—the truth is that both legal and illegal immigration from Mexico has dropped dramatically in the wake of the agreement.[14] In fact, over the last decade the number of Mexicans crossing the border into America has actually been smaller than the number crossing in the other direction. While the steep decline in Mexican immigration can't be solely attributed to NAFTA, the cultivation of Mexico as a formidable economic state with a healthy middle class, flourishing businesses, and a stable civil society probably deserves the lion's share of the credit—and there is no question that the trade deal was critical to fostering that growth, particularly once the 1994 Mexican peso crisis abated and NAFTA's benefits began to kick in.

That leaves us with jobs. Generally speaking, economists can agree that there are many benefits of trade: lower prices, more innovation, better international relationships, and so on. But it's hard to find an economist who thinks that free trade agreements are a truly effective tool for creating more jobs—they'll tell you that *trade* creates jobs, but not necessarily *free trade agreements* on their own. Despite that, as we now know, jobs are nevertheless the one issue that would come to define NAFTA's legacy. Ross Perot, the man most responsible for re-centering the NAFTA conversation around visions of idle autoworkers and abandoned factories, started the ball rolling with his prediction that the trade agreement would cost the U.S. an astonishing 5.9 million jobs—or about one of every twenty American jobs in existence at the time.[15] More recently, Senator Bernie Sanders accused NAFTA of costing 800,000 job losses nationwide in an exchange with Secretary of State Hillary Clinton during a 2016 Democratic primary debate in Flint, Michigan.[16] In 2018, after years spent referring to the agreement as "the worst deal in the history of the world," President Trump threw out the number of jobs lost due to NAFTA at "millions" in an interview with Sean Hannity.[17] And, lest we think that these dire assessments are in any way limited to the outmost wings of each party, even then-candidate Barack Obama once told a crowd in Lorain, Ohio, during the 2008 campaign that "one million jobs have been lost because of NAFTA. . . . I don't think NAFTA has been good for America—and I never have,"[18] a position he would later soften. His opponent at the time, one Hillary Clinton, also spent much of the 2008 primary distancing herself from the trade deal that had come into force during her husband's administration. While Republican leaders have historically faced less pressure to speak out against NAFTA due to not having to court the votes of labor, that, too, is rapidly changing: Republican *voters* have begun to oppose NAFTA at much, much higher rates than their Democratic counterparts.[19]

Perhaps most consequentially, the now quarter-century-long backlash to NAFTA has politicized trade in new, frequently nonsensical ways. The deal (like all trade deals) created winners and losers in the U.S. economy and earned its share of perfectly legitimate gripes, of course. But it also had the bad fortune of having been written on flypaper—or at least it feels like it was, since it has somehow managed to absorb twenty-five years' worth of blame for the effects of automation, innovation, and the emergence of the global workforce.

It's no surprise that NAFTA has turned into a punching bag for politicians to trot out every election cycle. For the last quarter century, candidates for office have been confronted by scenes similar to one Secretary Clinton encountered in February of 2008; campaigning in the tiny Appalachian town of Hanging Rock, Ohio, a fifty-three-year-old man working three jobs to make ends meet told her that "NAFTA is taking its toll. . . . It's absolutely devastated this county. It's just economically depressed. Manufacturing is void."[20] Across the Midwest, which today produces a larger share of the world's electoral votes than it does steel, politicians who fail to adequately denounce NAFTA can pretty much count on joining the ranks of the unemployed. The idea that the trade agreement shuttered factories and hollowed out working-class towns from Altoona to Oshkosh is more than just a theory there—it's the gospel truth.

Let's be clear from the outset: the pain felt by those communities is real. Many manufacturing jobs were indeed lost in the years since 1994; at least 80,000 industrial plants went dark in the two decades that followed, largely concentrated in the Midwest.[21] These are human tragedies—every single displaced job contains its own private tragedy of dreams diminished, of families thrown into uncertainty, of neighborhoods made weaker and dignity demeaned. The people whose lives have been blown about by job loss are justified for harboring resentments, for wanting answers, or even for pointing fingers. If those fingers have landed on the wrong culprit—and the question is an open one—the fault lies squarely with the politicians, media personalities, and interest groups who had the opportunity to tell them the whole truth, but discovered that it was easier not to. Some of those people in a position to be truthful may have believed that as the economy grew, it would naturally absorb those lost jobs—and it did, in a sense, just not the same jobs in the same places. Some may have just preferred not to deal with the cost and political messiness of taking care of displaced workers. Maybe it was a little bit "magical thinking"; maybe it was a little bit cynicism. Maybe there was a little bit of "pull yourself up by your bootstraps" ethos thrown in for good measure. Either way, the confluence of those attitudes certainly didn't help.

NAFTA's long second act as a scapegoat was made possible by the fact that it is impossible to accurately calculate the number of jobs lost or gained due to a trade agreement—rest assured, anyone who tells you otherwise is trying to sell you something (whereas I have nothing left to sell you now that you have presumably purchased this book). Economics is *famously* convoluted, and the forces controlling it have never been more complex at any time or place in history as they are right now in the United States of America. With hundreds of interconnected factors in play, we can never state with total certainty the exact reason for why jobs come or go—not in a world where technologies, tax incentives, currency fluctuations, interest rates, and even climate patterns can influence industry decisions. What we *can* do is examine the available evidence, look at trend lines, and analyze cause and effect in order to paint the best picture we can of what's been happening to U.S. jobs these past few decades.

We can start with what isn't in dispute: overall jobs, wages, and manufacturing output all increased substantially in the years after NAFTA. Beginning in 1994, wages in the U.S. manufacturing sector rose by 14.4 percent over the next decade (for context, they had risen at less than half of that rate, 6.5 percent, in the decade leading up to the agreement).[22] Manufacturing output climbed by 44 percent through the year 2000, and overall U.S. employment rose by more than 20 million between the dawn of NAFTA and the close of the millennium—even as those dreaded cheap imports from Mexico flooded into the marketplace.[23] If the late Ross Perot were reading this right now, he would probably be banging his head against the wall, screaming that the booming economy of the 1990s was all about the rise of the computer age, and had nothing to do with NAFTA. To that, I'd say he's mostly right—our economic growth was indeed sparked in significant measure by the ascent of the dot-coms and internet-powered financial services. But at the same time, inherent in NAFTA's calculus of winners and losers was the belief that what was best for the U.S. economy overall was facilitating the growth of higher-paying, higher-tech sectors in exchange for ceding ground on lower-paying, lower-tech industries. The dawn of electricity brought major economic progress, too—but it also hurt candlemakers. For better or worse, the prosperous 1990s were actually a potent demonstration of what the economy could look like when U.S. trade policy was weighted in favor of emerging fields rather than traditional ones.

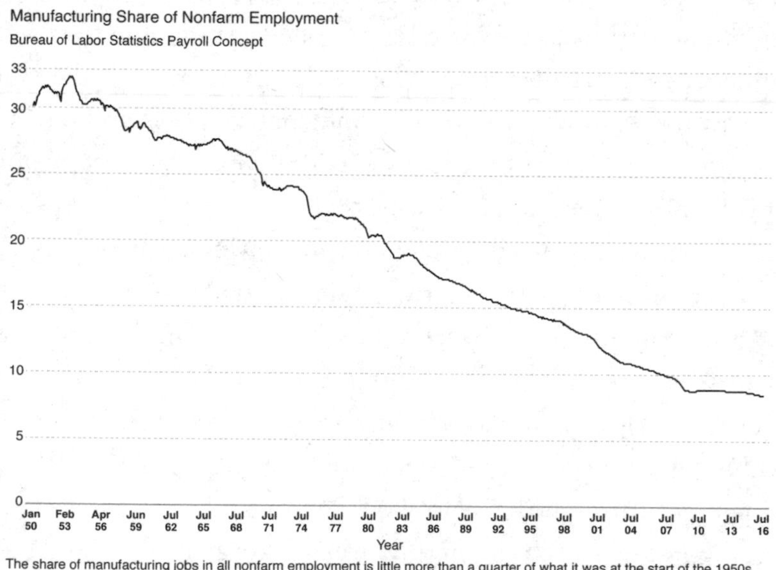

NAFTA: a trade deal so devastating that it started to destroy U.S. manufacturing jobs forty years before it came into existence.

The impact of NAFTA on manufacturing *jobs*—as distinguished from manufacturing output—is far less clear. Two charts help tell the story here. Take a look at the first chart above, which tracks manufacturing jobs as a percentage of all U.S. employment between 1950 and 2016. Without looking at the years along the bottom of the graph, can you spot the moment when NAFTA took effect?

Neither can I. While it's certainly possible that, without NAFTA, the steady decline of the manufacturing sector as a source of American jobs would have plateaued or somehow reversed itself, there's simply no substance to the argument that the deal created (or, frankly, even exacerbated) a problem that wasn't already in existence. "Now wait just one doggone Texas minute," Ross Perot might say to this, "what about *this* chart, which tracks the *total number* of U.S. manufacturing jobs rather than the share of manufacturing jobs as a percentage of overall employment?" Very well—let's have a look:

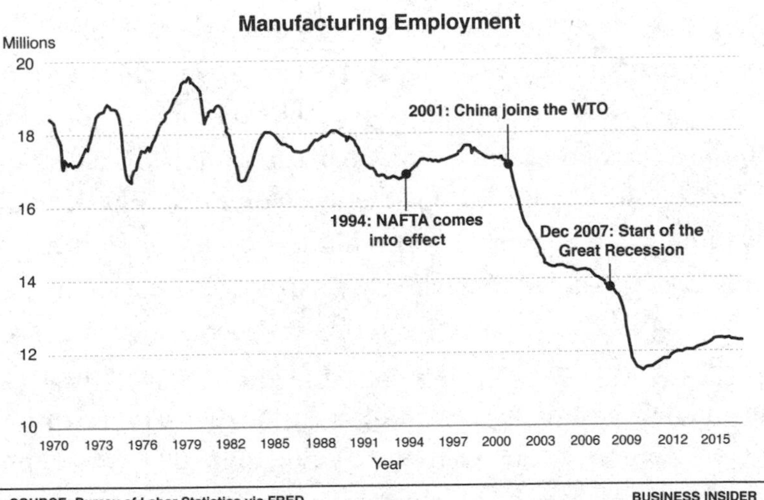

A murkier picture.

Our first chart shows an uninterrupted half-century-long decline in our manufacturing sector. Our second chart suggests a different story—one in which America begins hemorrhaging manufacturing jobs a handful of years after NAFTA comes into effect. But together, a new interpretation emerges. Manufacturing was already requiring fewer and fewer workers to get the job done—a phenomenon set in motion by advances in technology and automation. Consider this: today, with less than 10 percent of the U.S. workforce involved in manufacturing, we are producing more goods than we did in 1950, when more than 30 percent of workers made their living in manufacturing jobs. And that's a *good* thing—American manufacturing workers are more productive today than at any time in our history. NAFTA doesn't change that trend—the share of U.S. jobs engaged in manufacturing keeps declining. What it does is introduce a trade-off: as the loss of U.S. manufacturing jobs is accelerated, new jobs in rising sectors take their place.

If this is indeed the case, it's cold comfort to the lathe operator whose job moved overseas a decade before it might have otherwise been phased out by technology or other shifts in the market. For her, that's ten lost years of paychecks to send a child to college or take care of an aging parent—and the exciting new job opportunities that were created over that time probably didn't exist in her specific county. But for the workforce as a whole, trading away jobs in a declining sector for higher-paying jobs in areas that are *gaining* ground is an obviously smart move—the lathe operator may or may not be able to retrain for a second career as a solar panel technician or a programmer of 3D printers, but trade policies can help ensure that *some* American will. Once more, by helping to determine which sectors are vulnerable to foreign imports and which will have access to lucrative export opportunities, trade comes back as it always does to the creation of winners and losers.

The thing is, a growing economy will *always* create winners and losers—some products and sectors are always going to fall in and out of favor, just like certain cuisines do over time. All trade can really do is accelerate that process or slow it down by tinkering with supply—say, by making a deal that allows foreign competitors to enter the U.S. marketplace—and demand—by opening up an overseas market and its customers to American goods.

It's never easy to determine why winners and losers are created in the economy—and it's doubly hard once you factor in trade, because then you're factoring in the whole world! Because of that, we'll never know exactly how much the losers lost and the winners won because of NAFTA, or how much of what happened next was preordained much earlier by forces even larger than trade. Here, though, is what some of the most objective observers have to say. The popular perception of NAFTA leading directly to an increase in plant closures or a decrease in "made-in-America" industry is one that economists reject; in fact, factories shut down at essentially the same rate before NAFTA as they did after it.[24] U.S. industrial production grew by nearly 50 percent in the dozen years after NAFTA, even though it had grown by only about half that rate in the dozen years prior.[25] In 2015, the nonpartisan Congressional Research Service—an arm of the legislative branch long celebrated for its neutrality and credibility—issued a report on NAFTA assessing and synthesizing the findings of a wide breadth of studies that had come before. Their bottom line was not a bang, but a whimper: "In reality, NAFTA did not cause the huge job losses feared by the critics or the large economic gains predicted by supporters. The net overall effect of NAFTA on the U.S. economy appears to have been relatively modest."[26]

So What's with All the Commotion?

It's certainly the case that NAFTA's impact on the everyday lives of most Americans hasn't been anywhere close to as meaningful as, say, laws on overtime pay, the home mortgage deduction, or, frankly, our routine trade with China. No matter how you slice it, it's extremely likely that the only way the agreement has directly altered your day-to-day life is in the form of lower prices in the produce aisle or the car dealership. Let's take the most extreme anti-NAFTA claims at face value—say, the (baseless) charge levied by Donald Trump and others that the deal was responsible for a million lost jobs. That would amount to 40,000 jobs displaced per year since the agreement took effect. Over that same quarter century span, the U.S. added an average of just over 1.5 million jobs per year,[27] rendering that 40,000 loss relatively minor even before you account for jobs *created* by NAFTA, workers who lost a manufacturing job only to find work in another sector, and the positive impact on all workers caused by lower prices on everyday goods.

So if all NAFTA really did here at home was rearrange a few deck chairs, why then has it endured as one of America's tallest and most frequently zapped lightning rods for so many years? Part of that is due to the fact that wages have been slow to grow for decades in America—people naturally want something to blame. The country has created many more jobs than it has lost since NAFTA, but for workers concentrated in the hardest-hit areas, the new jobs that showed up didn't always offer the same wages, the same dignity, or the same sense of identity and purpose. Another part of the NAFTA blame game, though, is due to the ambiguity of economics and the poorly understood nature of trade. Most of us have very little knowledge of what trade agreements actually do, and better things to spend our time on than learning more about a complex and dry subject. Unfortunately, that gets exacerbated when our leaders fail to explain what the advantages of a policy might be. On a recent visit to Mexico, I heard over and over again from government officials and business leaders who lamented that U.S. politicians never made an effort to inform Americans about the benefits of NAFTA—we "left it on autopilot," as they put it, and are suffering the consequences today. When we lack firsthand knowledge of how a policy works, it makes it much easier for politicians to tell ghost stories about that policy in order to manipulate us in whichever direction they choose. The Affordable Care Act, for example, was deeply unpopular back when people were inundated with claims that it would institute death panels for grandma and grandpa, but as people gained personal experience with its actual effects, opinion turned sharply in its favor.

Trade deals never get the opportunity to introduce their real selves to the public in the form of free preventive health services or coverage for preexisting conditions, however. Studies have shown that clothing prices dropped by an estimated 7.5 percent after NAFTA[28]—let's be real: no shopper takes a moment to thank free trade for letting them buy an extra sweater. Instead, they think, "what a smart, savvy, shopper I am!" The savings that come from trade aren't put up on giant signs the way that shifting gas prices are, either—it's almost impossible for us to know when they've kicked in. Couple that with how difficult it is to prove causation for jobs gained or lost, and you have the perfect recipe for a political football. Politicians can, from time to time, claim that two plus two equals five—and some are embarrassed for being that shameless—but they have much more freedom to attribute all kinds of employment trends to NAFTA because, who knows, they *could* be right. After all, did you know that ever since

NAFTA was implemented, jobs for switchboard operators, travel agents, and Rick Moranis have been in steep decline? Damn you, NAFTA—is there nothing you won't destroy?!

While the murkiness of economic cause and effect and a general lack of interest among the public have made it easy for politicians to spin whatever NAFTA tales they wish, the biggest reason for the deal's longevity in our politics has to do with the who, what, and where of the workers it really did displace. Had NAFTA caused 100,000 restaurant workers in California, child care professionals in Mississippi, or lawyers in Massachusetts to lose their jobs over the course of twenty-five years, there is simply no chance that our political leaders would still be talking about it today. That the "losers" of the deal happened to largely consist of production workers in factories in electorally important states is enormously important to the NAFTA story, whether it makes us uncomfortable to admit it or not. Don't believe me? How many times have you heard politicians—including, but certainly not limited to, Donald Trump—expound on the plight of coal miners? How many borderline-romantic articles have been written about the fate of U.S. steelworkers?

Would it surprise you to learn that current estimates place the total number of Americans working in the coal industry at 50,800[29], and the total number of steelworkers at 140,000?[30] Yet in the retail sector, which accounts for nearly 16 million U.S. jobs and approximately zero percent of political conversations, 129,000 women—just women—were displaced in one year as recently as 2017 due to shuttered stores and the continued rise of online shopping.[31] There's an ugly truth at play here, which is that the job losses we tend to pay attention to as a society are almost always predominantly white and male. White men had something close to a monopoly on manufacturing jobs for many years, and as women and people of color gained greater educational opportunities and began to join the manufacturing workforce, that monopoly was broken up. That change happened to coincide with a period when wages stopped rising. And as many white men grappled with an erosion of status and power, the unfortunate reality is that many began to conflate the two trends, only one of which—stagnant wages—ought to have been seen as a threat. We see this still today, as hard feelings continue to brew among so many working-class white men who lump together economic resentment of trade and automation with cultural resentment of women, minorities, and immigrants seeking equal opportunity. The truth is that women and people of color have become more adaptable in our changing economy because they've had to be—they know that they won't get nearly as much attention paid to their plight. There is an element of white male privilege (and, full disclosure: I am one of those white males) that says "I shouldn't *have* to be adaptable—the world should adapt to *me*!" Though it isn't fair, we should acknowledge that there is a humongous gap between the attention we pay to a lone factory shutting down versus a dozen retail outlets shutting down—and, before long, it will be the only Gap left.

Put together, these factors can help explain why NAFTA has hung around in our national consciousness for so long, and why it has become the ultimate Rorschach test for both voters and politicians. It's been more symbol than substance since its inception, in fact: when the oldest sawmill in the country closed its doors in 1995 after conservation efforts resulted in it losing access to two thirds of its timber supply, politicians cited it as an example of NAFTA's cruelty (said the mill's former manager, Jerry Clark, "We didn't have any logs. . . . If anyone can find some legitimate connection to NAFTA in this, I'd sure like to see it").[32] The U.S. government even certified claims of NAFTA-related job losses for 874 workers who had been laid off when their factory moved to Mexico . . . in 1992, two years before the agreement took effect.[33] Like Bigfoot or the Abominable Snowman, NAFTA has seemingly always been out there in the wilderness, snatching up unsuspecting jobs in the dead of night.

For the last twenty-five years, during which time it has been an issue in every single election cycle, the vast majority of politicians have railed against the deal in order to win votes. And for a quarter of a century, those same politicians have done absolutely nothing but defend it once in office. Even Donald Trump, who could make a case to be the most prominent anti-NAFTA politician of all time (with apologies to you, Ross Perot), has followed this pattern. After years spent promising to alternately tear up or "renegotiate" NAFTA, in October of 2018 the White House announced that it had agreed to terms with the Mexican and Canadian governments on a successor to NAFTA: the United States-Mexico-Canada Agreement, or USMCA. Despite Trump's assurances that this was a "brand new deal," the USMCA does nothing to alter the underlying logic of NAFTA. It modernizes some provisions. It strengthens country-of-origin rules to help keep some inexpensive Asian auto parts out of North American supply chains. And it updates labor, digital, and intellectual property protections—essentially, it accomplishes with Canada and Mexico what the TPP deal that Trump pulled America out of had hoped to do with our Pacific allies (even lifting language nearly verbatim from the much maligned agreement). What the USMCA doesn't do is take a dramatic new stance on the side of American machinists or factory foremen. It is a replacement for NAFTA in much the same sense that the iPhone 8 was a replacement for the iPhone 7—a welcome update, but hardly a bold new direction.

It remains to be seen whether the USMCA's most crucial innovation—changing the name of the agreement—will excise

NAFTA from our political universe once and for all. That's not to say that the name change lacks significance! In March of 2019, I spoke with the recently appointed Mexican ambassador to the United States, Martha Bárcena. She astutely observed that replacing "North America" with the names of each country in the agreement was more than just a cosmetic change: it signaled a change in philosophy, from one of promoting prosperity and common goals across the continent to one that put the United States ahead of the other two parties in the agreement. Whatever becomes of the new NAFTA, it is a safe bet that politicians will not miraculously decide to start being up front about the trade-offs of trade deals. At the time that NAFTA was signed, there were a number of good strategic reasons for its passage that would prove beneficial to America and Americans over the long run. Realizing those benefits would hurt factory workers in many communities, we did not allow ourselves to be honest about the deal we were making—we glossed over the losses, and, later, turned around and pointed fingers. We could have done better, and we should have.

From NAFTA to China

On December 3, the president of the United States complained that America's recent tensions with China "spring from the antiforeign agitation which . . . lies deep in the character of the Chinese races and in the traditions of their Government," and, frustrated by China's response to trends in global commerce, called for "the adoption of measures insuring [*sic*] the benefits of equality of treatment of all foreign trade throughout China" in order to avoid "the imminence of peril to our own diversified interests." You'd be forgiven for assuming that these were the words of Donald Trump—in fact, they were delivered on December 3, 1900, as part of the fourth State of the Union address of President William McKinley.[34]

America's suspicious attitude toward China is as old as America itself, and has always been tied in—then and now—with ugly western stereotypes about the character of the Chinese people. Relatively isolated for much of the last two centuries, China's reputation for insularity and dormant power had endured long past the time when Napoleon was said to have delivered his famous assessment: "There lies a sleeping giant. Let him sleep! For when he wakes, he will move the world." As it turns out, Napoleon was right. China began to slowly reform its economic system following the death of Mao Zedong in 1976, setting the stage for a momentous awakening over the course of the decades to come—and scaring American politicians ever since.

What's different about China, from our perspective, is that for the first time in our history we're facing a true political *and* economic adversary all wrapped up in the same country—and that makes dealing with them much more complicated. Our economies depend on one another; we're going to have to figure out how to work together. We can label them a villain if we want, but they're a villain whose evolution over the course of this century has delivered substantial economic benefits to themselves. And let's not forget that they have also reduced the cost of living and held inflation in check—not to mention been a major customer—for their number one trading partner: the United States.

As we'll explore in the pages ahead, the grievances that lingered after NAFTA have shaped American politics ever since; Donald Trump did not create them, but he did take advantage of them to win the presidency. Nor are those grievances entirely unfair. Free trade agreements have made it easier for companies to globalize, and that has undoubtedly led businesses to become less invested in the strength of their hometown communities.

Companies can more credibly threaten to move overseas if they don't like the way that labor negotiations are going, while their ties to local schools, 4-H clubs, church groups, and so forth were weakened as a result of globalization, and this in turn loosened their ties to their neighbors. Today, our failure to tell the whole truth about that story still colors the way we approach the most important trade issue of our time: the rise of China. Whatever its fate in the years ahead, NAFTA will remain among the most important inflection points in U.S. political history, not because our policy changed—we were free traders before it, and we will be free traders long after—but because it brought jobs into the conversation unlike ever before, forever changing the way Americans think about trade.

CHAPTER 3

A Myth-Busting Interlude

In every aspect of our lives, there are myths that build up over time—stories and assumptions that get passed down as conventional wisdom, but aren't backed up by facts. It turns out that trade is no different. There are a number of stubborn myths floating around out there, let loose into the ether by politicians and interest groups who stand to benefit from keeping us ill-informed about trade. Before we venture out further into our story, we should take a moment to dispatch with those persistent myths once and for all, before they can further pollute our understanding of how trade works. Here, then, are eight of the most wrongheaded, infuriating, counterproductive fallacies that we tend to latch on to when it comes to the subject at hand.

Myth #1:
China Is Always a Villain When It Comes to Trade

China's entry into the World Trade Organization in 2001 turned out to be perhaps the most significant event in modern economic history. For China, joining the WTO put them on a level playing field with other economic powers, allowing them to trade and export on the same terms as everybody else. At the time, the western powers hoped that formally integrating China into the global marketplace would lead to the liberalization of its economy and ultimately make the country more democratic. This would prove to be at least a little bit true: the formerly closed country has now become our third largest trading partner behind Canada and Mexico, one of the top sources of tourism to America, and has begun to abide by some of the global trade rules and norms it had once flouted to win business.

That initial progress caused many to let out a sigh of relief—but then, something unexpected happened. While we were distracted in the early 2000s by the Iraq War, we didn't notice how aggressively China was moving on exports. Within a decade, they would pass us and Germany to become the number one exporter in the world. Before long, any hopes we harbored that China would emulate the West mostly vanished. They developed their own model—one marked by heavy-handed government engagement in the economy—and to our surprise, unlike the Soviet Union, they prospered as a result. They introduced concepts like private property and entrepreneurship, yet they have continued to lag behind in terms of personal freedom and liberty, as well as human and political rights—something that we did not fully anticipate. Rightly or wrongly, we believed that capitalism and freedom went hand in hand. It turned out not to be true. By the time the financial crisis struck in 2008, it was harder for us to argue that a thriving China or anyone else for that matter should be following our economic model.

For the most part, in attempting to influence China, what caught the world off guard was China's incredible capacity to influence the world instead. With the largest workforce on the planet, giant state-owned enterprises, and a desire to dominate high-value manufacturing sectors, it took very little time for China to become a formidable competitor for export business. That's been especially true in developing economies in need of new roads, airports, power plants, ports, mobile phone systems, and the like. China's big comparative advantage—remember, that's the edge a country has in some aspect of economic productivity which forms the basis of all trade—turned out to be price. Their price advantage, coupled with a large number of available workers, meant that China's entry into the WTO had a much bigger impact than that of other countries. And because of its size and the unique structure of its economy, the world has discovered that China has more tools at its disposal to corner markets than the rest of us do.

To give one example, consider this. The Export-Import Bank of the United States, which I ran from 2009 to 2017, is the American agency responsible for equipping U.S. exporters with financing. If Aquatech, a small clean-water treatment business in Pittsburgh, wants to sell wastewater technology to customers in Asia and Latin America, they need competitive financing to do it. But many businesses can't get that financing from commercial banks if their sales are too large, too small, or too risky—when that happens, they can look to EXIM for the government-backed insurance or loan guarantees they need to compete against foreign rivals. EXIM has done this work since 1934, and in all that time, the total amount of financing that the U.S. has provided for American exporters—more than eighty-five years' worth—was still less than the amount that China's four export credit agencies provided for Chinese exporters *between 2013 and 2014 alone*. So if a Chinese company is going up against an American company to sell locomotives to India, the Chinese company enters that competition equipped with an attractive, government-guaranteed financing package—giving it a major advantage right off the bat.

This aggressive export strategy has furthered the image of China as a trade villain, as have some of the other tactics it uses to gain an edge. Donald Trump is among those who have accused the Chinese of currency manipulation. What is currency manipulation? Simply put, it's when a government buys up large amounts of other countries' currencies to lower the value of *their* currency. Why would you do that? Well, it makes your goods less expensive in export markets, while making imported goods cost more in your country. Though China may have engaged in currency manipulation at one point, the consensus today is that their currency is fairly priced. China has also made liberal use of subsidies and a number of questionable practices in order to tilt the playing field in their favor: they require foreign companies who do business in the country to hand over technology and share their intellectual property—and they get away with it because, with nearly 1.4 billion people, they've got an enticing market that no foreign business wants to miss out on. They also provide low-cost loans to their own state-owned companies, and make it very difficult for foreign companies to bid on government projects—although, to be fair, we aren't much better on that last front. Most of our 50 states and many cities do entice businesses to operate inside their borders, but our federal government doesn't hand out subsidies the way that the Chinese government does. Combine that with the enormous scale of the economic threat they pose and a dash of long-standing xenophobia, and you have a perfect recipe for American politicians to paint China as underhanded.

It isn't just Donald Trump, either. Massachusetts Senator Elizabeth Warren has accused China of "demanding a hostage price of access to U.S. technology,"[1] a sentiment that Senator Bernie Sanders has echoed as well.[2] Chuck Schumer, the leader of the Senate Democrats, endorsed Trump's tariffs on China,[3] while fellow Democratic senator Ron Wyden has declared that China "has stolen our intellectual property, held American companies hostage until they disclose their trade secrets, and manipulated their markets . . . to rip off American jobs and industries."[4] Across the aisle, Republican senator John Cornyn has lambasted China for "circumventing our laws and exploiting investment opportunities for nefarious purposes."[5]

Have some of China's maneuvers gone too far? From an American perspective, yes—and plenty of other countries agree with us on that. In previous presidential administrations, we tended to give China a bit of a pass on how they do business because we needed their cooperation on other critical matters, such as handling North Korea, Iran, and climate change. Because building consensus on those sorts of issues is far less important to Donald Trump, he has felt free to take a harder line on some of China's trade tactics. But while Trump has made unfortunate, repeated, graphic assertions that China is "raping this country" on trade,[6] the reality is that America has *intentionally* ceded ground under his watch. Leaving the Trans-Pacific Partnership is the clearest demonstration of how America has walked away from a leadership role in global trade—we have abandoned our historic role of writing the rules of the road. Now, the Trump administration could push back by claiming that the president's approach *is* an effort to set the terms of trade: by making demands of China and threatening to impose tariffs if they fail to comply, he is attempting to change their behavior. Globally, everyone agrees that we want China to be a better actor, engaging in trade in ways that are more consistent with other industrialized nations. Up to now, the U.S. has done this in partnership with allies, and has provided leadership to guide the way. Under Donald Trump, the preference has been for America to go it alone (without pesky allies who might muddy things up) by using tariffs rather than joint action as the chief tool for influencing China. This reminds me of one of my favorite Winston Churchill quotes, which I saw inscribed in the Imperial War Museum on a recent trip to London: "There is only one thing worse than fighting with allies, and that is fighting without them."

We should not be surprised, then, that China chooses to operate by a different set of rules—why would they abide by rules that they had no role in creating and that we haven't insisted on enforcing? Fair or not, China has bet their future on exports; behavior our politicians call treacherous is, from their perspective, simply what's necessary to survive and prosper.

Myth #2: Bilateral Trade Deficits Matter

When it comes to our second myth, it isn't terribly difficult to figure out the person most responsible for spreading it around. As of the end of 2018, President Trump has tweeted about trade deficits thirty-seven times—that's more than he has tweeted about wages, Medicare, or his son Eric.[7] When he does tweet about trade deficits, he almost always appends the adjective "massive" to the phrase; he has cited trade deficits with China, Canada, and other nations as "killing our manufacturing sector," "costing Americans millions of jobs," "hurt[ing] the economy very badly," "one of our greatest national security threats," and evidence that countries are "robbing us blind" and "stealing our jobs." Five days after the 2016 Pulse nightclub shooting that took the lives of forty-nine people, Trump ended an especially ominous tweet with the lines: "Biggest trade deficit in many years! More attacks will follow Orlando." In speeches, statements, and Twitter dispatches before and after being elected, he has frequently blamed real and imagined trade deficits for an impossibly wide variety of challenges, often noting that he "will fix it fast—JOBS!"

But one tweet in particular, dating all the way back to the more innocent age of 2012, stands out as the most revealing: "'Right now, we are running a massive $300 billion trade deficit with China. That means every year. China is making almost $300 billion off the United States.' TimeToGetTough."[8] Looking back on this claim, it becomes easy to spot Trump's fundamental misunderstanding of what trade deficits are—a view that has no doubt been casually adopted by millions of Americans who automatically (and understandably) associate "deficits" with bad news. Trump confirmed this misapprehension while defending his proposed steel and aluminum tariffs in the spring of 2018, telling reporters in reference to our various trade deficits that "we lost, over the last number of years, $800 billion a year . . . . We got to [*sic*] get it back."[9]

It's hard to blame a person—any person—who knows little about trade for hearing the term "trade deficit" and assuming that it equates to lost money. I certainly once thought that bilateral trade deficits mattered as well—let's face it, the word "deficit" never connotes a positive. After all, the far more popular "budget deficit" is, indeed, a way of describing a financial shortfall. But a trade deficit is something else entirely: it simply describes the difference between the value of goods and services a country imports and the value of the things that it exports. Importing more from a given country than we export to it is not a measure of strength, weakness, solvency, fiscal irresponsibility, or anything else—nor is our money "lost" when we do so. As conservative trade expert Scott Lincicome put it to *The New York Times*, running a trade deficit with another country "doesn't really tell you anything about what the economy is doing, just like my bilateral deficit with my grocery store doesn't tell you anything about whether I'm in debt."[10] Larry Summers, the former treasury secretary and director of the National Economic Council, put it even more bluntly: "The trade deficit is a terrible metric for judging economic policy."[11]

In 2017, America's trade deficit with China on goods alone amounted to just over $375 billion[12] (or, as Donald Trump has repeatedly insisted on calling it, $500 billion[13]). We'll talk about this more in an upcoming chapter, but for now let's just lay out the basics of what that means. Far from flushing $375 billion down the drain, that money was spent by American families and businesses on electronics, furniture, clothing, and manufacturing equipment—as well as "intermediate goods," which are parts and nonconsumer pieces that get incorporated into products we make here. That money was also spent on things we don't make here at all; take our supply of penicillin, for example, 100 percent of which comes from China. And much of our trade deficit is due to our buying products we *intentionally* no longer produce in the United States because our economy has moved on to higher-tech goods and, especially, services. In fact, America ran a $40 billion trade surplus with China on services alone in 2017.[14] Over the last fifteen years, as our economy has evolved, we have expanded our service surpluses with Canada by more than triple, with Europe by a factor of 7, with South Korea by a factor of nearly 13, and with China from $1.6 billion to over $40 billion—a whopping *2,475* percent increase.[15] Complain all you want about China, but they are our third-largest customer in the world; our farmers and our service sectors rely on them to buy a lot of what America is selling.

In a world where services such as software, movies, television, music, banking, insurance, transportation, and education are becoming much more strategically valuable to economic growth than the number of goods we can produce in a factory, a trade deficit on physical goods simply shouldn't bother us. After all, services now account for more than 70 percent of U.S. jobs—a figure that is likely to keep rising. Even if we *did* want to place a higher priority on exporting more products than we import, trade deficits are nothing to get hung up on. Because they're attempting to measure the value of goods that pass between two countries, they tend to fluctuate for many reasons, including things like the relative strength of the U.S. dollar, changes in investment levels, and economic growth.

So we know that bilateral trade deficits don't matter—but what about *total* trade deficits: the ones we accrue not just with one country, but with all of them. Our overall trade deficit *can* have economic consequences if it gets too far out of hand. It's a little like wine in that regard: two or three glasses at dinner is fine, but two or three bottles becomes a problem! If our overall trade deficit rose beyond a few percentage points of our national GDP, that would be a bottle problem; today, however, we're still just indulging in a glass or two.

Of course, if you really want to understand how meaningful overall trade deficits are, you could just take a look at this chart.

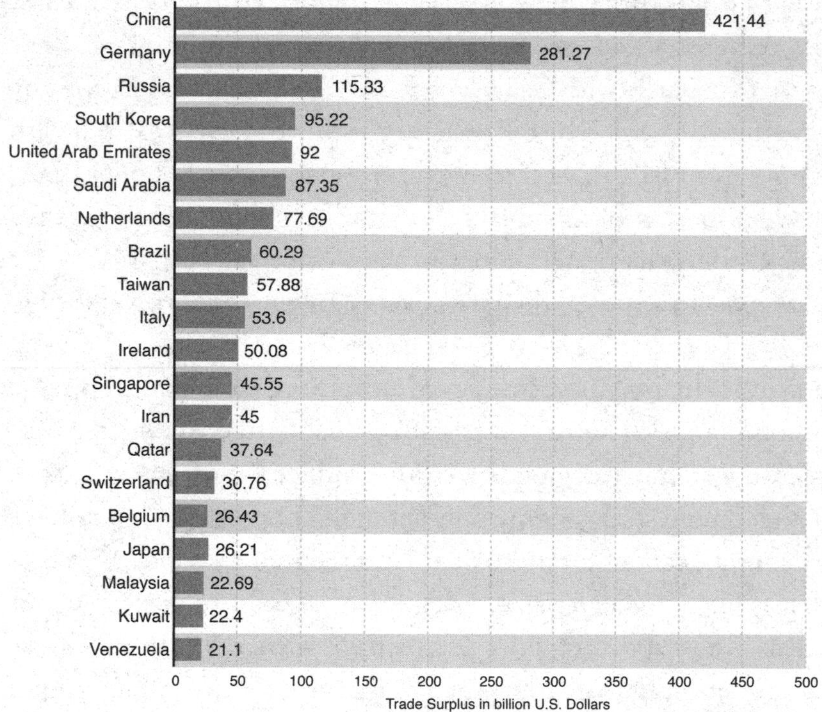

Be careful what you wish for, trade deficit hawks!

If it's so important to avoid trade deficits, well, these are the twenty countries that boasted the top trade *surpluses* in the world in 2017. A few have strong economies, to be sure—but would you trade the U.S. economy for Russia's, Iran's, or Venezuela's? I don't think so. In fact, I'm fairly confident that we wouldn't trade our economy with anyone on this list.

So the next time you hear a politician griping about how irresponsible we are for having allowed our trade deficits to build up, just remember that trade deficits are not debts that we have to pay back, scoreboards that show who's "winning" on trade, drains on our economy, or anything else of the sort. After all, every one of us probably has a large trade deficit with our barber or hair stylist! Sometimes desirable, sometimes regrettable, but almost always worthy of a great big shrug, these deficits are just another way for us to measure the difference between what comes into and out of our country in an increasingly interconnected world.

Myth #3: Tariffs Are Paid by Foreigners

Of all the myths and misstatements perpetuated by Donald Trump, this one has to be up there among the most baffling, most demonstrably false, and most frequently repeated. Tariffs, by their very definition, are a sales tax that a country imposes *on its own consumers and importers* for buying foreign goods—when the U.S. creates them, they get paid by U.S. citizens to the U.S. government, full stop. There's no debating this point; it's just a fact. Alas, that hasn't stopped President Trump from constantly and inaccurately arguing in the alternative. By my count, he repeated variations of this false claim nine times . . . just in the span of one particular week on Twitter—to say nothing of dozens of other instances before and since.

The idea that this myth needs debunking is curious—even diehard supporters of Donald Trump have conceded the absurdity of

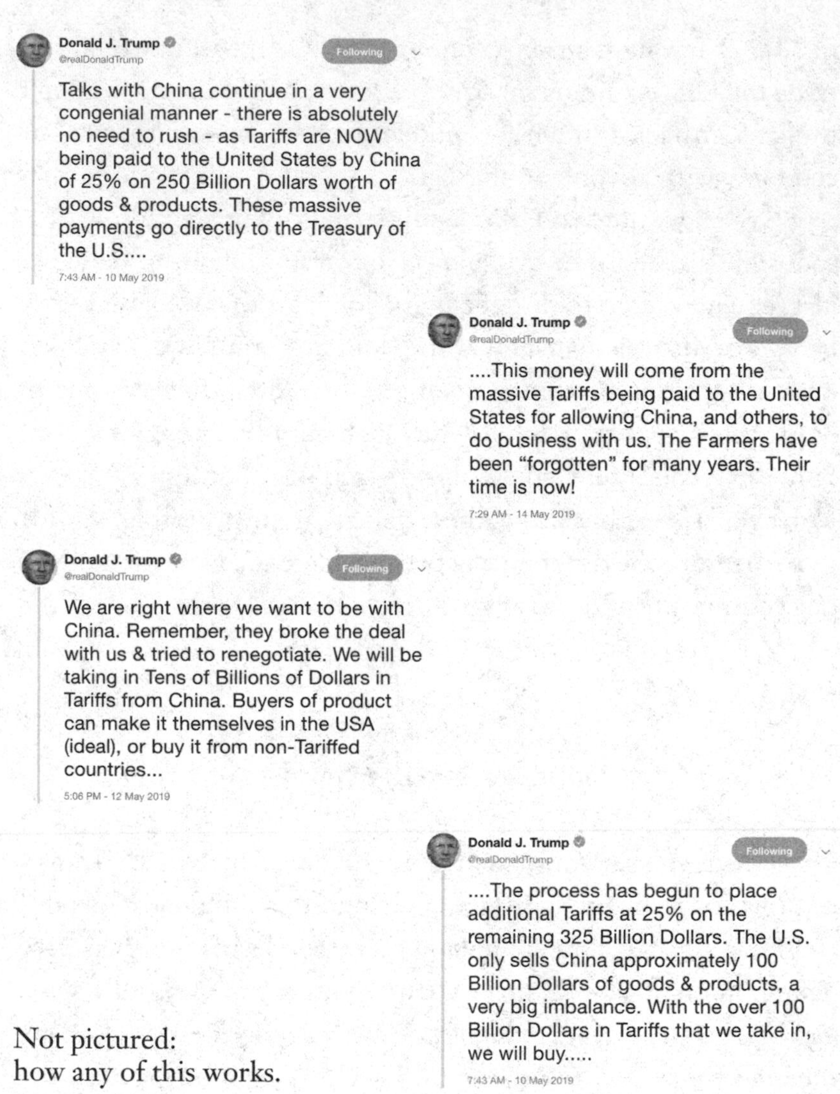

Donald J. Trump
@realDonaldTrump
Following

Talks with China continue in a very congenial manner - there is absolutely no need to rush - as Tariffs are NOW being paid to the United States by China of 25% on 250 Billion Dollars worth of goods & products. These massive payments go directly to the Treasury of the U.S....

7:43 AM - 10 May 2019

Donald J. Trump
@realDonaldTrump
Following

....This money will come from the massive Tariffs being paid to the United States for allowing China, and others, to do business with us. The Farmers have been "forgotten" for many years. Their time is now!

7:29 AM - 14 May 2019

Donald J. Trump
@realDonaldTrump
Following

We are right where we want to be with China. Remember, they broke the deal with us & tried to renegotiate. We will be taking in Tens of Billions of Dollars in Tariffs from China. Buyers of product can make it themselves in the USA (ideal), or buy it from non-Tariffed countries...

5:06 PM - 12 May 2019

Donald J. Trump
@realDonaldTrump
Following

....The process has begun to place additional Tariffs at 25% on the remaining 325 Billion Dollars. The U.S. only sells China approximately 100 Billion Dollars of goods & products, a very big imbalance. With the over 100 Billion Dollars in Tariffs that we take in, we will buy.....

7:43 AM - 10 May 2019

Not pictured:
how any of this works.

the claim. Larry Kudlow, the president's chief economic adviser, was forced to acknowledge in a May 12, 2019, interview—smack in the middle of the tweet-spree captured above—with Chris Wallace on *Fox News Sunday* that his employer had this one wrong. "It's not China that pays tariffs," Wallace reminded him, "it's the American importers, the American companies that pay what, in effect, is a tax increase and oftentimes passes it on to U.S. consumers." Kudlow's answer? "Fair enough," before cryptically hedging that "both sides will pay in these things."[16]

The impact of tariffs on American families was in the news fairly regularly in 2019—a fact that, by itself, is pretty astonishing. If you had told someone just a few years ago that Americans would soon have to deal with the consequences of tariffs, they probably would have looked at you as though you had told them that Americans would soon have to deal with the consequences of polio, the Y2K bug, or the Mongol Horde. And yet, here we are. Much of the media coverage of the Trump tariffs has focused on Midwestern soybean farmers, whose livelihoods have been hurt by the self-inflicted wounds of our trade wars. But it's worth taking a different angle on this myth to really understand the damage it causes—and why tariffs can be so difficult to kill.

The vast majority of Americans happen to be either parents or kids, which helps explain why one of the most common everyday products in our country is children's shoes. They're bought across regions, races, socioeconomic classes—you name it. And if you know anything about children, you know that their feet have an unfortunate habit of growing larger over time, making repeat purchases a necessity (shoes are also the one article of clothing that are not conducive to hand-me-downs!). While shoemaking was a historically important industry in the U.S., today about 98 percent of the footwear Americans buy is imported from overseas.[17] Even if we wanted to "buy American," our choices would be severely limited; our domestic shoe production is so low that a protectionist tariff couldn't do much to alter our purchasing behavior. With that in mind, you might expect U.S. tariffs on children's shoes to be nonexistent or at least extremely low—something in the range of the 1 or 2 percent tariff Americans usually pay on imported cars or toys.

It may surprise you to learn, then, that the tariffs we pay for children's shoes can run as high as a blood-curdling, pocketbook-shriveling *67 percent*! The average tax we pay for imported footwear—that is to say, essentially all of our footwear—is a still egregious 11 percent, or about ten times the average tariff on all imported goods.[18] Children's shoe tariffs are essentially a tax on parenthood, and a regressive one at that: the more expensive the shoe, the lower the tariff generally drops, meaning that lower-income families are the hardest hit. You'd think that a tax on parents would be among the easiest taxes to overturn, right? Wrong. Our children's shoe tariffs generate a cool $12 billion in revenue for the U.S. government, money that would have to be made up for with another tax or with spending cuts—and politicians are loath to do either.

The great irony in all this goes back to who else: Donald Trump. Before he was elected, the Trans-Pacific Partnership was poised to eliminate almost all tariffs between the United States and Vietnam, our number two source of shoe imports after China.[19] When Trump pulled America out of the deal, he pulled the plug on what would have amounted to substantial, immediate savings for American shoe-shopping families. Instead, Americans—not China or anyone else—are continuing to foot the bill for footwear tariffs, just as we do for all tariffs our government chooses to impose on us.

Myth #4:
Trade Agreements Are All About Jobs

On this one, you are ahead of the game. We know that trade, and exports in particular, can have a big impact on jobs—but we also know from our experience with NAFTA in chapter two that trade *agreements* often do not. Of course, these deals are often pursued *under the guise* of creating jobs, something they don't do very well. In reality, they are more often put in place to further diplomatic, geopolitical, or domestic policy goals as they are simply to strengthen the economy. But if the most important function of a trade agreement is to bring two or more countries closer together, couldn't we save an awful lot of paper by doing away with every page but the one with the signatures? Put another way, if trade agreements *aren't* all about jobs, then what are they about?

For a good example of what makes up a modern trade agreement, we need look no further than the Trans-Pacific Partnership—the deal proposed by Barack Obama and abandoned by Donald Trump that sought to strengthen the United States' position as the preeminent power of the Pacific. At more than 5,000 pages,[20] it's fair to say that TPP sought to cover quite a bit of ground (no surprise, as it was designed to integrate economies representing two fifths of the world's entire GDP). To begin with, it performed the classic trade agreement maneuver of lowering barriers to encourage the flow of trade between the twelve nations. Normally, lowering barriers means lowering tariffs—but tariffs were already low throughout most of the world following the post–World War II liberalization of trade (GATT—the 1947 General Agreement on Tariffs and Trade, another one of those brilliant acronyms designed to confuse—saw to that). So instead, TPP focused largely on tackling loopholes that countries had put in place over the years to keep out exports *without* raising tariffs. How clever—nontariff barriers!

Here's how they work. When a government wants to protect its domestic industries without being explicit about it, they'll often make creative use of things like labeling requirements, record-keeping regulations, and environmental and labor standards to effectively zero out foreign competition. If Australia wants to keep out Bolivian crops to protect its own farmers, a national law banning a certain mineral found in South American (but not Australian) soil will be just as effective at accomplishing that as a tariff or quota on Bolivian imports—and unlike tariffs and quotas, a mineral ban can be couched as a health issue to seem less belligerent. By disguising international trade restrictions as domestic safety or national security concerns, countries can often ward off scrutiny from international monitors without missing a beat. We're not innocent in this, either! The U.S. has "Buy American" regulations limiting the amount of foreign materials we can use on certain infrastructure projects, such as Amtrak lines and the San Francisco–Oakland Bay Bridge. Other countries, like Japan, have focused health restrictions on *frozen* beef in order to boost their domestic market. One of the objectives of TPP was to catch and curb those sorts of practices, which have sprung up around the world as the use of tariffs has become increasingly frowned upon.

Another area that modern trade agreements like TPP tend to focus on is greasing the skids for the trade of services (take note: we still aren't talking about jobs). As economies—and, especially, America's economy—have evolved to center more around services than physical goods, businesses in fields ranging from finance and law to marketing and entertainment have set their eyes on the vast majority of potential customers who happen to live beyond their own national borders. Because the rules of trade were largely written during eras when services were little more than a blip on the economic radar, a major goal of new trade agreements like TPP is opening the same doors to consultants, cloud service providers, IT support, and engineers that we've already opened to steel mills and lumberyards.

Modernizing the rules of the road eats up a lot of ink, and goes beyond just preventing service exports from being discriminated against. To further address the changing nature of trade, TPP sought to create a new set of guidelines governing digital commerce and intellectual property—the collection and analysis of user data has now become the most prized currency of large companies, so we need a system in place to responsibly safeguard it as it travels between countries. Much of TPP was devoted to doing just that (again: not jobs!). It was the first major deal to lay out ground rules for the importing and exporting of information. It was also among the first to include consumer privacy protections in recognition of the emerging risks of digital commerce—remember, Facebook, Google, and Amazon weren't on anybody's radar back when NAFTA was created. It strengthened rules around patent enforcement, protecting trade secrets, and the length of copyright terms. Controversially, it also extended those protections to the pharmaceutical field, potentially delaying the introduction of generic drugs to market where they might have otherwise lowered prescription drug prices—and drawing the ire of groups like Doctors Without Borders. (Just a reminder: when trade deals get attacked from the left for being overly friendly to corporations, the criticism is not always unfair.)

TPP wasn't just looking out for the poor, struggling pharmaceutical companies, though! To its credit, it also contained the most far-reaching environmental and labor standards in the whole history of free trade agreements. It specifically reduced tariffs on wind turbines and many solar panel parts to zero, strengthened protections around wildlife and endangered species, and required countries to raise the floor on marine conservation, sustainable fishing, logging, and pollution. It also set a hard line on child labor, instituted rules around employment discrimination, required baseline standards for workplace conditions and minimum wages, and forced countries who joined the agreement to permit their workers to unionize and collectively bargain.

Finally, because trade is obviously global, it comes up against the laws and regulations of many different nations—so a major component of any modern trade agreement involving a large number of countries is laying out how disputes will be resolved (and we're *still* not talking about jobs). This was especially tricky with TPP, which was designed in part to help businesses open markets and invest in other countries. The old adage of "let's make everything here and sell it to the rest of the world" doesn't hold up in the twenty-first century—everybody wants a piece of the action, and that means creating jobs in their countries, too. This is a tricky balancing act. For example, Ford has factories in twenty-one countries—we create the innovation and know-how here, but sometimes assembly has to happen locally to meet customs, regulations, cost considerations, and tastes if we want Ford to be able to sell cars around the world. America will get *some* of the jobs that come from those sales—but demanding that we get *all* of them simply won't fly today. Moreover, there's good evidence that when companies invest across borders and people in other countries work with and get to know Americans (and vice versa), it strengthens our international relationships. When we build things together, we become stronger friends and allies.

It's important to note that there are some people on the left and the right who are deeply worried about the complications of these global investments—after all, if a domestic business ends up in a dispute with a foreign nation, suddenly the ability of that country to govern everything within its borders comes into question. Enter "ISDS" . . . as if trade needed another abbreviation. Investor-state dispute settlement provisions are tools that permit companies to effectively sue governments by hauling them before arbitration panels rather than enduring long court cases. ISDS entered our lives due to NAFTA, when we became concerned that U.S. companies wouldn't be able to get a fair hearing in what were believed to be overly politicized and corrupt Mexican courts. As a result, it has been part of every trade negotiation we've embarked on since—and the rest of the world has largely adopted it, too. U.S. companies like having ISDS available as a security blanket, but it's fair to ask whether ISDS is necessary for every trade agreement; after all, Americans tend to be skeptical about subjecting ourselves to extraterritorial rules that we don't get to control—and not without good reason.

Critics of TPP like Senator Warren focused much of their ire on this aspect of trade agreements, arguing that when you empower foreign corporations to challenge decisions of the U.S. government in an ad hoc international justice system, you open the door to the weakening of our regulations. If, hypothetically, an overseas company successfully made the case that American environmental laws unfairly hurt their investment, an ISDS arbitration panel could, in theory, impose a hefty fine on the United States—which potentially could incentivize us to weaken those laws proactively. On the other hand, if an American company invests overseas and is treated unjustly—say, if Pepsi builds a plant overseas, and the host government then seizes it—the company needs a mechanism to safeguard its investment. That's not just a hypothetical situation, either; it's more or less precisely what happened to the Arabian-American Oil Company, a California-based business that came under the control of Saudi Arabia over the course of the 1950s, '60s, and '70s, ultimately becoming known as Saudi Aramco. To put this all in perspective, there are thousands of trade deals in effect throughout the world that have ISDS in place already—about fifty of which the U.S. is a party to—and we have only been challenged twenty-two times all told. And we are 22-for-22 in winning them, suggesting that these provisions certainly haven't been a major threat to our country. On the other hand, just because ISDS hasn't come back to bite us yet doesn't mean that it's the right thing to do. It's easy to see the provision as a form of corporate privilege—one that isn't available to labor.

So what about jobs? Wasn't this supposed to be about jobs? If you ever decide to peruse those 5,000 pages (something I don't recommend), you'll learn about the elimination of trade barriers, new standards for service exports, guardrails for the importing and exporting of data and digital information, labor provisions, environmental provisions, and rules about how disputes will be resolved. Trade agreements are a lengthy read, but as long as you don't hold your breath looking for the word "jobs," you should be just fine. In fact, you can see for yourself: search the full text of TPP, and you'll find exactly eight mentions of the word "job"—two of which are references to the names of the Australian and Japanese labor departments. So that's six mentions . . . in 5,000 pages. By contrast, you can find eleven mentions of jojoba oil, an extract used in cosmetics.[21]

Myth #5:
Trade Wars Work

"When a country (USA) is losing many billions of dollars on trade with virtually every country it does business with, trade wars are good, and easy to win." So began a tweet from the president of the

United States early on the morning of March 2, 2018. It would be followed a month later with the tweeted assertion that "We are not in a trade war with China," and finally, on June 2, with the claim that "When you're almost 800 Billion Dollars down on Trade, you can't lose a Trade War!" Within two weeks, the White House had announced that it would be imposing broad tariffs on more than $50 billion worth of Chinese products, including everything from medical equipment and airplane parts to fabrics and fish—an early salvo in what would escalate into, in the words of China's Ministry of Commerce, "the biggest trade war in economic history."[22]

Just as trade deficits bear little resemblance to budget deficits, I am pleased to report that trade wars are nowhere near as devastating as actual wars. That isn't to say that they don't also have *victims*, though—on the contrary, the major difference between trade wars and actual wars is that trade wars typically don't have *winners*. When Donald Trump enacted his first wave of tariffs on Chinese goods, China responded by upping their own tariffs on American soybeans, pork, aluminum, and other products, dealing significant damage to farmers in Kansas and autoworkers in Michigan. On September 17, 2018, Trump retaliated with even higher tariffs (that is to say, a tax) on $200 billion worth of Chinese imports—and China swung back the very next day, announcing a 10 percent tariff hike on $60 billion worth of American products.

When a country (USA) is losing many billions of dollars on trade with virtually every country it does business with, trade wars are good, and easy to win. Example, when we are down $100 billion with a certain country and they get cute, don't trade anymore-we win big. It's easy!

5:50 AM - 2 Mar 2018

It's not easy.

Of course, lest we forget, the problem isn't just other countries' tariffs hurting U.S. exporters; our *own* tariffs hurt American families by raising consumer prices here at home, too. Another word for a tariff is, of course, a tax. No victors—just victims.

While China and the U.S. began to cool off trade tensions by December 2018, plenty of damage had already been done. For starters, more than half of all American soybean exports are sold to China—and with access to their favorite market temporarily restricted, U.S. soybean farmers saw crop prices fall substantially in the summer of 2018, effectively crushing their profits for the year.[23] In fact, a number of farmers have even resorted to selling their soybeans at far lower prices to Mexican and Canadian middlemen—who then, because they're not in a trade war, can turn around and sell them off to China, keeping the profits. It's a story that repeats itself each time a trade war is initiated: governments engage in brinkmanship with one another, tossing increasingly severe penalties onto the pile, while exporters and consumers in both countries are left to grapple with the negative effects of shuttered markets: lost sales and higher prices. The long-term effects can be even worse, as trade wars create a sense of instability—causing other countries to wonder whether they really want to invest in and do business with a volatile trading partner.

In the worst case scenario, these tensions can grow into more serious conflicts—think the War of 1812, the Opium Wars, and the Great Depression. But even if a trade war manages to avoid bloodshed and bankruptcy, the results can still be devastating. Take the example of America's closest and most consistent ally, Canada—a friend so loyal that when the Florida orange crop was stricken with disease a few years ago and the hemisphere had little choice but to buy its oranges from Brazil, the Canadians immediately returned to the U.S. market as soon as the disease was eradicated (in order to help Florida growers recover). When Donald Trump initiated a trade war with our northern neighbors over steel, aluminum, and other goods, however, even the Canadians became fed up. They immediately imposed new tariffs on American oranges and went back to Brazil as their partner in citrus—despite the fact that this would raise the cost of oranges in Canada. The Florida orange industry employs about 75,000 people—and they have enough on their plate between hurricanes and crop diseases to worry about human-made disasters. Our alienation of Canada has already cost our orange growers millions of dollars and countless jobs, and left the industry teetering on the edge of solvency. "America first," indeed.

Myth #6: The Less We Import, the Better Off We Are

It's as simple a maxim as there is in economics: it's better to make more money than you spend. If I, a producer of solar panels, want to fatten my bank account, it stands to reason that I should do everything I can to maximize the number of solar panels I sell to others while also minimizing the amount of goods and services I purchase from them. As tempting as it may be to take that ironclad concept and apply it to the world of trade, however, economists will tell you that national import and export policies are a little more complicated than the rules by which we set our personal budgets.

A number of politicians—most notably, President Trump—remain stuck on the idea that the less we buy from foreign countries, the stronger we become. It's an easy logic to follow, and one that folds neatly into romantic notions about "made-in-America" products; after all, who *wouldn't* want to support U.S. workers while keeping our hard-earned dollars here at home? While there's certainly nothing wrong with wanting to buy American, the belief that we should—or frankly, that we even *can*—make everything we need and sell it to the world without shelling out for imports ignores some basic truths about the modern global economy.

As I mentioned in the introduction, if all trade between countries were to suddenly stop tomorrow, the United States would be in a better position than any other nation to survive. Survive? Yes. Well? No. Even if we were to *survive* in a world without imports, we probably wouldn't enjoy ourselves very much. An America that makes everything at home would be a land of $10 bananas, $100 shirts, and a diet limited by what's available season to season. You wouldn't have an iPhone to distract you or a laptop to stream TV on (just as well, as we'd miss imported shows like *Game of Thrones*, *Homeland*, and *Veep*). And if you think you could just trade in your Honda or VW for a Chevy or a Ford, think again—even the cars we think of as being classic American-made models rely on countless foreign parts to run; the waiting list for tires alone would be interminable given our meager supply of rubber. There are also resources we absolutely have to import if we want to stay on the forefront of innovation, such as the rare earth minerals used in our device screens, fiber optic cables, fuel cells, cancer treatment drugs—none of which occur naturally in the United States.

We'll explore the stories behind some of those products in the following chapters, but, for now, consider the blueberry. There was a time when blueberries were strictly a summer delicacy in the United States—and because Americans had limited exposure to the fruit, demand for them remained low. When we began importing blueberries from countries with different seasonal climates from our own (such as Chile, which now accounts for more than half of our blueberry imports[24]), it didn't put U.S. producers out of business or siphon consumer dollars out of the country. What it did was expand the American appetite by making blueberries available all year round, which in turn helped lead to more sales for domestic growers. Americans' consumption of blueberries has more than doubled since the year 2001, for example, tracking with a similarly steep rise in blueberry imports. The lesson of the blueberry is that trade is rarely a zero-sum game—imports don't always hurt homegrown industries, and can even spur them on to new heights by growing the market or prompting them to innovate.

The twenty-first-century economy is marked by increasingly complex products—many of which no one company and no one country can supply all of the parts for. Couple that with increasingly demanding consumer expectations around availability and price, and the idea that we can make and sell everything we need right here in America simply doesn't hold water. Want to stop buying aluminum from China? That's fine . . . but the U.S. automakers, construction companies, and airplane manufacturers who rely on inexpensive source materials won't be able to build, sell, or hire much without it—and they certainly won't be competitive. Tired of foreign produce crowding out American goods in the grocery store? Okay . . . as long as you're willing to say adios to year-round avocados. We've banished the idea of "seasonal" fruits—do we really want to go back to a time when we could only eat foods in the same season that they happened to have grown? Buying more from our friends and neighbors than we sell to them may not be the most popular idea on the surface, but when you look under the hood of our economy, there's no denying that imports have fueled our quality of life and empowered us to make the most of our strengths as a nation. And don't forget: when we buy from other countries and their economies improve, they in turn are able to buy more from us—supporting more jobs and industries here at home. That's why Henry Ford paid his employees well enough, and made his Model Ts inexpensive enough, that the workers who built them were able to buy one of their own—if you want to sell more, you better make sure that your customers are in a position to afford what you're making!

Myth #7: Trade Is Win-Win

The economy is not *win-win* . . . nor is trade. But in the wide world of trade-deal-related press conferences, it's possible that no phrase is more common than win-win. President Obama touted the U.S.-Korea Free Trade Agreement as "a win-win for both our countries" back in 2010.[25] The Japanese trade minister celebrated the announcement of a new deal with Russia as a "win-win" in 2016.[26] And when the United States-Mexico-Canada Agreement was announced in 2018, it earned a rare declaration of "win-win-win" from both the Mexican president[27] and the Canadian prime minister.[28] In fact, it might be harder to find a trade pact that *wasn't* described as "win-win" at the time it was forged than to find ten that were.

Zoom out far enough, and it's probably true that all trade agreements are "wins" for the countries that sign them: we know that whenever trade barriers are lowered and international sales increase, it boosts GDP, lowers consumer prices, and diversifies the marketplace. These wins become especially apparent as more and more developing nations open themselves up to trade. Consider this: today, developing countries account for half of all global trade. Twenty years ago, it was less than a quarter. Over that same stretch, as some of the poorest places in the world gained access to the fruits of trade, the total number of people living in extreme poverty (about $2 per day) was also cut in half.[29] The numbers are clear: more people have been lifted out of poverty in the last twenty years than at any other time in world history, and trade has a lot to do with that. Yes, it has extracted a toll on workers in our country, something we haven't addressed sufficiently, but it has benefited the world we inhabit greatly. And there's no reason we can't do both.

So if all you want to look at is the overall health of the global economy, there is no question that the chorus of "win-win" proclaimers is right—trade does indeed create an overall good for society. But the more you zoom in, the more apparent it becomes that there are holes in that net. Trade creates benefits in large part by reducing inefficiencies and spurring innovation—if America can buy foreign copper for less than it costs to mine it here at home, it will give a boost to our copper-reliant defense, electronics, and construction industries, each of which can turn the money they save on imported copper into more growth, more jobs, and lower prices. Critics are quick to point out, correctly, that those savings don't always trickle down to consumers—they sometimes end up as increased corporate profits. That's an undeniable win for our country on paper, and will show up in economic growth, employment figures, consumer purchasing power, and other measurements of success. But the "inefficiency" that this new trade arrangement corrected isn't an abstraction. It's people, families, communities—in this case, it's copper miners. Though we may have raised the standard of living in the aggregate—and helped create more jobs in electrical engineering than will be lost in the mines—it's entirely possible that we also hastened the demise of an industry along the way. For educational, geographical, or any number of other reasons, many of those miners won't be able to take advantage of the brand-new, cheap-copper-fueled semiconductor plants and HVAC companies. The communities built up around my mining towns will be hollowed out as local jobs disappear. Though the benefits of trade are often dispersed as small gains across broad swaths of the population, the fallout is frequently acute, severe, and narrowly focused on smaller communities that may have already been struggling in the first place.

Politicians, to the surprise of no one, have never done a great job of being candid about who loses as a result of these "win-win" deals—but somebody always pays the price. That every trade agreement creates winners and losers isn't an argument against trade; it just isn't a good one, at least, so long as trade makes people's lives better off on the whole. In fact, we celebrate these sorts of trade-offs all the time. Everybody cheers when a good report comes in showing that America added 350,000 jobs last month and the unemployment rate ticked down a few points. But the country never just adds 350,000 jobs—it's much more likely that 5,350,000 people found jobs last month, while another five million left theirs. While not all of the five million who left, lost, or switched their jobs were happy about it, Americans still treat overall gains as good news. It shouldn't be any different with trade. Trade would be better understood if we started acknowledging that even the best-intentioned deals are always going to leave somebody behind. If we're truthful about the trade-offs, we can finally have the honest, difficult conversations necessary to give the losers of our win-win agreements the support they need to pull themselves and their communities back up.

Myth #8:
Everything Donald Trump Says About Trade Is Wrong

Surprise! I won't blame you if you didn't see this myth coming, but it's true: Donald Trump, who so often has obsessed over trade deficits, called himself a "tariff man," taken aim at our economic allies, launched debilitating trade wars, derided "the false song of globalism,"[30] and unfairly demonized past agreements—yes, *that* Donald Trump—is sometimes right about trade.

To begin with, Trump does strike at something true when he centers his trade complaints around the idea of "fairness." No, other countries are not "unfairly" taking advantage of the United States—as the world's most powerful economy, we do a pretty good job of entering into agreements clear-eyed and strategically, whether voters know it or not—but the trade landscape does have inequities built into it. America is a capitalist economy with relatively high standards for labor rights, human rights, wages, and environmental protection; when we compete in the global marketplace, we take those values with us. Other countries operating under different systems have more leeway in the form of things like lower wage expectations or a higher tolerance for worker suppression—qualities that make for an uneven playing field when we compete against them for business. They also frequently have '"national champions." That's where governments put their finger on the scale to assist particular private or semiprivate companies so that they can better compete globally—Japan does this with Toshiba and Toyota, among others, while France does the same for Airbus. In fact, I remember vividly a meeting in Ottawa in September of 2013 to discuss export finance; my counterparts from other industrialized countries were stunned by the idea that we don't take the same approach. We as a country do not have national champions—we believe in the free enterprise system, and that U.S. companies will succeed if there's a level playing field. A lot of other countries . . . they don't mind if there's a little tilt! We come to the negotiating table with a different set of values and goals; whenever we work with nations that operate differently, we have to account for the fact that they're often thinking about their national champions as deals get negotiated. So some amount of unfairness will always exist; the world will never be perfectly aligned in terms of ideology or the development of every country's rights and economies.

A second area where Trump has a point comes from his critique of globalization—one that sometimes rings true among many union workers, Midwesterners, and the political left and right wings. Unfortunately, it's also a critique that, in its delivery, has become increasingly mired in explicit nationalism, implicit anti-Semitism, and anti-immigrant and anti-minority sentiments. Is it a coincidence that the last ad the Trump campaign ran before the 2016 election accused three specific "global" actors—financier George Soros, former Fed chair Janet Yellen, and Goldman Sachs CEO Lloyd Blankfein—of "put[ting] money into [their] pockets?"[31] Hmm . . . what do those three people, who are probably unfamiliar to most voters, happen to have in common? But I digress.

"Globalization has made the financial elite . . . very wealthy," Trump told a Pennsylvania crowd during a campaign stop in 2016, "but it has left millions of our workers with nothing but poverty and heartache. When subsidized foreign steel is dumped into our markets, threatening our factories, the politicians do nothing. For years, they watched on the sidelines as our jobs vanished and our communities were plunged into depression-level unemployment."[32] The real story, of course, is not so simple. As the world's number two exporter, the rising levels of income around the world made possible by globalization have benefited us enormously. When people move up the income ladder, they demand better food, infrastructure, cars, and so on, which America is eager to provide—and those exports support a ton of U.S. jobs. But even if we were to contend that globalization *has* delivered on its promised benefits, there can be no denying the fact that those benefits have not been distributed across the board.

Though the globalization of the economy has lifted more than a billion people out of poverty, much of that impact has indeed been concentrated in India and China—countries with huge populations that developed rapidly out of extremely poor conditions. That's a good thing, of course, but the remarkable scale of those success stories has also obscured the impact of globalization in other parts of the world. Enormous numbers of people left rural farming communities to join the manufacturing sector as part of that process, bringing themselves out of poverty, but also inadvertently depressing wages worldwide due to the growing size of the labor force. Trade enthusiasts are quick to point out that worldwide income inequality has declined in the era of globalization . . . but remove China and India from the equation, and the picture isn't quite as clear. The gap between the haves and the have-nots has widened, both on an international scale—between wealthy and poorer countries—and domestically in the United States and other western nations. By and large, globalization has helped three categories of people: rich people in rich countries, rich people in poor countries, and poor people in poor countries. What we have not done well is make globalization a winning proposition for poor people in rich countries. Part of that is because, too often, trade agreements have been influenced by those in a position to influence them: major corporations, politically powerful interests, and, yes, wealthy donors. Those hit hardest by global trade flows are far less likely to have a seat at the table to begin with.

It doesn't have to be that way. Critics of trade are right to decry a global race to the bottom—one in which countries that pay their workers the least and have the lowest corporate taxes are rewarded for hoarding the benefits of the global economy. And make no mistake: President Trump is right about the impact trade has had on many segments of our population as well as lower-income workers in developed countries around the world. Nor did Trump cause any of this—all he did was pull back the curtain on it in colorful terms. To ensure that trade serves the greatest number of people possible, countries should take a hard look at how their laws and policies might be increasing inequality and narrowing trade's positive impact. They need to do more—much more—to have the backs of those within their borders for whom globalization has not been a happy development. We'll explore a number of those ideas later in our story.

PART TWO

SIX PRODUCTS THAT MAKE THE CASE FOR TRADE

Now that we've gotten up to speed on the complete history of American trade, explored how the politics around it have evolved (and veered off track) over time, and dispensed with some of the most incessant myths on the matter, it's time to move on to the fun part. We know that trade is important—it utterly dominated the political conversation for most of America's first 150 years, after all, and has reemerged in heated moments ever since. We know that it inspires debate and evokes strong feelings among people of all ideological persuasions. But what we haven't talked about yet is what it looks like in *your* life—and isn't that the most important thing of all?

Our national conversations about trade, to the extent that we have any at all, tend to frame it as an abstraction—a force as high up, mysterious, and as large as the moon, capable of delivering prosperity or crushing whole industries from afar. But in reality, it's mostly little things that trade changes or makes possible in our lives—things so ordinary we might not even notice them. Trade can impact our quality of life almost imperceptibly, be it through a little money saved here or there, a wider range of choices, or a product we would not have otherwise had access to. What parts of your day—what experiences or outcomes—are being affected by trade without you knowing it? That's what we're going to find out next.

In this section of the book, we'll take a closer look at six perfectly ordinary products—each of which you'll be familiar with, and many of which you probably enjoy on a regular basis. The story of these six products is the *real* story of trade—the one that isn't measured in GDPs, manufacturing output, employment rates, or anything else you'd find at the Bureau of Labor Statistics. This is the story of your life, and mine, and everybody else's, and how trade colors our everyday experiences, large and small.

CHAPTER 4

The Spice of Life

If you were craving authentic Mexican food in the 1950s and happened to be in southern California, you might have paid a visit to a small, off-white adobe structure in the Anaheim Resort District. Two decades earlier, the proprietor—a San Antonio candy maker named C. Elmer Doolin—had a fortuitous encounter at a Texas gas station with Gustavo Olguin, a snack salesman from Oaxaca. After trying Gustavo's fried corn chips, Doolin quickly made him an offer on the patent and the machine that pressed them into shape.[1] He brought his new acquisition to Disneyland (where else?), and at the Casa de Fritos restaurant Doolin and his team pumped out innovation after innovation over the years, each one featuring a different take on his signature chip: Frito salad dressing, Frito meat sauce, Frito pie, the first widely marketed American tortilla chip (with the faux-Spanish name of *Dorito*), and the most popular treat of them all, a glorious taco-in-a-cup con-

Not pictured: actual Mexican foods.

coction Doolin aptly named the *Tacup*. It was simple, really—just black beans, ground beef, shredded cheese, and sour cream in an edible Frito bowl. But that little Disneyland snack would go on to become the dish we know and love today: the taco salad.

Of course, there was nothing "authentically" Mexican about the Tacup, the Dorito, C. Elmer Doolin, or anything else you might have found in Casa de Fritos. But as has happened with the cuisines of so many cultures before and since, Doolin's creations helped give the American people a taste for Mexican-inspired foods—and, today, the taco salad is one of the most ubiquitous meals in the country. We have immigrants to thank for the unparalleled variety of dishes available here in the United States. We have enterprising characters like Doolin to thank (or, perhaps, blame) for "Americanizing" and popularizing a number of foreign cuisines. Ultimately, though, we have trade to thank for the fact that any one of us, in any season, can order Pad Thai in Rhode

Island, Tikka Masala in Des Moines, or a taco salad in Alaska—even sushi in the supermarket, something I never imagined would be possible (or particularly appetizing) not so long ago.

Trade has delivered extraordinary benefits to our country through the years; even the most determined critic would have to admit that—whatever its flaws—it has lowered consumer prices, sparked new industries, and made our national economy stronger on the whole. But in terms of our sheer enjoyment of life, you would be hard-pressed to name a more satisfying consequence of trade than the fresh sushi roll, the midnight burrito, Nutella on toast—take your pick. So many of the ingredients we take for granted today would simply disappear from our grocery aisles, five-star restaurants, and fast food favorites alike were it not for trade. And while falafel and pesto may seem like a trivial matter, they are exactly the kind of choices that have made our country what it is over the last seventy years.

Since the dawn of the consumer age, no word has summed up America more succinctly than . . . *variety*. For a country forged by outcasts and dissenters, founded on promises of "freedom," and improved by wave after wave of immigrants and refugees from every nation, what else could the United States become but the land of a million options? Modern American freedom, after all, isn't just the freedom to speak, vote, or assemble—it's also the freedom to eat mangoes in December, to choose between dozens of cheeses, and to get extra guacamole. We fulfilled that destiny in the years after World War II, as a surge of new, young families with income to spend set their sights on household products, cars, and an endless stream of groceries. In 1975—after the western world had begun to lower trade barriers, but before the first free trade agreements were written—the average U.S. supermarket carried just under 9,000 different products. By 2008, that number had mushroomed to nearly 47,000.[2]

No shortage of sociologists have explored how that boom of consumer choices has shaped what it means to be an American. Ted Ownby, a historian and author at the University of Mississippi, has described it in terms of four distinct "American Dreams." The first, the *Dream of Abundance*, is the abiding vision of America as a land of plenty—a "material paradise" of stocked pantries and teeming shelves. The *Dream of a Democracy of Goods* is the notion that product choices can help "flatten out differences among people of diverse backgrounds" by allowing them to transcend their status through the things they shop for and own (everybody wears blue jeans, after all). The *Dream of Freedom of Choice* is the liberation that comes from choosing between those 47,000 items in the grocery store; as Professor Ownby puts it, "Whether they are fascinated with the stores themselves or shop in catalogs that encourage people to imagine how goods will help them become new people, the process of selecting goods allows shoppers a pleasure in redefining themselves." Finally, the *Dream of Novelty* conveys our desire to experience the new, be it an exotic fruit, a foreign fashion, or an upgrade from the iPhone 8 to the iPhone X. "Together," Ownby writes, "the four dreams assume a future full of progress" for America, wedding prosperity, inclusiveness, choice, and forward momentum into a singular American Dream—made possible by variety.[3]

Perhaps no moment better demonstrates just how significant variety is to American life than one that occurred in the fall of 1989. Boris Yeltsin, the populist Soviet agitator who would later become the first democratically elected president of Russia, had embarked on a well-publicized goodwill tour of America; over the course of nine days, he visited a pig farm in Indiana, lectured at three universities, appeared on *Good Morning America*, and circled the Statue of Liberty twice by helicopter (prompting him to remark sarcastically to an aide that he was "double free").[4] While preparing to leave Texas after touring the Johnson Space Center, Yeltsin made an impromptu stop at a Randalls supermarket near the Houston airport. Leon Aron, his biographer, describes what happened next:

> Outside, the Soviet visitors looked for the customary crowd and queue, but found neither. On entering the store, they were dazzled by the "profusion of light" and a "kaleidoscope-like," "spell-binding" multitude of colors. Yeltsin asked a salesperson how many different products they had in the store. Around 30,000, she said. They examined cheeses and hams, began counting varieties of sausages—and "lost count." The myriad of sweets and cakes were "impossible for the eye to assimilate." . . . And all this unimaginable splendour to be found in a "provincial" store, "not in New York!" . . . Yeltsin was in "shock." . . . For a long time, on the plane to Miami, he sat motionless, his head in his hands. "What have they done to our poor people?" he said after a long silence.[5]

Boris Yeltsin, pudding pops and the end of the Soviet Union

Yeltsin's advisor, Lev Sukhanov, identified their unscheduled visit to Randalls as the moment when "the last prop of Yeltsin's Bolshevik consciousness decomposed."[6] Fifteen months later, after years of economic decay behind the Iron Curtain, the Soviet Union would formally disband. Its dissolution was due in no small part to intense pressure on the Communist regime from within—an upheaval led most vocally and forcefully by Boris Yeltsin. Years later, when a colleague asked then-President Yeltsin what the biggest factor was in turning him against the Soviet system in which he was raised, Yeltsin answered bluntly: "America and its supermarkets."[7]

Did America's variety of cookies really crumble the Soviet Union? Well, not exactly—the full story is much more complicated than that, of course. But the Yeltsin episode demonstrates just how powerful a force variety can be, how central it is to our culture, and what it must feel like to see the (literal) fruits of an open economy when all you've ever known is a closed one. That variety touches our lives every day in ways we may or may not always appreciate; when we drive a foreign car (or even, as we'll later see, a supposedly "American" one), eat a foreign food, or choose a new laptop or cell phone from among a range of options, we are quietly taking advantage of the benefits of our globalized economy.

Consider, once more, the taco salad. Everybody knows that they are delicious—although not everybody knows that they aren't actually of Hispanic origin (that includes President Trump, who memorably tweeted during the 2016 presidential campaign, "Happy #CincoDeMayo! The best taco bowls are made in Trump Tower Grill. I love Hispanics!"[8]). Like chop suey, corned beef and cabbage, fortune cookies, and Häagen-Dazs ice cream, the taco salad follows in a long tradition of American foods masquerading as imported cuisines—we even invented dipping bread in olive

oil at Italian restaurants, which the Italians only later began to adopt. By looking at the taco salad's ingredients, we can better understand some of the hidden ways that variety—and, in particular, our reliance on a variety of *sources*—improves our enjoyment of life. We can also learn more about how trade makes that variety possible by lowering prices, introducing new options, supplementing American production, and filling in seasonal gaps in our farming sector.

With apologies if you are a vegetarian, lactose intolerant, or even just counting calories, let's assume that an average taco salad contains nine basic ingredients: black beans, ground beef, romaine lettuce, tomatoes, onion, avocado, shredded cheese, sour cream, and a tortilla shell (we'll leave out any other fixings and spices for simplicity's sake). As C. Elmer Doolin knew well, you could technically produce all nine of these items without having to import a thing—once you've imported the *idea* of Mexican food (and concocted a dish that was never really Mexican to begin with), you could cobble together Iowa corn, North Dakota beans, Montana beef, Arizona lettuce, California tomatoes and avocados, and cheese and cream from Wisconsin. But could you cobble them together in the winter? Could you make enough to meet the needs of hundreds of millions of taco lovers nationwide? In other words: could you ensure U.S. consumers the variety that is *their birthright as Americans*?!

Not even close. We can start with the tomato, the second-most-consumed vegetable in the United States (after the potato . . . and you can blame the Supreme Court for classifying the tomato as a vegetable rather than a fruit—but that's another story for another book).[9] Despite being prolific producers of tomatoes ourselves, America still imports 60 percent of our supply—almost all of it coming from our NAFTA partners, Mexico and Canada.[10] And our taste for foreign tomatoes has only grown stronger through the years; while we shipped in about 1.6 billion pounds' worth in 2000, by 2016 we had more than doubled our national import intake to over 3.6 billion pounds.[11] This influx of relatively cheap tomatoes has more than offset declines in states like Florida—second only to California in production—where tomatoes can't be grown in the winter, and helped satisfy Americans' insatiable appetite for tacos, pizza, pasta sauces, ketchup, and so much else. Without trade, we would never come close to generating enough tomatoes to meet that sort of demand.

Let us turn to lettuce, another staple food made permanently accessible because of trade. The U.S. produces more than eight billion pounds of the stuff,[12] and exports about twice as much as it imports[13]—but because nearly 99 percent of American lettuce grows in a small portion of just two states,[14] it makes our domestic supply especially vulnerable to drought and disease. We don't need to look back very far to see the reality of that risk; 2018 saw multiple *E. coli* outbreaks linked to romaine lettuce grown in the vicinity of Yuma, Arizona, a quiet city of about 95,000 people. Ordinarily, that wouldn't be a problem . . . except that nine tenths of all U.S. lettuce grown between November and March comes from the Yuma region.[15] If you enjoyed a taco salad—or any other sort of salad—in 2018, it's likely because leafy green Mexican imports arrived just in time to save lettuce's bacon. The lesson? Even when domestic production is high for a particular item, trade can help guard against unexpected shortages.

It's a similar story for the other ingredients we named. The U.S. consumes more beef than it produces (as you might expect, we lead the world in both raising and eating it)[16]—so we depend on imports from Australia, New Zealand, and Canada to keep our taco salads fully stuffed.[17] We also ship in roughly 31 million pounds of black beans[18] and up to a billion pounds of onions each year,[19] the latter of which we obtain mostly from free trade agreement partners Peru, Chile, and Mexico. Corn is an interesting case—we are by far the number one producer of it in the world, with over 90 million American acres dedicated to corn farming—because even though we grow an astounding 360 *million tons* of corn each year, nearly all of it is genetically modified.[20] The overwhelming majority of U.S.-grown corn gets processed into animal feed (either at home or abroad), oils, fuels, or sweeteners like corn syrup; because U.S. shoppers tend to be skeptical about genetically modified foods, we actually have to import additional corn from Romania, Turkey, the Netherlands, and other countries in order to meet demand—and that's the corn you're just as likely to find in your tortilla shell.

As for sour cream and cheese, trade is admittedly less of a factor in our enjoyment (at least when it comes to the type of cheese you might find in your taco salad). That's partially because we produce far more milk than we could ever consume—and partially because the American dairy industry enjoys a level of government protection unmatched by just about any other sector. Yes, while tariffs may have largely become persona non grata after World War II, the United States has not been above getting a little creative to ward off competition from foreign cows. One of the tools we've used to do that—with apologies for feeding you yet another dose of alphabet soup—is called a "TRQ," tradespeak for tariff-rate quota. The way it works is that a quota is set for a given type of product under which tariffs are very low (so as not to look like naked protectionism), but above which tariffs are extremely high. Imported butter, for example, would go from no taxes at all to being taxed at about 80 cents per pound after reaching the quota—more than one third of its market price.[21] The effect is that, in a crowded American dairy market, the TRQ essentially blocks any imports from entering the country once the quota has been hit . . . and the quota is kept low enough, at about 2 percent of all dairy produced, to keep everything *except* for sought-after foreign cheeses from making it to our shores and stores.[22] If you like delicious French, Italian, and Spanish cheeses, you're in luck—but if you've never seen foreign milk in your corner store before, this is part of the reason why.

That leaves us with the avocado, so popular across America today that it's hard to imagine they weren't always here in abundance—although, notwithstanding their popularity, I could never convince my mother to enjoy them. It wasn't so long ago that avocados were little more than a seasonal, regional delicacy; as late as the 1990s, you were unlikely to find one outside of California, and only then during the summer months. From that starting position of near-total obscurity, avocados caught on with a vengeance; in the year 2000, Americans consumed a record of just over one billion of them. By 2005, that number had nearly doubled—and it more than doubled again by 2015, when we collectively ate about four and a quarter billion avocados (holy guacamole, indeed).[23] What explains that rapid, ongoing avocado ascendance from Los Angeles novelty to a mainstream fact of life in every American town? Why, trade, of course.

California had been growing a limited number of avocados since at least 1871, when a judge from Santa Barbara managed to acquire three trees from Mexico.[24] A half century later, a high school dropout from Wisconsin was captivated by an illustration of an avocado tree in a magazine; the young man pooled his money together (along with a generous loan from his sister), and purchased a small plot of land in the La Habra Heights neighborhood of Los Angeles County. Without any special training, this amateur grafted together a number of preexisting avocado seed varieties to form a new breed, one which happened to greatly improve the taste and resilience of the fruit. That lone strain, traceable to a single tree which died in 2002 after seventy-six years of life,[25] now accounts for about 95 percent of all avocados eaten in North America[26]—all thanks to the luck and ingenuity of that young man from Wisconsin, Rudolph Hass.

The Hass avocado returned to its ancestral roots in Mexico, but favorable growing conditions south of the Rio Grande meant that far more Mexicans than Americans were able to enjoy the delectable concoction for a long time. Between 1970 and 1999, the United States was the second-largest avocado producer in the world, growing an average of just over 150,000 tons of avocados per year—in Mexico, however, the average output of about 530,000 tons per year dwarfed ours.[27] Despite Americans' newfound love of avocados in recent years, our capacity to grow them has actually *decreased* over time; in 2017, for example, we grew only 132,000 tons of them, slipping to tenth place in the world after our long reign as number two.[28] Our supply didn't keep up with our tastes—but imports did.

The real story of what fueled our love affair with avocados goes back to NAFTA. In the years before the trade agreement, the U.S. had severely restricted the importing of Mexican fruit, but our new partnership opened the door to a slow, planned loosening of trade barriers beginning in the late 1990s and culminating with the complete removal of all tariffs and quotas in 2007.[29] That easing of trade restrictions coincides almost perfectly with the rise in popularity of the avocado in America; the more that trade barriers were chipped away, the more exposure and demand ticked upward. And while in the year 2000 only about 40 percent of the billion avocados eaten in the United States were grown in places like Mexico, the Dominican Republic, Colombia, and Peru, by 2015 about 85 percent of the more than four billion avocados we ate were imported.[30]

The ramifications of that policy shift on Mexican fruit—a minor appendix in a mammoth agreement—are hard to overstate. Avocados are *everywhere* in America today, from Burger King Whoppers to ritzy Manhattan restaurants, from hipster ice cream shops to fancy cosmetic scrubs. Industry groups estimate that we smash nearly 140 million pounds of avocados into guacamole on Super Bowl Sunday alone.[31] No dish has become more synonymous with millennials than avocado toast, thanks in large part to Australian millionaire Tim Gurner's suggestion during a *60 Minutes* interview that the generation's love of the pricey, popular brunch item was responsible for their low homeownership rates—a viral moment that led to widespread mockery online.[32] All told, the average American now eats more than seven pounds of avocados per year,[33] or nearly twenty typical Hass avocados. That's more than triple the amount that we consumed less than two decades ago[34]—and today, a higher percentage of Americans regularly eat avocados than they do cherries, raspberries, asparagus, or pears.[35] In fact, the buttery green ovals have become so ubiquitous that they've even given rise to avocado fatigue, prompting a backlash from online tastemakers who argue that the fashionability of the once hip fruit is already "over-cado."[36]

At its core (or, rather, its pit), the meteoric rise of the avocado in American culture is simply a modern, sped-up version of a story that has been replicated hundreds of times before. Chocolate, coffee, and tea were once imported luxuries; pineapples, cumin, fennel, and Sriracha were at various points in our history just curiosities with exotic-sounding names. It's important to note that this story is more about trade than it is specifically about trade *agreements*; we've adopted (and regularly import) plenty of foods and products from countries like Vietnam, with whom we don't have a formal free trade deal. It's also worth noting that none of this has crushed U.S. agriculture in the way that many manufacturing industries have been hurt by globalization—by and large, American farmers have benefited enormously from gaining access to global customers, 95 percent of whom live beyond our shores.

Trade has been the unsung hero in creating the variety that has come to define our culture—not only in the food we eat, but in the products we use, the cars we drive, the entertainment we enjoy, and the jobs we do. Go into your local grocery store sometime, and try to see it the way that Boris Yeltsin must have seen it: Brazil nuts next to Chinese walnuts next to cashews from India; Peruvian carrots alongside broccoli from Mexico; lamb from New Zealand and salmon from Canada; spices from every corner of the world. These are the sorts of choices that can only exist in an open, globalized economy; for whatever harms that trade may bring to industries undercut by foreign competition, the ampleness of our produce aisles and deli counters must be part of the equation, too. This is the dream of abundance, the dream of a democracy of goods, the dream of freedom of choice, and the dream of novelty all rolled into one—although, regrettably, we know that these dreams have not been made available to all Americans in all parts of the country. For better or worse, however, they are the dreams that, more than any other, now define life in America.

One man who understood these ideas well was Winston Churchill. When a young Sir Winston was made First Lord of the Admiralty just prior to the outbreak of World War I, his chief concern was ensuring that British warships would be able to withstand the firepower of the German fleet. The advent of the torpedo had added weight to vessels in the form of offensive and defensive steel, and speed was at a premium. Churchill was faced with a choice of whether to continue to run his country's ships on coal—which Britain produced a great deal of—or to run them on oil, which lasted longer, generated steam more quickly, and produced less smoke, allowing ships to simultaneously accelerate faster and be less visible to enemy vessels from afar. The only problem was that Britain didn't produce any oil at all. Churchill's decision to move the Royal Navy from domestic coal to imported oil was widely criticized at the time, including by military leaders; many in Britain could not conceive of trading away national self-reliance for an objectively better choice. But he persuaded Parliament, and, before long, all new British vessels were fueled by imported oil—a decision that helped ensure the Allied powers' supremacy over the Germans for the duration of World War I.[37]

The lessons of Churchill, of Yeltsin, and of the taco salad are one and the same: if you want to stay on the forefront of success, of variety, of might, and of the good life, you have to look beyond your own borders. You have to import. There is a strength and resilience that comes from integrating the best elements of multiple cultures that no country, however self-sufficient or determined, could ever hope to achieve on its own. And while there may be something vaguely patriotic in the notion of an all-American taco salad—with Iowa corn, Montana beef, California tomatoes, and all the rest—the version we ended up with is, like oil over coal in British battleships, simply better. Because it contains Romanian corn, Mexican tomatoes, Peruvian onions, and so forth, it is more available, more affordable, and more reliable to all of us than it would ever otherwise be. We've mingled together the best and most resilient ingredients from all over the world so that everybody has the freedom and variety they need to make a choice—in the end, what could be more American than that?

CHAPTER 5

The Most American Car on the Road

Now that we've talked about tomatoes, onions, avocados, and lettuce, the time has come to turn our attention to lemons. No, not the yellow fruit—we'll get to yellow fruit in the next chapter. I speak not of citrus, but of Citroëns (and Fords, Chevys, and Chryslers, too). Those of us who were born prior to the 1960s probably remember the automotive variety of lemons well; those who are a little younger than that may be asking themselves, "'what in the world is he talking about right now?" A lemon, for the uninitiated, is a new car that rolls off of the dealership lot so riddled with manufacturing defects that it's essentially a dud—a surprisingly common occurrence prior to the mid-1970s, but one that is unthinkable today.

No one knows for sure why we began calling defective cars

lemons, but it may trace back to early-twentieth-century British slang (and the experience of purchasing one would certainly leave a sour taste in your mouth). I'm old enough to recall a time when lemons were just a fact of life—something you hoped beyond hope not to get saddled with when you visited the dealership. If you were one of the unfortunate buyers who happened to get stuck with one, you'll remember it well: the engine would start smoking; the car would break down on the way home; parts would stop working after a matter of days. I once owned a 1965 Buick Skylark convertible that, when you turned it off, would keep sputtering for a few minutes and make some pinging noises before finally screeching to a halt. The color: "champagne mist." And my friends uncharitably snickered that my car certainly *miss*-(t). My dad's '57 Mercury station wagon wasn't much better. For a long time, there was very little that you could do about a situation like that but eat the costs and chalk it up to bad luck.

Recourse arrived in 1975. That's when President Gerald Ford signed the Magnuson-Moss Warranty Act—the first so-called "lemon law"—allowing consumers to seek legal remedies if a car they purchased failed to live up to the seller's warranties. Connecticut became the first state to pass a lemon law of its own in 1982 to raise standards even higher, and today all fifty states have a version on the books to protect unlucky buyers from getting stuck. But lemon laws just provided an avenue for disgruntled car buyers to get their money back—they didn't do anything to improve the quality of vehicles. After all, to be clear, most lemons were the result of manufacturing slipups by otherwise reputable automakers—not intentional efforts to dupe consumers. So why is it that lemons are now a thing of the past? Would you be surprised if I told you that the answer to that question is that beautiful, five-letter word, *T-R-A-D-E*? You wouldn't?

The first foreign automaker to import cars into the U.S. is

believed to have been Volkswagen, which first brought its Beetle to America in 1949—just four years after the close of World War II—and sold a grand total of two (yes, *two*) vehicles that year.[1] It would be joined by British entrants like Jaguar, Austin-Healey, and MG in the early 1950s before Toyota and Nissan quietly made their own initial jumps across the ocean toward the end of the decade.[2] The luck of the Beetle would begin to turn in 1955, when the creation of the Volkswagen Group of America—a North American headquarters initially located in New Jersey—helped the German automaker jump from two vehicles sold in 1949 to about 50,000 by 1957.[3] When my dad traded in his cursed Mercury station wagon and bought a 1961 red Volkswagen bus—picture the family van featured in the film *Little Miss Sunshine*—it was just about the only foreign car we ever saw on the road. But it was cheap, saved on gas, and carried a lot more than our old Mercury. It also came without a gas gauge, meaning that we had to write down the mileage on a card taped to the dashboard so that we would know when to refuel! Fortunately, American automakers would later adopt the minivan, innovate on it, and make it an institution of our own. For the most part, though, Americans were still mostly intent on buying American at that time. In 1960, the "Big Three" automakers (GM, Ford, and Chrysler) made up about 90 percent of the U.S. market share—a figure that doesn't even include other domestic companies like the American Motors Corporation—and by 1970 that number had only dropped down slightly, to 82 percent. Today, that percentage has slipped all the way down to the 40s.[4]

What really killed the lemon wasn't laws—it was the rise of serious foreign competition and advanced manufacturing techniques, each of which took root in America during the 1970s. All those years spent insulated from overseas competitors had allowed U.S. automakers to get lazy; until the Japanese and the Germans arrived, they had no real incentive to control costs or improve quality. A late friend of mine who served as president of both Ford and Chrysler, Paul Bergmoser, once told me that American auto executives were so confident about their control over the marketplace, they had no qualms about inviting Japanese auto executives to tour their assembly plants—they weren't the least bit worried about foreign competition eating into their customer base! This attitude was shortsighted, of course, but it was also a disservice to American consumers who went years without benefiting from the innovation that open competition tends to spark.

We've already discussed in chapter one how the arrival of Japanese automakers transformed the marketplace and lit a fire under Detroit. By the middle of the decade, Honda, Toyota, Nissan, Mazda, and Subaru had already become firmly associated with quality in the minds of American car buyers. But what was truly revolutionary about these imports wasn't the models themselves, but rather the way in which they were assembled—using precision engineering, aided by robotics, with a relentless focus on quality. They empowered their workers, too. Automakers instilled concepts like *kaizen*, Japanese for "improvement," a principle under which employees were encouraged to offer recommendations to make the manufacturing process better. Andon cords—suspended lines that resemble what you might pull on a public bus to request a stop—gave every worker the power to halt assembly if they noticed something amiss. Mixed production lines also allowed Japanese automakers operating in America to produce different kinds of models on the same assembly line, which offered greater flexibility and responsiveness to consumer demand. To this day, many assembly lines in Ford and GM plants go unused because they lack this ability—in fact, it's one of the big reasons why facilities end up getting shuttered and why there is so much unused capacity.

Because our trade policy during those years allowed for an influx of imports to compete in the U.S. market—and because Americans soon discovered that other countries like Japan and Germany had developed more appealing cars—the only way for the United States to keep up was by playing copycat. In time, Detroit's manufacturing capacity quickly grew more sophisticated and more automated, though it was still playing catch-up into the 1990s. This process cost many U.S. autoworkers their jobs, but it brought us higher-quality, more reliable domestic cars—and ultimately rendered lemons a distant memory. That transformation was deeply painful for many workers and their families left behind by new manufacturing practices—but by forcing us to innovate and grow stronger, in all likelihood, it may have saved the American auto industry and the jobs it supports from becoming completely overtaken by overseas competitors.

It's easy to forget what a marvel today's cars really are. As automakers from Japan, Germany, South Korea, Britain, America, and other nations pushed each other to win customers through the years, they discovered that the competition made each of them better. Safety and performance have reached heights that were once unimaginable. Vehicles now routinely run for well over 100,000 miles. Cars are probably the first product that comes to mind for most Americans when they think about imports and exports. They also happen to be a perfect demonstration of how global trade has led to better products. The road to better, safer, more durable vehicles has been a bumpy ride—and, somewhere along the way, the notion of the "American car" vanished.

There's No Such Thing as an American Car

The Ford Mustang. The Chevy Corvette. The Cadillac Eldorado. You'd be hard-pressed to name more iconic symbols of life in twentieth-century America than these classic, all-American cars. The automobile occupies a place in our culture that is more than just central—it's downright romantic. Decades of movies, music, literature, and art have fueled our obsession with cars; they are the modern incarnation of our "Manifest Destiny," monuments to our unique national ambition, our love of exploration, and that most American of freedoms: the freedom of the open road. How much do we love our cars? But if I asked you to guess the most all-American car available in 2018—that is to say, the vehicle with the highest portion of American parts, labor, and assembly—you'd just be spinning your wheels naming Fords and Chevys. According to the National Highway Transportation Safety Administration (or NHTSA, a federal agency that is charged by law with publishing made-in-America vehicle ratings each year), the most American car of 2018 was in fact—drumroll, please . . . the Honda Odyssey.[5]

Yes, the Honda Odyssey! Assembled in the heart of Lincoln, Alabama, with an American engine and an American transmission, the Odyssey topped the charts in 2018 with an estimated 75 percent of U.S. content. Well, technically, because of a quirk in the law, our government includes both U.S. *and Canadian* content in its made-in-America determinations—perhaps an indication of the seamlessness of our supply chains and manufacturing processes. Parts move so freely between the two countries that even our government can't differentiate what came from where—remember, walking from Detroit to Ontario wouldn't even make a dent toward getting your 10,000 steps in. Look down the list, and you'll have to go through a half dozen Hondas at the top of their ratings—including the Civic, the Pilot, and the Acura MDX—before you get to . . . a German car, the Mercedes-Benz C-Class Sedan. It's only after this that you'll find the first "American" entry in the list of 2018's most American cars: it is, indeed, the Chevy Corvette, coming in with a respectable 67 percent of U.S. content.[6] Keep going, and the story is the same—you'll find yet more Hondas, Toyotas, Hyundais, Nissans, and Mercedes surrounding the occasional Ford or Buick.

In fact, right after the Odyssey comes the Honda Ridgeline, named the North American truck of the year at the 2017 Detroit Auto Show. Like the Odyssey, the Ridgeline is assembled in Alabama and designed in southern California. Its engine and transmission are both American-sourced, and its engineering and testing—also known as "research and development"—happens at Honda R&D Americas in Raymond, Ohio, which employs 1,600 locals. The Ridgeline doesn't sell as well as the Ford F-Series, but even in the hyper-American world of pickup trucks, the Ridgeline fits right in—and tops the charts. The reason for the discrepancy between the cars we think of as being "American" and the cars that are actually built here using American-made parts is one of the most frequently overlooked—and one of the most critically important—elements of the modern economy: the global supply chain.

A supply chain, at its core, is simply the path that a product takes as it is being created—it's the network of raw materials, natural resources, parts, ingredients, labor, and any other stops along the way that an item makes before it becomes a finished product ready for the market. More and more frequently, these supply chains are referred to as "value chains," a reflection of the fact that they include research and development, engineering, and other nonphysical elements. That's true with trucks like the

Manufacturers	Makes	Carlines	Vehicle Type on Part 567 Certification Label	Percent Content US/ Canada
Honda Motor Co., Ltd.	Honda	Odyssey	MPV	75%
Honda Motor Co., Ltd.	Honda	Ridgeline AWD	Truck	75%
Honda Motor Co., Ltd.	Honda	Ridgeline FWD	Truck	75%
Honda Motor Co., Ltd.	Acura	MDX AWD	MPV	70%
Honda Motor Co., Ltd.	Acura	MDX 2WD	MPV	70%
Honda Motor Co., Ltd.	Acura	TLX AWD	PC	70%
Honda Motor Co., Ltd.	Honda	Civic 2D	PC	70%
Honda Motor Co., Ltd.	Honda	Civic 2D	PC	70%
Honda Motor Co., Ltd.	Honda	Civic 2D	PC	70%
Honda Motor Co., Ltd.	Honda	Pilot	MPV	70%
Honda Motor Co., Ltd.	Honda	Pilot	MPV	70%
Mercedes-Benz USA	Mercedes-Benz	C-Class Sedan (C300/C300-4M)	PC	70%
General Motors LLC	Chevrolet	Corvette	PC	67%
General Motors LLC	Chevrolet	Volt	PC	66%
Honda Motor Co., Ltd.	Acura	RDX AWD	MPV	65%
Honda Motor Co., Ltd.	Acura	RDX FWD	MPV	65%
Honda Motor Co., Ltd.	Acura	TLX AWD A-Spec	PC	65%
Honda Motor Co., Ltd.	Acura	TLX FWD	PC	65%
Honda Motor Co., Ltd.	Acura	TLX FWD	PC	65%
Honda Motor Co., Ltd.	Acura	TLX FWD A-Spec	PC	65%
Ford Motor Company	Ford	F150	Truck	65%

According to the U.S. Department of Transportation, it just doesn't get more American than this.

Honda Ridgeline, electronics like the iPhone, and any other complex product you might use. When I served as chairman of the Export-Import Bank, and we would finance the sale of American planes to Ethiopian Airlines or Kenya Airways, there was a common misconception that our support was only helping to create jobs at Boeing—one of the largest companies in the world. But an airplane doesn't spring fully formed out of corporate offices in Chicago or a plant in suburban Seattle. To build their products, Boeing relies on more than 13,000 suppliers in every state in the country—and those suppliers, many of which are small businesses, in turn rely on Boeing for the big orders that allow them to hire and grow in their own communities.[7] The supply chain for a single aircraft includes thousands of links in places like Plainview, New York (where Cox & Company builds electric de-icing equipment), McMinnville, Oregon (where Meggitt Polymers makes rubber seals for the wheel wells), St. Charles, Missouri (where LMI Aerospace, a factory I visited, manufactures wing flaps), and Canton, Ohio (where Canton Drop Forge molds landing gear parts).[8] There are also plenty of items, including, for example, metal parts used on the exterior of John Deere tractors, that travel back and forth between the U.S. and Mexico several times before they are finally assembled and sold. We live in an age when so many products, from children's toys to "smart" TVs to cars and airplanes, contain both hardware and software components that are growing more complex by the day. Appreciating supply chains is crucial to understanding where the things we use actually come from.

The idea of a *global* supply chain is hardly new; it dates as far back as the eighteenth century. And some of it is pretty ugly. Perhaps the worst global supply chain began when West Africans were abducted, brought to the Americas, and forced to grow sugarcane on Caribbean plantations. The sugar was then liquefied into molasses and shipped to distilleries in New England to be converted into rum. The rum then traveled to Europe to be exchanged for other goods, which in turn were used to barter for slaves in West Africa, completing this infernal cycle. Less evil global supply chains would gain popularity throughout the Industrial Revolution, when advancements in steamships and other forms of transportation made it more practical to make use of components from different countries. It also became much less expensive, too—between 1840 and 1910, the cost of shipping freight across the Atlantic dropped by 70 percent as the introduction of regular shipping schedules helped make trade and transit more reliable.[9] The real breakthrough, however, was much more recent. The period after World War II brought together technology, trade agreements, and economic integration, making global supply chains an almost seamless proposition. Those Boeing 737s, for example, don't *just* depend on local tool and die shops in small towns across America. Because of the ease of trade and shipping, they also save on flight deck panels from Tianjin, China, electrical wiring from the Netherlands, and window seals from Germany.[10]

Of course, the reverse is true, too: plenty of products we probably think of as being "foreign"—sold by foreign companies in foreign countries—are produced using American parts, services, or natural resources . . . meaning they help support American jobs, too. Walk past Sun Fiber, a polyester manufacturing and recycling business that has created more than 300 jobs in Richburg, South Carolina, and you probably wouldn't realize that it's a subsidiary and supplier to a much larger company: JN Fibers of Zhejiang, China.[11] Sylvania, Georgia, is a town of about 2,500 people—and it's also home to the SV Pittie textile plant, a recently constructed $70 million factory that in time will create 250 jobs in the community.[12] The "SV" in that name stands for ShriVallabh Pittie, a centuries-old textile conglomerate in Rajasthan, India, to which the Georgia plant will supply labor and cotton products. There are many more examples of these sorts of small and midsized domestic businesses that function primarily as suppliers to foreign companies—and their impact on U.S. communities is no less real than the impact of the "American" factory or farm across the street.

Regardless of which direction they flow in, global supply chains have become the norm for a whole host of products, including seemingly simple goods. It wouldn't be uncommon for an American pencil manufacturer to keep costs down by using Brazilian cedarwood, Chinese paint, and Indian graphite, for example.[13] But if relying on international parts is a valuable cost-saver for basic products, it has become utterly essential for more complex machines like modern vehicles. Check out the VIN (vehicle identification number) plate on your car sometime, and you'll see what I mean—it's usually located on the interior of the dashboard, along the driver's-side door jamb, or under the hood. The first digit of your VIN will tell you where your car was assembled; if you see a 1, 4, or 5, that means that it was built in the United States. If you happen to drive a Ford Fusion, a GMC Terrain, or a Lincoln MKZ, however, your first number is probably going to be a 3—each of those cars is usually assembled in Mexico. Ford Focus drivers might be surprised to see a W in place of an initial number—that's because that particular model is more often built in Germany (the W is actually for "West Germany" . . . it turns out that VIN codes aren't updated as frequently as you might think). The Ford Edge and the Chevy Equinox start off with a 2, to let you know that they were made in Canada; the L that might lead off the VIN of your Cadillac CT6 means that it was assembled in the People's Republic of China.[14] Are you getting the picture?

Volkswagen was the first automaker to recognize the benefits of global sourcing, constructing the first of several assembly plants in Mexico as early as 1961. Before long, just about every major competitor would follow in their footsteps. As trade flows increased, import barriers fell, and the race to build ever-more efficient, high-performing, cost-effective vehicles heated up, a curious mosaic of moving parts began to take shape. Quintessential American cars like the Ford Mustang started using transmissions from China. The 2018 Buick Cascada—an ostensibly American car produced by a German subsidiary of GM—was assembled in Poland with a Korean transmission and an engine from Hungary.[15] And by 2018, not only was the Honda Odyssey the most "American" car on the road—the largest U.S. auto exporter by value for five years in a row had been none other than BMW (remember, that "B" is for Bavaria, not Baltimore), which builds some of the best German SUVs money can buy at its 1,150-acre plant in Greer, South Carolina.[16] That's right: when a German citizen wants to buy a BMW SUV, imagine their surprise when they discover that they'll have to get it imported from America! And keep in mind, anytime an automaker uses a transmission from China or an engine from Mexico, those parts can themselves contain smaller components from a host of different countries, including ours.

In fact, the process of building cars has become so globalized that, realistically, no country can produce a quality, affordable car entirely on their own. We saw a dark demonstration of that reality in the days after the September 11 terrorist attacks, when our borders were temporarily shut down due to the national security threat. Without the ability to bring in foreign engines, transmissions, shock absorbers, and hundreds of other components, it only took three days before there were no American manufacturers capable of assembling a single car. Setting self-reliance and the romance of the American automobile aside, it's important to remember that these foreign parts ultimately make our cars better, cheaper, and more reliable. It's also an open question whether there has *ever* been a true "all-American" vehicle—it's possible that the Model T may have qualified, but it wasn't long after World War I that the earliest U.S. automakers began building manufacturing plants in Canada.[17]

As you might expect, the completely global nature of automobile production has blurred the lines between what we might consider imported and domestic cars. That evolution has taken the idea of "buying American" and turned it on its head—not only in the auto industry, but across a wide spectrum of purchases we make every day. That's important, because buying American is an idea that many U.S. families consciously strive to uphold—one national survey from *Consumer Reports* found that 78 percent of Americans were more likely to buy a product if they thought it was made in the United States.[18] One senior Obama administration official relayed to me how he repeatedly complained to his wife about her preference for buying Honda Odysseys—the family is on their fourth in a row. He used to tell her, "why can't you find a nice Chevy or Ford?" When I told him about the Department of Transportation naming the Odyssey the "most American" car, he said that he wasn't looking forward to that night's dinner conversation.

That patriotic impulse to buy American is a mile wide, but it may also be an inch deep. An Associated Press poll conducted during the 2016 presidential race—a period when the issue of globalization was especially front and center—revealed that most of us actually value low prices over "made in the USA" labels. While about three quarters of us *say* that we want to buy American, the poll found that only 9 percent of us truly go out of our way to do so.[19] When asked to choose between an $85 pair of pants made in America and a $50 foreign-made pair, two thirds of those surveyed said definitively that they'd go for the less expensive option—regardless of their income level.[20] Despite our apparent preference for saving money, the desire to buy American-made goods remains strong. Not only is it our overwhelming inclination as individuals—it also represents an important part of our national identity as a country that *makes things*.

So what makes a product truly *American*, anyway, in an era when even our pencils are globally sourced—to say nothing of our cars? To gain some perspective on this, I sat down with

Frank DuBois, chair of the International Business Department at American University's Kogod School of Business. In an effort to add clarity around the question of what really determines the "American-ness" of our cars, Professor DuBois created the Kogod Made in America Auto Index in 2012 as an alternative ranking. His research provides further proof that none of us are ever *just* buying American when we shop for a car. Not a single vehicle on the 2018 version of either the Kogod index or the Department of Transportation list clocked in with more than 76 percent U.S. (or Canadian!) content. And DuBois expects that ceiling to drop even further as more and more companies take advantage of big increases in Chinese, Indian, and Thai auto parts production and exporting. And yes, for the curious: the *least* "American" supposedly American car is the Chevrolet Spark, with a whopping *one percent* of U.S. or Canadian content![21]

It's perfectly natural to take a look at this state of affairs and lament the fact that America has lost the ability to build a powerful machine on its own—we no longer have the option to "go it alone." But that's not how I see it. In early 2019, I visited a company called Rassini—a manufacturer of vehicle brakes, and the number one supplier of lift springs that can be found in many "American" pickup trucks. Rassini's cutting-edge operation makes the cars we buy from GM and other domestic automakers safer, more innovative, and more affordable. They are a major boon to U.S. drivers . . . and they are located in the city of Puebla, Mexico. Rassini is the perfect example of why while going it alone may remind us of our cowboy past, it makes even less sense today than it did in times gone by. Our dependence, and everybody else's, on global supply chains has allowed us to make much better things, often for far less money. That extends well beyond pencils, cars, and airplanes to cover a huge swath of products and services, too. The controversial trend of moving customer support call centers to India, which began in earnest around the year 2000, is part of this phenomenon as well. That shift has allowed companies to offer 24/7 support—something that isn't easy to do across America's multiple time zones. Of course, it has also become the poster-child of "outsourcing," the deeply unpopular practice of corporations shipping U.S. jobs overseas to save a buck.

From a company's point of view, outsourcing jobs on the assembly line or in a call center is no different from the idea of the Ford EcoSport using an engine that was built in Chennai, India. After all, both are just ways to cut costs by shifting the supply chain to take advantage of less expensive foreign parts or labor. But we're not just replacing American steel and graphite—we're replacing people who live in our own communities with those half a world away. Global supply chains have been instrumental in making remarkable, affordable products widely available to American families. But too often in their rush to improve products and increase profits, companies have treated American workers the same way they've treated American parts: as interchangeable. The pace of change has been fast and frightening, and the replacement of American workers with the "other"—that is to say, foreign workers—has added to the fear and resentment that many Americans feel about globalization.

That last point is what fuels so much opposition to globalization on both the political right and left in America. Critics of trade have every right to be protective of American jobs, of course, and can't be judged for prioritizing the success of families in Hershey and Sheboygan over that of families in Hyderabad and Shenzhen. Proponents of trade would argue that they are being protective of American jobs, too—even if that sometimes means ceding lower-wage jobs to other countries in order to cultivate different, often higher-skilled categories of jobs here at home. Unfortunately, pro-trade politicians haven't always been candid about that point—and when they *have* been, it usually hasn't been well-received. When Bill Clinton informed the country that the average eighteen-year-old American "will change jobs eight times in a lifetime" during a 1992 presidential debate, for example, the public was not exactly enthusiastic to hear it.

The reality is that we couldn't simply turn off the spigot of the global economy even if we wanted to. Today, virtually every American industry has already become irreversibly intertwined with the rest of the world. Even the special black paint used by Ford, GM, and other automakers for car exteriors is imported from Fukushima, Japan—it had to be temporarily halted after the nuclear disaster in 2011. It would be easy to pursue protectionism—and temporarily safeguard the jobs of American autoworkers—if all we had to do was ban every foreign company or slap large tariffs on outside steel. But it's Ford and Chevy, not Honda and Nissan, that rely on a lot of that foreign metal to stay competitive. And it's the Toyota Camry—America's best-selling car for most of this century, built in Georgetown, Kentucky—that is believed to have created more U.S. assembly line jobs than any other. A 2011 ABC News investigation found that the Camry created 20 American manufacturing jobs for every 100 cars sold, compared with 13 for the Ford Escape.[22] All told, supposedly "foreign" automakers employ about 130,000 Americans, most of whom are concentrated in communities in Kentucky, Ohio, Michigan, Tennessee, and South Carolina.[23] What will restricting imports or otherwise pulling back from the world do for them?

Tariffs: A Circular Firing Squad

This brings us right back to tariffs, the weapon of choice for U.S. protectionists for more than 230 years. You'll recall that tariffs were actually a fairly effective tool during the early years of our republic—an essential one, in fact, given that they were basically America's only source of tax revenue. Back when Alexander Hamilton and his compatriots were making the case for tariffs, there were clear reasons to put up barriers to foreign competition: our industries were in their infancy, and, like a caterpillar in a cocoon, needed to be kept safe from the world until they could grow strong enough to take flight on their own. Back then, of course, the products we made weren't as complicated—we could source all of them, including the labor, right here at home. Goods were simply simpler, and only rarely crisscrossed borders during the production process. But in a modern world of mature, highly competitive U.S. industries that require long, intricate global value chains, it's hard to even conceive of a tariff that would be helpful to some group of American workers without hurting others.

Take tariffs on steel, for example—like the ones that President Trump imposed in 2018. Trump proclaimed at the time that the hefty tariffs would "discourage companies from laying off their workers"[24] by making it costlier for U.S. businesses to purchase foreign steel. And he was right! The tariffs really *did* discourage companies from laying off their workers—steel companies, that is. In November of 2018, Steel Dynamics of Fort Wayne, Indiana, announced that they would begin construction on a new flat roll steel mill expected to support 600 new jobs somewhere in the American Southwest. Trump took to Twitter later that week to crow that "Steel JOBS are coming back to America, just like I predicted."[25] What Trump probably did not predict, however, was the impact of his tariffs on *other* types of companies, and more specifically on the global supply chains U.S. businesses rely on to make sales and hire American workers.

The most prominent example of this was, again, the domestic auto industry—the same import barriers that cleared the way for Steel Dynamics to expand also hammered companies like GM, which faced a $1 billion increase in production costs largely as a consequence of the new tariffs on the raw materials they depend on to build their cars.[26] In June of 2018, GM warned the Trump administration that these tariffs—and the trade wars they would inevitably provoke—would lead to "less investment, fewer jobs, and lower wages,"[27] a prediction that top White House trade advisor Peter Navarro dismissed as mere "smoke and mirrors."[28] A few months later, on November 26, the very same day that news broke about Steel Dynamics' plans to build a new mill, that warning came true. GM announced that morning that it would be closing four U.S. plants and slashing 14,000 American jobs, or almost 25 times the number of steel industry jobs projected to be created by the new Steel Dynamics facility.[29] There were certainly a number of factors that went into GM's decision—but tariffs were among them. The bottom line is that, essentially, we started this particular trade war by killing off 14,000 jobs for the potential of adding 600—you do the math on whether that constitutes a good idea. The following day, Trump tweeted that he was "very disappointed with General Motors" and would be "looking at cutting all @GM subsidies"—a curious threat, given that no such subsidies exist.[30]

The consequences of the steel tariffs extended far beyond just Steel Dynamics and GM, of course. For starters, June saw America's largest nail manufacturer lay off sixty employees in Missouri. The summer trade war prompted Milwaukee-based Harley-Davidson to shift jobs overseas to help stave off a $2,200 spike in the cost of every motorcycle it sells in Europe.[31] Shortly after opening its first-ever American manufacturing plant in Ridgeville, South Carolina, Swedish automaker Volvo—owned by a Chinese parent company—announced that Trump's steel tariffs could force the company to go back on its promise of creating 4,000 new jobs there.[32] Smaller businesses and suppliers have been hit hard, too. Jane Hardy, the CEO of Brinly-Hardy, a 180-year-old lawn care equipment manufacturer in Jeffersonville, Indiana, told *The Washington Post* that she was forced to lay off seventy-five employees as a result of the tariffs, calling her company and its workers "collateral damage."[33] TV manufacturer Element Electronics shuttered a plant—and 126 jobs—in Winnsboro, South Carolina, due to "the new tariffs that were recently and unexpectedly imposed on many goods imported from China."[34] So many companies, large and small, have already announced layoffs and factory closings stemming from the tariff fallout. And many more have canceled plans to invest or expand, cut back on employees' hours, or even furloughed parts of their workforce—from door lock shapers in Michigan, to electric bike designers in North Carolina, to lobstermen in the Florida Keys.[35] Add this all up, and for the 170,000 steelworkers in America being protected by tariffs, there are 6.5 million Americans working jobs that depend on steel who are hurt by them.

While it's impossible to tally the exact number of U.S. jobs lost or gained due to the tariffs, the GM numbers alone suggest that the losses are dramatically outpacing the gains. For what it's worth, the U.S. Chamber of Commerce estimates that trade actions initiated by the Trump administration in 2018 could ultimately cost America as many as 2.6 million jobs.[36] When it comes to the steel and aluminum tariffs specifically, estimates vary: economists at the pro-free-trade Trade Partnership Worldwide expect that they will bring about a net loss of 470,000 jobs,[37] while those at the protectionist Economic Policy Institute claim that total losses will only amount to 5,000.[38] No serious study or projection made so far is suggesting that the tariffs will lead to a net *increase* in American jobs—the position of President Trump. This is the reality of the modern economy—the way we produce most goods and services today has become so intermingled that it's nearly impossible to do so without triggering unintended consequences across other sectors. When we interrupt global supply chains in the name of "America First," we set a wildfire that can quickly escalate in ferocity and spread to parts of the economy we never imagined would be touched. We also run the risk that as a place to do business, the U.S. will be seen as unreliable and unpredictable.

So what does all of this mean for the future of "buying American"? To begin with, it means that we all have to reconsider our assumptions about what defines things as being "American" or not. If we want our choices to support U.S. jobs, we need to think harder about every link in the chains that make up modern products. A good place to start might be by test-driving a Honda Odyssey. We also need to stop thinking of economics as a zero-sum game in which a blow to a competitor's fortunes automatically means a win for us; gone are the days when boosting the profits of a U.S. industry was as simple as turning away British ships at the harbor or placing a ban on Chinese steel.

Somewhere along the way, the globalization of our economy changed the math—we still compete with other nations, of course, but to a growing extent we also depend on *their* success for our own. Indeed, that interdependency was a major rationale for globalization, the idea being that weaving our economic fortunes together would promote stability and peace. As the world's number two exporter, America stands to benefit enormously from the success of other countries—the more that people around the world enter the global middle class, the more they buy from us, fueling job growth and prosperity here at home. And while trade has always been premised on the idea that, at its best, it is a rising tide that lifts all boats, today, through global supply chains, we've tethered our boats together just to make sure. That connectivity has proven to be a strength, whether it's improving the quality and affordability of our cars or simply delivering us a better American pencil.

CHAPTER 6

The $10 Banana

What did you have for breakfast today? Cereal? Oatmeal? If so, there's a decent chance you put some fruit on top. Whether you prefer berries, a banana, or something else, you can bet that international trade had something to do with the breakfast toppers we all take for granted today. *Why is that*, you may ask. Well—let's take a glance at the history surrounding America's foremost fruit.

When people hear the phrase *banana republic*—once it's clear that they're not talking about the clothing store—it probably conjures up images of dictators donning sunglasses and full military regalia, lawless tropical islands, political corruption, and disarray. But the term actually goes all the way back to 1901. That's the year when celebrated American writer O. Henry—whose work I remember from high school—published *Cabbages and Kings*, a collection of stories that included one titled "The

Admiral" about Anchuria, a fictional Central American nation with an economy that revolves around a single crop. O. Henry described Anchuria—modeled on the six months he had spent in Honduras—as a "small maritime banana republic," coining a term that would go on to have a life of its own.

Contrary to popular belief, countries don't become banana republics just by virtue of being chaotic, crooked, or otherwise unstable. The phrase refers specifically to economies that are so reliant on a single export that they've fallen under the thumb of private companies that control the crop in question. The result is a country with extreme income inequality subject to widespread exploitation of both the crop and the workers who cultivate it. The corporations maintain power by delivering piles of money to an upper echelon of business leaders, government officials, generals, and the like, who in turn allow the corporations to squeeze the working class and do whatever they want with the lucrative crop that funds their lifestyle. Technically speaking, *that's* what makes a country a true banana republic. When O. Henry coined the phrase, he had a very specific corporation in mind: the United Fruit Company—which years later would come to be known as Chiquita.

A century ago, the United Fruit Company represented everything insidious about global economics. One of the earliest successful multinational corporations, its roots traced back to a New York businessman named Minor Keith. Keith's family had been granted a contract from the Costa Rican government to construct a railroad from the nation's capital, San José, through a treacherous stretch of jungle to the eastern port city of Limón. Working conditions were brutal; it was said that of the 700 men who took part in the project—many of whom were inmates Keith had arranged to have shipped down from a New Orleans prison—a mere 25 survived all the way to Limón.[1] To cut corners on his workers' meals, Keith had banana plants sown along the route—but when the Costa Rican economy crashed and the government could no longer afford to pay Keith for the work, the fate of the railroad was uncertain. In lieu of money, Keith accepted President Próspero Fernández Oreamuno's offer to hand over 800,000 acres of Costa Rican land—all of it tax-free—along with a ninety-nine-year lease to operate the railway.

Keith's team finished laying the tracks in 1890, but, not surprisingly, passengers didn't flock to the route—the railroad turned out to be a boondoggle. He soon discovered, however, that owning a vast expanse of tax-free banana plantations and an empty train to carry them to the coast presented a lucrative opportunity of its own. Keith may not have been admirable, but no one could accuse him of not being resourceful—and I should note that his tactic of building a railroad in order to win access to the surrounding natural resources is the same playbook China is following when it comes to development in Africa today. It wasn't attractive then and it certainly isn't now. Keith started three separate companies dedicated to exporting bananas, eventually expanding his operations up and down the Caribbean coast; his empire would later join forces with a Boston-based importer to become the United Fruit Company. With an eventual 3.5 million acres of land—about the size of Connecticut—spread across the region, a vast network of radio and railway holdings, and near-total control over the most vital commodities of Colombia, Honduras, Jamaica, Belize (known then as British Honduras), and a number of other countries, United Fruit held extraordinary influence over Central American and Caribbean politics. It became the largest landowner in Guatemala—where it also ran the national postal service. In addition, it became the single largest employer in all of Central America; today, that title is held by Walmart. Locals took to calling it "El Pulpo"—and no, that isn't

Spanish for "the pulp." It's Spanish for "the octopus," a reference to the fact that the company had its tentacles just about everywhere in the region. And in each new market it entered, it used threats, kickbacks, and bribes and all sorts of unsavory activities to keep presidents and dictators under their thumb, while exploiting workers mercilessly without anyone saying a word. Its best customer for bananas: America.

Just a few generations before the banana would become the most widely eaten fruit in the United States,[2] it was generally considered by the small number of Americans who had heard of it to be an unusual, unaffordable curiosity—a bizarre crop grown in exotic lands. Until United Fruit cracked the code on refrigerated train cars and freighters, up to then, transporting large quantities of fresh fruit across long distances was virtually impossible. Exacerbating the transportation issues was the fact that bananas bruise easily, need to be picked by hand, and spoil quickly as compared with other fruits. To overcome those problems, the company made use of global supply chains—often ruthlessly. Not only did they control the land, the labor, the trains, the media, and the governments that oversaw their banana production, but they also assembled a veritable armada of company-owned vessels to safely and speedily transport their product to the United States. As if the colonialist overtones were not explicit enough, these ships came to be known as "The Great White Fleet."

Andrew Preston, whose Boston Fruit Company had merged with Minor Keith's to form United Fruit, believed that the unfamiliar banana held the potential to become "more popular than apples" among the American public—and he was right.[3] A vast network of ice-filled warehouses across the United States allowed for broad distribution with limited spoilage, while a relentless marketing effort centered on children firmly installed the banana as a healthy choice. Most crucially of all, bananas were remarka-

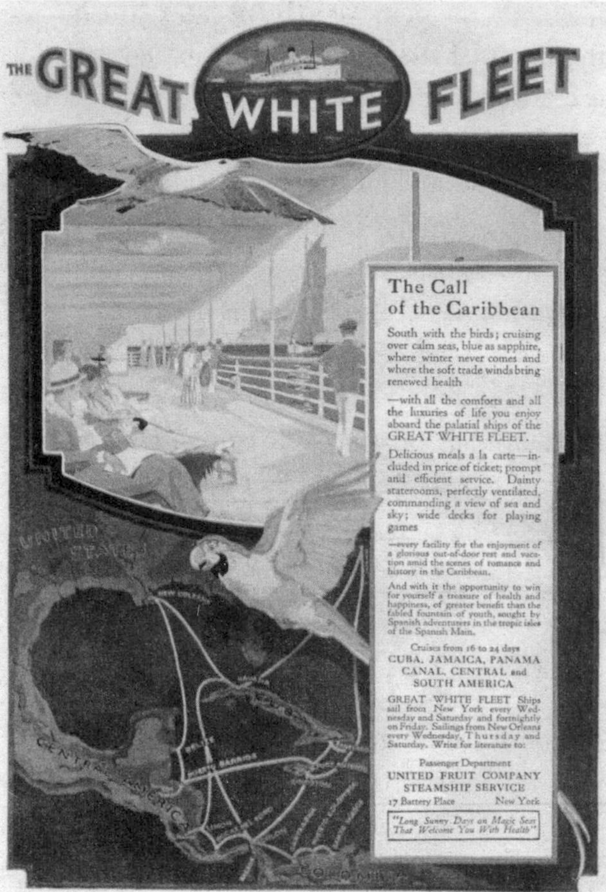

United Fruit Company posters: just a little on the nose.

bly cheap from the day they arrived in America—something that was only possible due to the tight grip that United Fruit held over the people and places that produced them. We were able to enjoy plentiful and inexpensive fruit, but there was a cost . . . just not one that America incurred. As country after country in Central America was reduced to the status of a banana republic—leading to riots, coups, bloodshed, and stunted economic growth—the United States was falling ever more in love with a fruit that would

Bananas . . . wholesome—and then some!

arguably become the most successful import in our nation's history. Perhaps it shouldn't surprise us, then, that the United States had difficult relations in many Latin American countries in the years since—the shadow of colonialism runs long.

The impact of the banana was profoundly different in the United States and Latin America—a rising tide did *not* lift all boats, and the proof of that is in the art. In the U.S., bananas have become the subject of lighthearted works of pop culture, from the enormously popular 1923 novelty tune "Yes! We Have No

Bananas" to Harry Belafonte's 1956 rendition of "Banana Boat Song (Day-O)," the latter of which had originated as a much more solemn call-and-response folk song favored by United Fruit Company field workers in Jamaica. Banana peels became the most valuable prop in the world of slapstick comedy, musicians from George Gershwin to Gwen Stefani have incorporated bananas into popular song, and Andy Warhol's pop art print of a banana for *The Velvet Underground & Nico* remains among the most recognizable album covers of all time. Carmen Miranda, a Brazilian entertainer who became one of the biggest stars in Hollywood in the 1940s, famously wore a hat made largely of bananas for the 1943 Busby Berkeley musical *The Gang's All Here*.

America's first experience with bananarama.

It was so popular an image in American culture that the United Fruit Company adopted a cartoon version of Miranda in her banana hat as their logo the following year. Half a century later, after changing ownership multiple times, the company would be renamed in honor of this Miranda-inspired character—already known to generations of Americans as Miss Chiquita.

While bananas have become a mostly comic symbol in the country that voraciously devours them, they have inspired far more tragic reflections in the places that grow them. Gabriel García Márquez, the Nobel Prize–winning Colombian writer, set a major portion of his acclaimed 1967 novel, *One Hundred Years of Solitude*, against the backdrop of striking banana plantation workers who are slaughtered by a nefarious American fruit corporation—a plot based on the real-life *Masacre de las Bananeras* ("Massacre of the Banana Workers"), in which thousands of United Fruit Company workers were killed in Ciénaga, Colombia, while on strike in 1928. Chilean poet Pablo Neruda, another of South America's most revered artists, offered a more brutal assessment of the banana industry's impact in his 1950 poem "La United Fruit Co.," a common English translation of which reads in part:

> The United Fruit Company
> reserved for itself the most juicy
> piece, the central coast of my world,
> the delicate waist of America.
>
> It rebaptized these countries
> Banana Republics . . .
> it abolished free will,
> gave out imperial crowns,
> encouraged envy, attracted
> the dictatorship of flies . . .

With the bloodthirsty flies
came the Fruit Company,
amassed coffee and fruit
in ships which put to sea like
overloaded trays with the treasures
from our sunken lands . . .

. . . a corpse rolls, a thing without
name, a discarded number,
a bunch of rotten fruit
thrown on the garbage heap.[4]

I share this story not because it reflects well on global trade—it obviously doesn't—but rather because it is vital for us to understand and grapple with the human and national tragedies that trade has at times left in its wake. Confronting the legacy of the United Fruit Company does more than simply help us learn how bananas made their way onto our breakfast tables. It also forces us to be honest about trade's darkest potential trade-offs, a number of which have in reality been truly horrific and left lasting scars. Some of those who are opposed to global trade today are old-school protectionists; some are politicians looking to foment outrage; some are nationalists with reasons of their own. But a great many are conscientious, rational dissenters who look at stories like this one and say: this is what *actually happens* when multinational companies become entangled with government trade policies. They're not wrong—but it's also not that simple. And it's only by understanding the worst episodes from trade's past—including the story of the banana as well as others, such as the Atlantic slave trade—that we can responsibly chart a course for the future of global economics. These stories remind us that this future must be approached with the humanity and dignity of all

people foremost in our minds. We'll take a clo
the ways we might build that future later on i

It's important to remember that you and I
too—you are, at least, if your family is amc
U.S. households that will purchase a banana
cans' favorite fruit took a regrettable route to our shores, but
is no denying the fact that, once it arrived, it almost immediately became just as American as baseball or apple pie. Whether prized for their nutritional content or indulged in as a dessert (and we can thank a young pharmacist in training from Latrobe, Pennsylvania, for inventing the banana split in 1904), bananas have become so deeply ingrained in our lives that one study claims that the average American now eats an impressive twenty-seven pounds of them per year—how about them bananas! We grab one for breakfast on our way out the door in the morning, mash one up for the baby, bake banana bread on a weekend afternoon, or order a strawberry banana smoothie at McDonald's. I like to bring one with me anytime I give a talk or teach a class on trade—not only because they illustrate the impact of imports so clearly, or because almost every hand goes up when I ask how many people in the room have eaten a banana that week. I also do it because, let's face it, what other prop is available everywhere for about 19 cents?

It's that last point that matters most when it comes to the role of the banana in our everyday lives. Unlike so many products that have been with us for more than a century, the banana—which was inexpensive from the moment we began importing it in significant quantities—has actually gotten *less* costly over time. According to the Department of Labor, the average price of bananas in the U.S. was about 15 cents per pound in 1947,[5] roughly equivalent to $1.70 in today's dollars. Of course, if you're paying $1.70 today, you're getting ripped off—in 2017, a pound of bananas cost only 56 cents, less than a third of what it went some seventy years earlier. And keep in mind that the banana n't like a computer or a microwave that can be improved upon or made more efficient in order to lower prices over the years.[6] In fact, had an American consumer from the 1950s walked into any Trader Joe's grocery store in the country in 2018, probably the only thing that wouldn't shock them would be the sign indicating that individual bananas cost a mere 19 cents.[7]

One major reason for that remarkable consistency is bananas' own remarkable consistency: unless you happen to do your vacationing on small Indonesian fruit plantations, it's very likely that every banana you've ever eaten has been a precise genetic clone of each other one. That's because, for more than fifty years, the only variety available in the United States has been the bright yellow Cavendish banana—which, in addition to being relatively easy to

A bunch of savings.

pick and pack, reproduces asexually, unlike most fruits and flowers . . . so it never varies. That is to say, every Cavendish grows and ripens at the exact same rate as—and tastes identical to—all of its forebears. And that predictability in the process helps keep prices low. For those who don't believe that every banana is the same, just know that any variance in the quality or look of a banana that you've encountered is due either to *when* it was picked, how long it's been sitting on a shelf, temperature, and other factors that set in *after* it was picked.[8] All of us take it for granted that bananas are cheap, just as all of us take it for granted that we can find one in every corner store. That's just the reality of life in America.

But what if that wasn't true? One of the most important things we can learn from the banana is what the world would look like if our trade policies happened to bend in a different direction. If something were to take place that disrupted our trade relationships with Guatemala, Ecuador, Colombia, Costa Rica, or Honduras—the five countries that now make up almost the entire crop of bananas that we import—everyday life in America could abruptly become a little less a-peeling. All it would really take to deprive us of our bananas would be for one or more Central or South American leaders to decide that the U.S. was ripping them off—the exact sort of accusation, by the way, that Donald Trump has regularly levied against other countries. If America and, say, Colombia were to get into a trade spat and begin to impose tariffs on each other's major exports, the immediate effect would be that the number of bananas likely to be imported to the United States would drop. Prices would start to rise a little bit as the supply thinned out; increased demand for bananas amid news of a trade war would push costs even higher. Many Americans probably wouldn't notice right away—but as that 19 cent Trader Joe's banana crept closer and closer to a dollar, some families would begin opting for cheaper alternatives.

Over time, as fewer stores were reliably stocked and prices continued to rise, the banana would be downgraded from a humble, ubiquitous staple of our lives to more of a specialty fruit—the tier of the papaya and the kiwi. Lower-income households would eventually lose interest in the banana as a staple food altogether, and other banana-exporting countries might very well decide that it made more sense to take their business elsewhere—perhaps to another partner that proved a little more hospitable to trade, such as Canada. Chiquita, the successor corporation to the United Fruit Company, would be forced to announce layoffs at its headquarters in Charlotte, North Carolina, threatening the livelihood of its 20,000 employees (you see—imports *do* create jobs). Its chief rival, California's Dole Food Company, would suffer as well. Before long, America's most popular fruit would return to its roots as a luxury item as we adapted our diets to reflect the depleted supply. There would be no more songs, no more splits, no more smoothies, and no more school lunches. And that, my friends, is how you end up with a $10 banana.

All of this may sound like science fiction, but the truth is that we are already seeing a variation on this story playing out today. The banana's frequent breakfast buddy, the orange, has been a signature American export for more than a century—although, like the banana, it isn't native to our country; it's believed that Christopher Columbus brought the first orange seeds to North America in 1493 (not 1492—he came back). Today, however, the future of Florida's most iconic crop is very much in doubt. Beginning in 2005, a citrus disease struck America that turns orange skins green, making them completely inedible. Over the following decade, Florida growers' production dropped by more than half.[9] Because the supply of U.S. oranges had suddenly become limited, the price of Florida orange juice shot up substantially, from about $4.50 a gallon to $6.71.[10] Since the beginning of this century, orange production has plummeted, prices have skyrocketed, and disease and natural disasters have decimated Florida's crop—Hurricane Irma alone destroyed half of the state's orange supply in 2017.[11] The once proud Florida orange is following the script of our imaginary $10 banana.

None of this means that Americans have soured on oranges—Brazil has filled in the gap to become the world's largest producer, as well as its hottest exporter. In fact, Brazilian companies have benefited so much from the decline of the U.S. orange industry that they've purchased a significant financial stake in every major Florida orange juice operation still in existence in order to corner the market on "American" OJ. The two largest U.S. orange companies, Pepsi-owned Tropicana and Coca-Cola–owned Minute Maid, have both sold off juice and processing plants to Brazilian interests.[12] The result is that supposedly Floridian orange juice is now frequently not from Florida at all—more and more, it's from Brazil, leaving some companies to subtly shed their "Florida orange juice" labels. As the price of 100 percent *actual* Florida orange juice pushes northward to $6 or $7 per carton domestically, companies have slyly reduced the size of their containers, in some cases shaving seven ounces off the size of some containers you'll find at the store.[13] The Florida orange is also on the verge of becoming extinct as an American export. Trade wars with China, Canada, and Europe launched in 2018 are driving some of our most reliable partners further into the arms of the Brazilian orange industry, too. The U.S. exported as much as 151,000 metric tons of orange juice in the 2010–2011 season—that works out to roughly 335 million 8-ounce glasses, or about one for every person in America. But the number dwindled to less than one third of that—an estimated 45,000 metric tons—for the 2017–2018 harvest.[14]

Strictly speaking, it wasn't trade policy that caused the Florida orange to decline. But the fate of this once thriving industry does provide a glimpse of what a world of high trade barriers might look like. If a trade dispute, quota, or trade war were to prevent the United States from importing Brazilian oranges, and if trends in the Florida orange industry were to continue, it would not be a stretch to imagine America as a nation of $10 oranges—or, frankly, of no oranges at all. And if our country were to keep gravitating back toward protectionism, as it has begun to do under the watch of President Trump, it wouldn't just be our nation's most iconic fruits that suddenly became more expensive or disappeared entirely from our lives. A whole host of products that have grown so commonplace in our culture that they now *seem* to be entirely American—even though in reality they depend on imports—would follow suit. We've already talked about how quickly our domestic production of cars would cease without imported parts. Laptops and cell phones, too, would be nearly impossible to come by. Good luck finding a television, a men's dress shirt, a Barbie doll, or an American flag—we have nearly all of these items shipped in from overseas. Gerber baby food, Rawlings baseballs, Converse shoes, Fender Stratocasters, and even Levi's jeans are among the iconic "American" products that are made entirely in other countries.[15] In a world of high trade barriers, they would either vanish entirely from our stores or appear only sporadically in the form of new, exorbitantly priced made-in-America editions.

Talking about imports is taboo—we haven't had a national conversation about it. You see, politicians *hate* talking about imports; we have brainwashed the public to feel that it's un-American to like and celebrate foreign products on principle (unless you are an elite globalist, that is). Everybody knows that cheap imported goods undermine U.S. jobs and American-made products, after all . . . right? So instead of touting the value of imported goods when they talk up trade's benefits—bananas that cost less than a quarter, year-round tomatoes, less-expensive clothing, toys, electronics, and so on—politicians focus on the far more popular side of the equation: exports, which people rightly equate with American jobs. Believe me—I get it. I spent eight years in government as one of our chief cheerleaders and deal makers on U.S. exports, and nothing makes me happier than sharing those success stories. But because nobody ever makes the case for how *imports* also improve our lives by lowering prices and keeping inflation at bay, our negative feelings about them only become more deeply entrenched over time.

This is borne out in recent surveys on trade, which has always been an issue where our opinions tend to fluctuate pretty wildly as compared with polling on taxes, immigration, or other major topics of the day. Why is that? I suspect that it's because trade is less well understood on the whole, so it's easier for us to be swayed by fleeting debates and our feelings about whoever happens to be in the White House. Bruce Stokes, formerly at the Pew Research Center, tracks our attitudes on trade over time; in the first question on his survey, he asks people to complete the sentence "trade with other countries is . . ." with either *good* or *bad*. In their spring 2018 findings, Americans chose *good* over *bad* by a margin of 74 percent to 21 percent—a 13-point pro-trade jump from just four years earlier. Surveys from Gallup support this finding as well—both Republicans and Democrats have grown increasingly fond of trade in the wake of the 2016 election. Yes, it's true—trade does seem to be growing more popular in America! But a closer look at our responses shows that there is a fair amount of skepticism about the *specific* impact of trade on our lives.

When asked about the effect that trade has on U.S. jobs, just over a third of people in the Pew survey said that it "creates" them, another third said that it "destroys" them, and a quarter said that it doesn't make a difference either way. That great big collective shrug shouldn't be terribly surprising given how we tend to talk about trade—and my guess is that the group who opted for the *does not make a difference* response also includes most of our economists! The same results held when people were asked about trade's impact on wages: remarkably, 31 percent of Americans said that it increases them, 31 percent said that it decreases them, and 30 percent said that it has no impact at all—an almost perfect split! What's unusual about both of these questions is how far the public has shifted *in favor of trade* just since 2014—a period, you'll recall, that featured a presidential race in which Donald Trump, Hillary Clinton, and Bernie Sanders all spoke forcefully against the major trade issue of the day, the Trans-Pacific Partnership. In 2014, half of Americans said that "trade destroys jobs," while only 20 percent said that "trade creates jobs"—only four years later, Americans are evenly divided. The same story holds for wages: in 2014, three times as many Americans believed that trade hurt wages as helped them . . . four years later, those numbers are evenly split.

It shouldn't surprise us that our attitudes about how trade impacts jobs and wages are a little bit hazy. We know that jobs in export fields do in fact pay better on average than other jobs, but it's only natural that our views on how trade impacts jobs and wages depend on whether we are personally seeing a benefit or not. But the impact of imports on consumer prices? That *is* entirely clear. There is no debate whatsoever among economists—whatever their position on trade—about the fact that imports lower the cost of our food, clothing, household items, and everything else. That's why the most interesting finding in Bruce Stokes's work comes from the question of whether trade lowers or raises prices: just over a third of us say (correctly) that it decreases them, while another third believe that it somehow *increases* them. If there's one thing that economists can agree on, it's that trade reduces prices. Yet the idea that imports lower prices has failed to take root among the public, simply because no politician wants to be caught saying something nice about foreign goods. This isn't just an American phenomenon, either. Pew asked the same question in twenty-seven countries, and in only *two* of them did more than half of people express a belief that trade lowers prices: Israel and Sweden. There is a silver lining, though. Even though the number of Americans who got this question correct was fairly low, at least we were still ahead of every other country but those two. It seems that, no matter where you travel, precious few politicians are willing to explain why your daily banana costs 19 cents instead of $10—and isn't it ironic that harboring a little xenophobia about foreign goods is a trait that just about every country shares?

The truth is, it's unlikely that you or I will ever have to live in the world of the $10 banana. However much Donald Trump relishes his self-proclaimed role as a "tariff man," his commitment to protectionism is most definitely at odds with mainstream opinion in modern America. There simply isn't a line of tariff men or women waiting to follow him down that particular road. Even if there were, twice as many Americans now say that tariffs hurt the economy as the number who believe that they help. The coveted bloc of Independent voters, whom politicians love to court, oppose tariffs by a margin of 56 to 16 percent, according to Pew. In other words: voters understand that tariffs are effectively just taxes being placed on *them*. Apart from the occasional exception made for dairy products or steel, the fact is that the battle over American protectionism was fought long ago—and tariffs lost in a landslide. Cheap imported goods are thankfully here to stay.

But just because we may never see the $10 banana doesn't mean that we should ignore it. In fact, it's precisely *because* cheap imported goods are here to stay that we must account for them when we think and make decisions about trade. The price of our food, our clothes, and the products we use every day has an undeniable impact on our quality of life—and that's before you get into the cultural importance of bananas, iPhones, and so much else in our country that we only get to enjoy thanks to trade. We tend not to pay much attention to the declining costs of many of the things we buy—when we do notice it, we tend to just think of ourselves as smart and savvy shoppers. When it comes to gas prices, we plaster them up on billboard-sized signs, fret over every 10 cent hike and celebrate every minor reduction, and hold our politicians to account for shifting prices they most likely have nothing to do with. But we don't seem to ever apply that same focus to just about anything else we purchase—though maybe we should.

Consider this. In the year 1900, American households spent 57 percent of their income on food and clothing. By 1950, just a few years after the western economies began to integrate, that number had dipped to 42 percent. A few years into the new millennium that number had fallen to a mere 17 percent.[16] What could have caused this? Probably a number of factors had a role to play, including the rise of automation. But the first wave of trade deals like NAFTA, China's entry to the World Trade Organization, and the dismantling of tariffs in most of the world certainly had something to do with it. Make no mistake: this decrease in the cost of food and clothing wasn't simply a "benefit" of global trade—that was a bona fide revolution. As America continues to struggle with stagnant wages, exorbitant health care costs, housing crises, and extreme income inequality, imagine just how much harder life would be without imports. Indeed, where would working families be but for the existence of inexpensive fruits and vegetables, T-shirts, baseball mitts, backpacks, and all of the other easily ignored items that populate our day-to-day lives? While exports occupy most of the attention that politicians pay to trade, it's those dreaded imports—from the banana on up the line—that truly color what it means to be an American today.

CHAPTER 7

How Do You Like Them Apples?

We've talked tomatoes. We've talked lemons. We've talked bananas. We might as well keep working our way down the produce aisle, right? And what better topic to take on than Apples—after all, statistically speaking, there is almost a 50 percent chance that there is an apple within just a few feet of you right now.[1] Don't believe me? Check your pocket. Yes, just as a lemon can be a car, an apple can be a phone . . . an iPhone, more precisely. In fact, Steve Jobs occasionally worked in an apple orchard near McMinnville, Oregon, around the time that he met Steve Wozniak and the two came up with the idea for their Apple Computer Company. He even helped design an early logo for their company depicting Sir Isaac Newton and the famous apple preparing to give in to gravity and strike him on his melon. Today, few products provide a better demonstration of how trade can be

The state of the art in 1976.

used to spread technology, spur innovation, and widely disperse both the costs and the benefits of human progress than Apple's iPhone.

If you would, take a minute to consider your phone . . . not to stare at the screen, but to marvel at all that it stands for. The modern smartphone is a self-contained smorgasbord of human needs and desires—it is unlike anything our universe has ever seen. Though it's easy to take our devices for granted now that they've become so intimately and intensely wrapped up in our daily lives, it's worth it to take a quick step back and acknowledge what it is we're really talking about here. As I write this, there is a three-by-six-inch rectangle sitting in my jacket pocket that provides me with instantaneous access to the entire accumulation of human knowledge to date. In less time that it takes you to read this sentence, it can connect me by text, voice, or pristine video to friends on the other side of the world. It functions as a state-of-the-art camera and photography studio, contains a comprehensive and interactive map of the world, and can house tens of thousands of my favorite songs—Broadway show tunes included! If I ever wanted to, I could use it to watch a live soccer match taking place in Senegal. If I point it at the night sky, it can tell me what constellation I'm looking at. I could ask it to bring me an order of delicious steamed dumplings, a new pair of shoes, or a stranger willing to drive me wherever I'd like to go, and they would all soon arrive at my doorstep. There's even a flashlight! Oh, and did I mention that this device retails for something in the neighborhood of $999—roughly the cost of one ticket to see *Springsteen on Broadway*, a new fender for your car, or five nights in a mid-range Cleveland hotel?

My point is this: the smartphone isn't just another product. It's the pinnacle of human invention—at least so far. Less than a decade after it was first introduced, the smartphone has already changed the way Americans seek knowledge, entertain themselves, track their health, date, communicate with loved ones, manage their money, and so much else. It has allowed us to connect to—and disconnect from—the world to astounding, sometimes terrifying effect. It has become the primary way that our politicians speak to us. And however easy the device makes it all seem, the truth is that getting it into your hands requires the ideas, resources, and labor of people on six continents. Yes, the story of the iPhone is a story made possible by trade; these little rectangles in our pockets are a miracle—and, at times, a menace—that simply could not exist absent a free-flowing, globalized economy.

It's a story that begins in California in 2004, when Steve Jobs first gave the green light for Apple to begin moving into cell phones—a market that, while booming, was at the time plagued by design flaws and plenty of headaches for consumers.[2] I, for one, had one of the early mobile phones . . . it was the size of a shoe box and not much lighter! Their plans were ambitious: they wanted to create a single product that could simultaneously function as a phone, a computer, a camera, and an iPod—the wildly popular music device Apple had first released in 2001—and package it all in a small, light body with a touchscreen, Wi-Fi connectivity . . . and a price point that was appealing to the average shopper. There was no road map for this sort of project; not even in the most fantastical works of science fiction had a product like this ever really been imagined before. It was such a bold proposal, in fact, that the Apple brain trust wasn't even sure how to go about building it—when they first started out, Jobs split his staff up into two separate teams: one to create an iPod that could make calls, and another to shrink a Mac down to the size of a phone.[3] The shrunken-Mac team won out—the iPod's distinctive wheel-based interface didn't work quite as well on a cell phone, due in no small part to the fact that it conjured up the antiquated feel of a rotary dial.

Building a product this sophisticated would never be possible within the confines of California—or anywhere else, for that matter. While most of us probably assume that iPhones are conceived in America, assembled in China, and shipped back across the Pacific to us, the reality is far more complicated. From the very beginning, Apple has relied on one of the most intricate global value chains in human history in order to deliver on the promise of its iPhone. In 2013, photojournalist David Barreda teamed up with *Foreign Policy* editor David Wertime in an attempt to map out the iPhone's globe-trotting production cycle. They located 748 iPhone suppliers in dozens of countries—from Australia to the Philippines to Israel to France to Brazil.[4] But the gyroscope that makes it possible for your screen to flip from horizontal to vertical with a simple turn of your wrist? That comes from

STMicroelectronics, a company based in Geneva, Switzerland, with manufacturing facilities in Italy and France.[5] The chip that allows your phone to understand and interpret your movement—say, for a fitness tracker app, or to save power when the device is sitting idle? It's the brainchild of a semiconductor manufacturer in the Netherlands called NXP.[6] The paper-thin, light-resistant, scratch-proof glass that makes for a near-perfect touchscreen? That comes from Corning, a company founded before the Civil War and situated in a town of 11,000 in western New York State.[7] And your phone wouldn't work at all without a rare earth element called tantalum, a metallic powder capable of holding especially high electrical charges—a necessary component for powering the tiny circuit boards that bring smartphones, tablets, and other modern devices to life. Tantalum comes from a rare, jet-black mineral called coltan, which is extracted by hand in often brutal conditions by miners in Rwanda and the Democratic Republic of Congo. In recent years, Apple and other companies have faced increased scrutiny to ensure that they are sourcing their coltan ore from mines that meet baseline human rights thresholds.[8] While there remains room for improvement on that front, coltan mining stands as another example of just how complicated the ethics and economics of trade can often be.

We know that trade has made many products cheaper, stronger, more innovative, or more accessible by influencing supply and demand; it lowers the price tag on our clothing, allows for more durable car parts, and provides us with blueberries in the wintertime, as we've discussed. But its impact on smartphones and other gadgets has been far more profound than that: by weaving together the technologies and resources of many nations, trade has made these products *possible*. American audio chips, Korean batteries, Congolese minerals, Japanese cameras, German accelerometers—the iPhone might well be the most truly global product yet devised by humankind.[9] And as trade continues on its long-range trajectory of becoming increasingly open and easy, the iPhone also provides a glimpse into the future of product development. The global economy is still in its infancy in many ways; we've just begun to explore what we can achieve when we put our international heads together. The truth is, we have no idea what other marvels we could invent when thousands of people from dozens of countries make unique contributions toward a common goal—particularly when it comes to emerging technologies.

In his famous book on globalization, *The Lexus and the Olive Tree*, columnist Tom Friedman expounded on a theory that he had first introduced a few years earlier in *The New York Times*. Popularly known as the "Golden Arches Theory," Friedman's idea was that, in his own words, "no two countries that both had McDonald's had fought a war against each other since each got its McDonald's."[10] As adages go, it would prove to be short-lived. *The Lexus and the Olive Tree* first hit bookstores in April of 1999, just weeks after the Happy Meal–loving NATO countries began launching air strikes against Yugoslavia—destroying several McDonald's restaurants in Belgrade, as well as Friedman's maxim. Other conflicts have called the Golden Arches Theory into question before and since. The United States invaded Panama to depose Manuel Noriega back in 1989, for example, which—like the 2006 war between Israel and Lebanon and the 2014 Russian incursion into Ukraine—was a conflict featuring plenty of Big Macs on all sides.

Friedman would eventually update his theory, replacing McDonald's with Dell, the Texas-based computer company. As it turned out, it wasn't enough that two countries shared a taste for global burgers—to truly keep the peace, nations needed to be even more economically intertwined than that. Specifically, the

Dell Theory states that "no two countries that are both part of a major global supply chain, like Dell's, will ever fight a war against each other as long as they are both part of the same global supply chain."[11] That is to say, what really brings countries together isn't having access to the *outputs* of global capitalism—fast food restaurants, Walmarts, and so on—but rather having a piece of the *inputs* . . . also known as a piece of the action. When a meaningful portion of your economy is tied to the success of workers in other nations, it makes governments think twice before upsetting the apple cart, be it by waging war or otherwise aggravating one another. There's simply too much at stake. The economies of the United States and China are so intertwined by value chains that they serve as guardrails against the escalation of disputes—our recent trade squabbles notwithstanding. Compare that with our relations with Turkey, for example, with whom we don't share nearly as much connective tissue in terms of supply chains, tourism, young people studying in each other's countries, and so on. The result, I believe, is a relationship between us that is far more brittle. Global value chains can help keep countries from going off the rails with one another, but for developing countries they can also create a dependency on huge foreign companies that can sometimes lead to exploitation.

Nobody knows whether Friedman's Dell Theory will prove true in the long run—there's more to maintaining international harmony than simply economics, after all. But as products like the iPhone continue to be developed and brought into our lives, it's worth considering what impact these vast, global supply chains will have on our relationships with people from around the world. That consideration cuts both ways, too. While integrating our economic fortunes with another nation may help keep our friendship strong, it's also the case that when we become too dependent on those connections, we might be inclined to overlook bad behavior that we would otherwise rebuke. Throughout our history, there has been a pretty glaring difference in the way we respond to, say, human rights abuses when the perpetrator happens to be a government with whom we're economically linked. Put another way: if we're relying on you to sell us oil or assemble our laptops, we're more likely to let a few things we don't agree with slide. It's difficult to say whether those negative consequences ultimately outweigh the positive outcomes of global supply chains—namely, fewer wars and more openness and understanding between economically cooperating countries. But both the negatives and positives should be factored in when we think about the long-term implications of the iPhone and trade more generally.

Deficit, Schmeficit

There's an equally important lesson that iPhones can teach us about trade, and it has to do with bilateral trade deficits. We've already talked about some of the myths surrounding these trade deficits back in chapter three—as you may recall, they're about as useful for determining the health of trade relationships as they are for determining the weather. As a quick refresher, though, a trade balance between two nations measures the value of goods and services sold from country A to country B versus the value of goods and services moving in the other direction. The country that buys more than it sells is running a *bilateral trade deficit* with the country that sells more than it buys. To take a simple, zoomed-in example: I run one of these trade deficits with my barber, Omer, because I repeatedly purchase the service of a haircut from him, while he *never* purchases anything from me. And we're both okay with that! Of course, that deficit doesn't tell you much of anything about the state of either of our finances. By the same token, the $378 billion trade deficit we ran with China in 2018 doesn't offer us much information about the strength or weakness of the U.S. economy.

But even beyond the barber problem, trade deficits are an unreliable measurement of economic health for a number of other reasons, too. For one thing, they can be easily distorted by factors that go beyond a simple tally of imports and exports. When the U.S. dollar goes up or down in value, for example, our trade balances fluctuate in turn—a high dollar renders American exports more expensive and foreign imports cheaper. So even if the number of things we've bought from overseas hasn't changed one bit, when the dollar becomes more valuable, we probably buy more imports and sell fewer exports—making our trade deficit "worse." But is that a bad thing? In fact, any change in exchange rates, inflation, or how much people in a country save or invest all have an impact on trade surpluses and deficits. So that $378 billion trade deficit with China isn't just a poor metric for determining the strength of our economy . . . it's also an imprecise number that could be relied on to make bad policy choices.

The journey of the iPhone illustrates yet another shortcoming of trade deficits—one that renders them especially laughable as a trade policy talking point. Despite the fact that the iPhone was invented and designed in America, is powered by Central African minerals, and is brought to life by European and Asian technologies, it is nevertheless classified as a 100 percent Chinese export. For the purposes of calculating our trade deficit, it wouldn't matter if 99 out of every 100 iPhone suppliers were located in downtown St. Louis—the nation that gets credit for the product is whichever one "substantially transforms" it last. And because the overwhelming majority of iPhones have their final assembly done in China, the value of all of those Swiss gyroscopes, Dutch motion chips, Japanese retina displays, and American glassware gets assigned to the Chinese economy. What makes this calculation so misleading is that the iPhone's assembly—which is largely handled by the Taiwanese company Foxconn, the world's largest contract manufacturer of electronics—is estimated to represent just 3 to 6 percent of the cost of building each phone, or about $8 to $20 for every iPhone X.[12]

Donald Trump and others have made a big deal of our large trade deficit with China, suggesting that it is a source of economic weakness for the United States. We've ticked through a number of reasons why that argument doesn't add up. But it's also worth noting that Trump's rationale seems to be premised on the idea that a $378 billion trade deficit with China is akin to us just forking over $378 billion directly to them each year—perhaps in the form of an oversized novelty check delivered by Ed McMahon to President Xi Jinping's front door. That isn't speculation on my part, either; in the past, President Trump has tweeted in regard to our bilateral trade deficit with China that "every year . . . China is making almost $300 billion off the United States."[13] Once again, he has gotten tripped up on the issue—this is the equivalent of claiming that your local gas station "made $20 off of you," but completely ignoring the fact that you also got to put $20 worth of gas in your car.

It's also an argument that becomes more absurd when you factor in the case of the iPhone (including the *literal* case of the iPhone, which often comes from Singapore[14]). The price of an iPhone can vary dramatically based on its model, memory, and features, but let's say that a more or less typical one retails for about $999. It's been estimated that, in 2017, just over 69 million iPhones were sold in America.[15] Because the trade deficit uses factory costs rather than retail sales prices to determine the value of imports, it assumes that iPhones contribute about $16 billion to our trade deficit with China. We don't know the exact number because it's proprietary to Apple; it could be somewhat lower or higher depending on the actual average price of all phones that happened to be sold each year. What we *do* know is that the number is certainly in the range of tens of billions of dollars, all of which gets factored into our $378 billion deficit with China as Chinese exports to America.

This, of course, is despite the fact that every time a $999 iPhone gets sold to a U.S. customer, that money doesn't get wired directly to Beijing. Global information provider IHS Markit has estimates that for every iPhone X that gets sold, $110 is sent to Samsung, the South Korean conglomerate that makes the iPhone's displays (as producers of the Galaxy series, they also happen to be Apple's chief rival in the smartphone market).[16] Another $44.45 is spoken for by the iPhone's memory chip suppliers: Toshiba of Japan and SK Hynix of South Korea.[17] China, however, earns only an estimated $8.46 for the labor and parts it supplies.[18] A little goes to Singapore; a little goes to Brazil; a little goes to Italy . . . a little goes to Corning, New York . . . and the vast majority of it goes to Apple Park in Cupertino, California. The iPhone may be calculated as a Chinese import, but most of the money Americans spend on it doesn't travel very far from home. So it is that our trade deficit with China is artificially and substantially inflated, all because it happens to be the last stop in one product's long global supply chain.

Arch Frenemies

Many of us have become so primed to see China as a trade villain that we'd probably be surprised to learn that, at least when it comes to the story of the iPhone, they're really more of an unsung ally. President Trump has consistently called on Apple to produce the iPhone entirely in the United States—speaking from the White House Rose Garden in January 2019, for example, he told reporters: "Don't forget this—Apple makes their product in China. I told Tim Cook, who's a friend of mine, who I like a lot—make your product in the United States. Build those big, beautiful plants that go on for miles, it seems. Build those plants in the United States."[19] This is a stance we might expect to hear from any American politician, of course; more plants in the U.S. means more jobs in the U.S., after all. Or perhaps Trump has a special interest in Apple moving its assembly to our soil—perhaps it would make the iPhone more secure? *The New York Times* reported in October 2018 that Trump's own aides have repeatedly warned him that Chinese intelligence agents routinely listen in on his personal iPhone calls.[20] Trump denied the truth of that particular story . . . and, appealing to Trump's loathing of the *Times*, a spokesman for China's Ministry of Foreign Affairs put out a statement describing the report as "fake news," while cheekily explaining to the U.S. president that, "if there are concerns about Apple calls being listened-in on, then you can change to Huawei phones."[21]

The thing is, Apple *did* flirt with building its products in America once upon a time. In 2012, President Trump's dear friend Tim Cook announced that his company would start constructing a

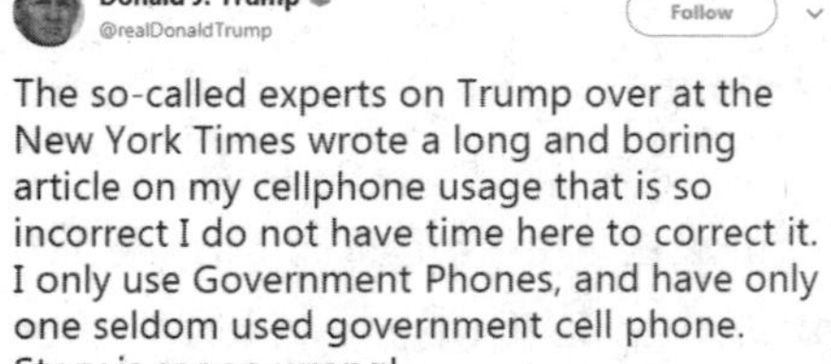

Can you hear him now?

line of Mac Pro computers in Austin, Texas.[22] It seemed like a watershed moment for U.S. electronics manufacturing—but the whole plan fell apart when Apple realized that American suppliers couldn't provide enough of the tiny, customized screws that were required to assemble each computer. Because of the screw shortage, parts had to be ordered in from China; tests and sales of the first Texas-made Macs were postponed by several months, throwing cold water on the dream of made-in-the-U.S.A. computers that has yet to dry off.

The fact of the matter is that, even if we did have those little screws, Apple simply can't move all of its assembly to the U.S.—not if it wants to build an iPhone that a decent chunk of Americans can actually afford. That's because, when it comes to this particular product, China isn't "ripping us off" in the least. What they're doing is sharing the cost of making the iPhone with us and the rest of the world—and helping reduce its price for consumers everywhere. In return for carrying their portion of that cost, they receive a bevy of poorly paid assembly jobs in their cities, as well as the aforementioned $8.46 per phone. What they don't receive are the profits, which largely flow right back to America. So if Apple *were* to insist on bringing its assembly operations to the United States, America wouldn't stand to gain very much. Sure, that $8.46 per phone would go toward paying U.S. rather than Chinese factory workers, but because our wages are much higher here, it couldn't pay very many of them. Hiring enough American workers to keep production up would force Apple to raise the cost of the iPhone . . . which in turn would drive down sales as customers opted for cheaper alternatives, hampering the company's ability to maintain its U.S. workforce. Furthermore, the fact is that America simply doesn't have a modern, well-developed electronics manufacturing infrastructure in place. Even if we did, we ceded the entire field of electronics assembly to Asia decades ago, and it would require substantial investment and time to get our country up to speed and essentially jump-start the industry from scratch. All told, between labor costs, the fact that most electronic components are already made in Asia, the efficiency and agility of Chinese factories, and China's much larger contingent of engineers, it's estimated that building a single iPhone in America would cost about $73—more than nine times the $8 it takes to build one in China.[23] It just doesn't make sense.

The other obstacle to moving iPhone and other tech manufacturing work to the United States is that the *manufacturers*—that is to say, not the Apples of the world, but the firms that handle the actual production—are opposed to it, too. The good people of Wisconsin got a firsthand look at exactly what it takes to entice an electronics manufacturer to come to America not long ago, and the results haven't been pretty. In 2017, President Trump and then-Governor Scott Walker became intent on convincing Foxconn to build a plant in the Badger State—yes, that would be the very same Foxconn that handles the assembly of most iPhones. The Taiwanese company was reluctant, of course; for all the reasons enumerated above, it just doesn't make much sense for a giant electronics manufacturer to set up shop in a relatively high-wage, relatively labor-friendly country half a world away from most of the parts they need. But Walker was determined to make it happen, whatever the cost. He ultimately lured Foxconn to Wisconsin, but not before offering them a record-smashing package of financial sweeteners and other incentives.

After announcing the deal alongside Trump at the White House in July of 2017, Walker signed the multibillion-dollar incentive package into law that September, immediately making Foxconn the biggest foreign beneficiary of state subsidies in American history.[24] Trump came to Racine County to help Walker and then–Speaker of the House and local congressman, Paul Ryan break ground on the new facility—a $10 billion flat-panel display factory expected to be larger than ten football fields. As you might expect, there was plenty of premature celebration in the air. "Frankly, they weren't going to come to this country," Trump said of Foxconn at the announcement ceremony, quite accurately. "I hate to say it, if I didn't get elected, they wouldn't be in this country."[25] Walker, too, would crow via Twitter that, "Foxconn is bringing 13,000 high-tech jobs to Wisconsin—the biggest jobs announcement in our state's history!"[26] A new state-of-the-art factory, and thousands of new American manufacturing jobs—what could go wrong?

As it turned out: plenty. Between extremely generous tax breaks, credits, rebates, property abatements, grants, and other state subsidies, Walker had put Wisconsinites on the hook for up to $4.8 *billion* in taxpayer dollars in order to land the deal.[27]

June 2018: President Donald Trump participates in a groundbreaking ceremony in Mt. Pleasant, Wisconsin, for a new Foxconn facility. From left: Wisconson's first Foxconn employee, C. P. Murdoch; Governor Scott Walker; Trump; Foxconn Chairman Terry Gou; and Speaker of the House Representative Paul Ryan.

The state already offered remarkably low taxes for manufacturing companies—they don't tax manufacturing profits at all. So convincing Foxconn to come required going the extra mile: the good people of Wisconsin will have to pay, literally writing the corporation checks for as much as $200 million each year for fifteen years in a row.[28] The project was expected to create about 3,000 jobs in the southeastern part of the state, a number with the "potential to grow" to 13,000 at some point in the future.[29] But even if we were to take the higher figure as a sure thing, the potential $4.8 billion price tag for securing those 13,000 jobs meant that Wisconsin was forking over nearly $370,000 for each one. Wisconsin's Legislative Fiscal Bureau, the nonpartisan agency charged with analyzing programs on behalf of the state legislature, projected that taxpayers wouldn't realize a return on their governor's investment until *at least* 2042, a full quarter century after the deal was struck.[30] And to make room for Foxconn, Wisconsin is trying to force dozens of homeowners to sell their houses and farms to the state by using—or, as many have argued, abusing—eminent domain laws.[31] For residents like Joe Janacek, who has lived in his Racine County home for nearly thirty years, and Kim and James Mahoney, who had just finished building their dream house when Foxconn arrived, the attempted land grab has been an ongoing nightmare.[32]

It remains to be seen what will become of the Foxconn experiment. Will the new plant fulfill its promise to become a wellspring of jobs and economic opportunity, transforming a static region and offering a path forward for American electronics manufacturing? Or will the problems that have already begun surfacing since the deal was struck continue to mount? The scope of the taxpayer burden is unprecedented. Private property has been seized. Air pollution laws and conservation rules protecting Lake Michigan have been circumvented—Governor Walker granted special permission for Foxconn to siphon seven million gallons per day from the Great Lakes, violating an agreement signed by eight governors in 2008.[33] In short, a lot of Wisconsin's chips have been pushed into the center of the table in the hopes that this Taiwanese company will prove to be a good bet.

There is no doubt that bringing manufacturing jobs to the American heartland is a good thing—and it's catnip for politicians. But as the Foxconn deal demonstrates, the situation is often not that simple. On the day that ground was broken on the project in the summer of 2018, the unemployment rate in the area was a minuscule 3 percent[34]—Racine County has been struggling not because there aren't any jobs, but rather because wages have remained stagnant for years. So if those 13,000 factory jobs really do materialize, it's an open question whether they'll put more money in the pockets of local workers. There's also the issue of automation, which is just as prevalent in electronics manufacturing as it is in other sectors—including in many of Foxconn's Asian facilities. How long will those jobs last? Not to mention the fact that the promises made by companies like Foxconn often have a history of fizzling out. In 2013, in fact, Foxconn announced plans to build a $30 million technology factory in central Pennsylvania that would employ 500 local workers. Ribbons were cut, projections were made, local real estate prices went up—but the project disappeared without a trace.[35]

In November of 2018, Governor Walker lost his bid for a third term by a margin of one percent—with Foxconn serving as a major issue in the election, as you might expect. Two months later, the company announced that it had fallen short of its 2018 jobs target: of the 1,040 local workers they had vowed to hire by the end of the year, they had filled only 178 positions.[36] Still eligible for their billions in incentives if the project moves forward as planned, Foxconn notified the Wisconsin Economic Development Corporation that they "have adjusted [their] recruitment and hiring timeline."[37] On January 30, 2019, a spokesperson for Foxconn revealed that the company was reconsidering their plans to build a manufacturing facility at the Wisconsin site, and may instead end up using the space as a research center rather than an assembly plant.[38] Referencing the relatively high cost of building high-tech display screens with an American workforce, the spokesperson told Reuters that, "in terms of TV, we have no place in the U.S. . . . we can't compete," adding ominously: "In Wisconsin we're not building a factory. You can't use [the word] factory to [describe] our Wisconsin investment."[39]

Only time will tell what that may ultimately mean for the people of Racine County, but one thing seems clear: investing in tax breaks for electronics manufacturers may not be the smartest approach to securing Wisconsin's long-term economic health. As we'll explore in the next chapter, a better industry to invest in may be one that Governor Walker's administration saw fit to make devastating cuts to during his tenure—the public university system, the strength of which directly impacts service exports, job opportunities, and the state budget. I share this story not to impugn the leaders who thought that the Foxconn project would be an economic victory—or at least a political one—but because it so perfectly illustrates why making our iPhones in China is actually a good deal for the U.S. As painful as it may be to acknowledge it, the truth is that China is well positioned to quickly, cheaply, and effectively manufacture mass quantities of electronics, and we simply aren't.

In China, factories can be built, opened, or adapted to new purposes at speeds that make American heads spin. With a pool of eager factory workers and engineers that dwarfs ours—and far less formal hiring practices—they can put tens of thousands of people to work quickly. Land is cheaper and more plentiful, component parts are closer by, a well-developed supply chain already exists, government support is generous and forthcoming—and that's before you even get into the "advantages" that we don't like to talk about. Many Chinese factory employees work sixteen-hour shifts in troubling circumstances for less than a dollar per hour in pay. To maximize the time they spend working, some live in on-site dormitories, crammed into small rooms stacked with more than a dozen beds.[40]

America couldn't replicate those conditions—nor should we ever want to. Our values have informed our own laws and norms around wages, workers' rights, environmental protections, and so much else over the course of our history. We should be proud of that, even if we have much more progress to make on each of those fronts. We should also acknowledge that, in exchange for those standards we've set, we have most likely forever traded away the ability to compete in certain industries. Projects like the Wisconsin Foxconn plant sometimes pan out and sometimes fail, but, in the long run, we already know that America will never lure electronics manufacturing back from Asia. Of course, we should also be candid about why that is, and clear-eyed about the conditions in other countries that allow us to enjoy our iPhones and other gadgets at such low prices. And we should remember that China isn't the enemy here—in reality, they make these products possible, yet don't reap a large share of the benefits. The lesson of iPhone, then, is clear: if we Americans were ever left to our own devices, we'd be left without very many devices of our own.

CHAPTER 8

A Matter of Degrees

For twenty-two years, one of the bloodiest conflicts in human history raged on in what may well have been among the most desperate and most dangerous places on earth. In the shadows of the Nuba Mountains, astride the blue and white tributaries of the Nile, the Second Sudanese Civil War claimed the lives of two million people, displaced millions more, and unleashed horrific episodes of abduction, enslavement, and massacre from its start in 1983. Though African hostilities are rarely covered in the American media, you probably did hear about some of the tragedies that emanated from this war. Among them were the Darfur genocide—one of the worst humanitarian crises in modern history—and the orphaned and indoctrinated child soldiers whose rehabilitation journey has been chronicled in films like *Lost Boys of Sudan* and books such as Dave Eggers's *What Is the What* in the years since. The Sudanese government was led by strongman Omar al-Bashir—finally ousted in 2019—who had overseen the perpetration of countless war crimes. The rebel opposition fighting on behalf of the country's ethnic and religious minorities, known as the Sudan People's Liberation Army, was led by a man named John Garang. Half a world away, a small, bipartisan group of U.S. lawmakers had been searching for years for some opening that could help lead to a breakthrough in the region. And when a crack in the hostilities offered them the first opportunity in two decades to initiate peace talks, they found the opening they needed: John Garang happened to be in possession of America's most important export.

Garang was a Dinka villager, born into poverty and orphaned at ten, who would go on to command a force of rebel warriors. But before he found himself at the center of a bloody civil war, he found himself in the center of Iowa—first as an undergraduate student at Grinnell College, and later as a graduate student earning his PhD in agricultural economics from Iowa State.[1] At Iowa State, Garang befriended a classmate named Brian D'Silva, who became interested in the challenges facing Garang's homeland, and even traveled with Garang after graduating to teach briefly at a Sudanese university.[2] Decades later, D'Silva—now a U.S. government advisor focused on development in South Sudan—became part of a select group working with a handful of members of Congress to bring attention to the civil war. Because of his university connection and friendship with Garang, he was able to help facilitate an official visit by a Garang-led rebel delegation to Washington. Later, he convinced Garang to host U.S. representatives Frank Wolf and Donald Payne in southern Sudan.[3] The group successfully lobbied President George W. Bush to involve America in bringing an end to the war, and—long story short—U.S. officials were able to help broker a peace agreement in 2005, curtailing much of the crisis and leading to the creation of South

Sudan as the world's newest nation following an independence referendum in 2011.[4]

The U.S. export Garang possessed—the most important, I would argue, that our nation produces—was an American education. We have no way of knowing how long the Second Sudanese Civil War might have raged were it not for Garang's openness to—and connection with—Americans. But we do know that his exposure to the United States made a number of the steps on the path to peace possible. Yes, when foreign students come to America to study at our colleges and universities, it gets counted as an export—a *service* export, to be precise. When a German buys an American SUV, they send money into the U.S. economy in exchange for a physical good. By the same token, if a German student comes to study at MIT, their tuition dollars are flowing into the U.S. in exchange for a nonphysical benefit: the service of an education. And though the dollar value of that education export—about $42 billion in 2018[5]—pales in comparison to the money we make from, say, electrical machinery or aircraft exports, the *true* value of exporting American education is incalculable.

Garang is far from the only important world leader whose time earning degrees in America helped foster closer relations with the U.S. As of 2019, Japan, Israel, Colombia, Kenya, and Singapore are all led by heads of state who once studied at American schools—to say nothing of influential former leaders like Pakistani president Benazir Bhutto, Filipino president Corazon Aquino, South Korea's first president, Syngman Rhee, and Israeli prime minister Golda Meir. When a heated battle for control of the Greek government broke out in 2011, it was a showdown between two men—Prime Minister George Papandreou and opposition leader Antonis Samaras—who had been roommates almost forty years earlier at Amherst College in western Massachusetts. Had they driven twenty minutes up the road after graduating, they might have bumped into King Abdullah II of Jordan, who was attending the prestigious Deerfield Academy as a high schooler. All told, the State Department estimates that almost 300 current or former world leaders have studied at American institutions, a number that does not even include the countless U.S.-educated legislators, policymakers, social leaders, artists, and other influential figures who don't happen to have been heads of state.[6]

These connections have not always resulted in perfect diplomatic relationships between former students' home countries and the United States, of course—plenty of future nefarious figures have marched across American gymnasium stages to receive their degrees. The very same college—Amherst—that produced Greek's squabbling leaders and Prince Albert of Monaco also taught current president Uhuru Kenyatta of Kenya, who would go on to be called before the International Criminal Court in The Hague under suspicion of crimes against humanity. On the whole, however, there's little doubt that exposing hundreds of thousands of young foreigners to our education system every year has helped create a pipeline of American values and international friendship with the rest of the world. That's something I saw firsthand when I served as chairman of the Export-Import Bank of the United States; foreign officials who had been educated in America seemed to be more eager to do business with U.S. companies. It isn't just about presidents, prime ministers, kings, and queens, either—for generations, rank-and-file citizens from every country have come to the U.S. to seek knowledge, forge friendships, and experience our culture, and have returned home to infuse their communities with a greater understanding of American life.

It's hard to overstate how important this has been to America's influence in the world—even if it's impossible to ever really quantify the impact. The ability of the United States to help shape world events has always required more than just military might or economic clout. It requires what political scientists call *soft power*: the capacity of a country to guide global affairs toward the outcomes it desires without invading or coercing anybody—something out of step with the current administration. American soft power has always been at work, advancing our interests quietly. When young Chinese protesters fought to bring democratic reforms to their country in Tiananmen Square in 1989, students at Beijing's Central Academy of Fine Arts constructed a thirty-foot model of the Statue of Liberty—which they called the *Goddess of Democracy*—to win support for their reforms. Everyone in the world who watched as soldiers destroyed the students' statue knew what Lady Liberty, the American icon, stood for. Soft power is Boris Yeltsin being overcome by his visit to that well-stocked Houston supermarket, and flying home to dismantle the Soviet Union. It's Kim Jong-il's obsession with Hollywood movies, and his son Kim Jong-un's love of American basketball stars.[7] It's hundreds of thousands of East Germans, stuck behind the Berlin Wall, lining up to buy a shipment of Levi's blue jeans in 1978.[8] It's every piece of culture—be it a hamburger, a pop song, a cool car, or a shared experience—that breeds familiarity and improves the reputation of America among the people of the world.

Few instruments of soft power are more effective than an American education, which tends to ingrain legitimacy and respect for the United States among foreign students who come to discover what our country is all about. It's an export that pays enormous dividends for us in terms of our long-term diplomatic and economic relationships throughout the world. There's a common refrain that American products are sought after because of their reputation for quality, but what often goes unspoken is that they are also frequently sought after because of their cultural cachet. That cachet is impossible without exposure—the sort that makes a can of Coke, a Yankees cap, Beyoncé's mezzo-soprano, or the Statue of Liberty instantly recognizable and relatable nearly everywhere in the world.

The 2017–2018 school year saw a record number of international students enrolled in American colleges and universities—nearly 1.1 million, which is more than twice as many as the United Kingdom, the next most popular host country.[9] In addition to the fuzzier long-range benefits we've talked about, the U.S. State Department estimates that the presence of these foreign students injects a total of about $42 billion and supports 450,000 jobs into the American economy each year.[10] Because most of these students pay their own way and are ineligible for U.S. financial aid programs—the Institute of International Education estimates that 82 percent of foreign undergraduates fund their own tuitions through family wealth or work earnings[11]—they also allow schools to offer more generous financial aid and loan forgiveness programs to American students than would otherwise be possible. That is to say, every time an international student is able to pay full freight, it increases the chances that a lower-income domestic student will be able to get the support they need to go to college. As my friend Congresswoman Donna Shalala, who previously served as president of the University of Miami, told me, "university budgets are built on foreign students." The former president of New York University, John Sexton, put it to me more bluntly: "Foreign students who pay full tuition are the narcotic of higher education."

Unfortunately, however, this is not an area that has been trending in the right direction for America of late. While plenty of international students are still attending school in the U.S., the number of *new* students entering each year has been threatening to crater. After years of rapid growth, 2018 marked the second year in a row that the United States saw a decline in new international students entering American schools as undergraduates.[12] After a drop-off of a few percentage points for the 2016–2017 academic year, the rate of decline doubled in the year after that.[13] The ascension of Donald Trump to the presidency—and the wave of restrictions on skilled-worker visas, tightening of immigration rules, and inflammatory "America First" rhetoric that followed—is at least partially responsible for the sudden downturn in international college applicants.[14] But, as CEO Allan Goodman of the Institute of International Education told me, this is a problem that has been exacerbated by a number of factors, including ever-rising tuition costs and the seemingly endless, tragic stream of shootings in American schools. Most of all, Goodman says, it has been exacerbated by competition.

Where the United States has shed some of its appeal for foreign students, Australian, Canadian, and European universities have eagerly filled the gap. Seizing on America's nativist turn, Canada now offers permanent residency status to international students who work in the country for one year after earning their degree from a Canadian school—an incentive that can often take a decade or more for those hoping to achieve the same status in the United States.[15] At the moment, about half of all Chinese and Indian students attending overseas universities do so in America—they choose to spend their dollars and expand their minds here because of the quality of our schools.[16] Right now, in fact, there are more American-trained PhDs teaching in China than in the United States. But faced with hostility from U.S. leadership and waning prospects for working and living in America as temporary residents or future citizens, how much longer will the world's best students keep making that choice?

It may seem like a minor story in the grand scheme of things, but if our country were to continue losing out on international students, it would carry grave consequences for the U.S. economy, our capacity for innovation, and our place in the world. To be sure, America still boasts the most impressive colleges and universities in the world—on quality alone, they will always be a draw. But they are also kept afloat by a fragile funding structure, one that is increasingly dependent on there being a steady stream of applicants who can pay the full cost of tuition. Should that stream dry up, the quality of education our schools offer will drop in turn—as will the diversity of backgrounds and perspectives in our classrooms, which contribute enormously to the college experience. Our workforce will be weaker for its lack of educated immigrants, who will build their lives and offer their ideas in Toronto, Paris, London, and Berlin. And both the citizenry and the future leadership of who knows how many countries—including the John Garangs yet to come—will hold no special regard for or relationship with the people of the United States.

The good news is that it wouldn't take much for this story to have a happy ending. But reversing this recent trend will require us to take education seriously not just as a domestic issue, but as a critical U.S. *export*. We should be selling American higher learning as aggressively as we sell American construction equipment and aircraft—after all, the profits are ultimately far greater, and the product is second to none. Schools already have a compelling financial interest in attracting young people from foreign countries. American students, too, have both a financial and an educational interest in drawing in more international classmates, whether they realize it or not. But the fact of the matter is that *all* Americans have a vested interest in this issue, regardless of their past, present, or future educational pursuits. Our country benefits every time we impart our values, raise our credibility, and forge relationships in the world, particularly with young people from other nations. And every once in a while, the young person getting to know America better will grow up to be a key partner in bringing about peace, democracy, prosperity, or some other goal we share.

It's a Small World, After All

Education isn't the only unexpected export that doubles as a way for America to strengthen its reputation in the world. In fact, our number one service export, directly responsible for generating over half a trillion dollars for our economy and more than five million jobs, is tourism.[17] In 2017, an estimated 77 million foreigners traveled to the United States on vacation—a figure that equates to nearly a quarter of our total population.[18] While France and Spain attract a slightly larger number of tourists than we do each year, those who visit the U.S. spend *three times* as much money here as they do in either of those countries—that might have something to do with the cost of Disney World passes versus the price of admission to the Louvre or a front row seat for the Running of the Bulls.[19]

Tourism may not create as lasting or as meaningful a connection between America and its visitors as higher education does, but it sure is lucrative. Still a relatively young industry, international tourism wasn't able to flourish—at least not in the U.S.—until the dust had settled on World War II and air travel became a mainstream part of life. While attractions like Steeplechase Park in Coney Island and Disneyland in California had drawn local families for years, it wasn't until Disney World opened near Orlando, Florida, in 1971 that Americans began to recognize the true potential of global tourism for what it was: big business. And I do mean *big*. At thirty-nine square miles, Disney World is nearly twice the size of Manhattan; it employs about 74,000 people—a labor force roughly equal to the entire working population of Santa Fe, New Mexico.[20] Each year, more than six million foreign tourists flock there, enough not only to help make Disney World the most visited resort on earth, but to propel the unlikely city of Orlando to set the record for the most visitors ever to come to a U.S. city in one year.[21]

Whether they're interested in Disney's Magic Kingdom, Times Square, the Grand Canyon, or the Las Vegas Strip, tourists who come to the United States—also known as "foreign customers who purchase the U.S. export of an enjoyable American experience"—help goose our economy and burnish our image in the world. But just as we've seen a decline in new international students entering the United States since 2017, we've seen a similar slump in tour-

The mouse that roared.

ism over the same span. All across the world, international travel is booming; destinations like Europe, Southeast Asia, Australia, and Canada have all enjoyed an incredible swell of foreign visitors of late. The United States, on the other hand, is one of only two developed countries to experience a drop-off in tourists over the last few years—the other is Turkey, which has recently been beset by coups, crackdowns, and chaos.[22] The trend isn't good.

The fact is, America's share of international tourists has dropped precipitously since 2016, costing us an estimated $32.2 billion in tourist spending and 100,000 American jobs, according to the United States Travel Association—think of that as export sales opportunities we lost out on to other countries.[23] This is particularly troubling given that the value of the dollar went down in 2017. With the dollar low, we'd expect *more* tourism, since it provides foreigners with a friendlier exchange rate. Instead, even as tourism grew worldwide by 8 percent, here in America it fell by more than 6 percent—a trend that we can only hope will soon reverse itself.

Usually when we talk about "barriers" to the free flow of trade, we're talking about things like tariffs and quotas we impose on foreign goods. But service exports like education and tourism have barriers of their own. For generations, America has been an attractive destination for students and visitors not only due to the prestige of our schools or the splendor of our sights, but because we've tried to cultivate an image of our country as a place that is welcoming of all people. So what changed at the end of 2016 to send our education and tourism exports spiraling in the wrong direction? Again, there's no need to beat around the bush here: this slump largely belongs to President Trump. Take a look at the chart below, which tracks the percentage of people in twenty-five countries who view the United States favorably over the years 2016, 2017, and 2018.

Little overall change to U.S. image in Trump's second year, but in most countries a dip from Obama era

Favorable views of U.S.

	End of Obama presidency* %	2017 %	2018 %
Mexico	66	30	32
Netherlands	65	37	34
Germany	57	35	30
Canada	65	43	39
Sweden	69	45	44
France	63	46	38
Italy	72	61	52
Indonesia	62	48	42
Brazil	73	50	55
Spain	59	31	42
UK	61	50	50
Argentina	43	35	32
Philippines	92	78	83
Australia	60	48	54
Japan	72	57	67
Tunisia	42	27	37
South Korea	84	75	80
Poland	74	73	70
Nigeria	66	69	62
South Africa	60	53	57
Greece	38	43	36
Hungary	62	63	63
Israel	81	81	83
Kenya	63	54	70
Russia	15	41	26

*Obama presidency figures are based on the most recently available data for each country between 2014 and 2016.

Source: Spring 2018 Global Attitudes Survey. Q17a.

PEW RESEARCH CENTER

From Russia (and Kenya) with love.

It's not a pretty sight. Nowhere has our image been more badly damaged than in Mexico, America's second-best export customer and our top source of tourists. Though Pew wasn't able to conduct this particular poll in China—the leading country for young people coming to the U.S. to study—the abrupt increase in Chinese students choosing British or Canadian universities, combined with Trump's 2018 trade war with Beijing, is probably evidence enough. This loss of trust and goodwill in America is, in effect, a *nontariff barrier* that holds us back from exporting the amount of education and tourism that we're accustomed to. Other nontariff barriers set in motion by the Trump administration that may have stymied these vital U.S. industries include—but are not limited to:

- Imposing "travel bans" that single out Muslim countries, which either discourage or outright restrict prospective students and tourists from coming to America;
- Repeatedly portraying Mexican and Central American migrants as "rapists" and "killers," and separating families seeking asylum at our southern border—both of which serve to paint America as a cruel and racist nation;
- Reportedly referring to Haiti and African nations as "shithole countries" in a meeting with senators to discuss immigration policy, which, well . . . see above;
- Inviting government shutdowns, which convey an image of instability and chaos to the world;
- Pulling America out of the Paris Climate Agreement—to which every other country in the world has signed on—which portrays the U.S. as a country unconcerned about the planet we share.

And so on. The purpose of this list is not to flog Donald Trump—it's to point out some of the unexpected ways that U.S. exports, and, consequently, U.S. prosperity, can be diminished by actions that seemingly have nothing to do with trade policy. As we discussed in chapter three, service exports are critical to the future of the American economy—and, on the whole, they are an area in which we've excelled. Just as we've managed to tear down more traditional barriers to trade over the years, it's essential that we find a way to quickly tear down these nontraditional barriers as well; if we can't, we'll risk being left behind in the race to lead on the biggest service export of all.

Trouble's a Foot

While attracting visitors and conferring degrees to foreign students is something we need to be focused on today, there's a different type of degree we ought to be paying attention to if we want to remain in sync with the world of tomorrow. That's right—our future success doesn't just rest on bachelor's, master's, and PhD degrees, but on Fahrenheit and Celsius degrees as well. Take away Belize, the Bahamas, the Cayman Islands, and Palau, and the U.S. is alone in the world using Fahrenheit to measure the temperature outside. Take away Liberia and Myanmar, and we're the only country that hasn't adopted the dreaded metric system. No, we don't need to switch our thermometers over to Celsius anytime soon—nor do we need to give up our yardsticks, mile markers, and 12-pound bowling balls in favor of metersticks, kilometer markers, and . . . 5.44311-kilogram bowling balls. But we do need to think seriously about some of the areas where the United States has fallen out of step with the rest of the world, including in the realm of basic things like weights and measures. After all, what good is having access to an innovative piece of foreign technology if I can't plug it into an American electrical outlet? How can I sell furniture to another country if they use different sizes of screws? I ran into this issue at the Export-Import Bank, helping U.S. businesses win deals to build energy infrastructure in the sub-Saharan region as part of the Obama administration's Power Africa initiative. A problem we ran into is that the U.S. uses 60Hz power (think: 120 volts), while almost every country in Africa uses 50Hz (220 volts)—American companies could sell transmission lines and some other components, but our different electrical standards hampered much of our ability to effectively export to the region. At some point in the future, we'll have to grapple with a number of those inconsistencies—either by conforming to meet global standards, or by encouraging the globe to meet ours.

As we look to the future of trade, we should begin by acknowledging that the central battle that has defined it for hundreds of years has now been all but won. Tariffs are still a part of our lives—maybe they always will be, here and there. But the days of widespread high tariffs impeding the free flow of trade are essentially over; Donald Trump's trade wars notwithstanding, tariffs are on their way to becoming a relic of a simpler time. As modern trade agreements finish off the last of the world's remaining, already low tariffs one by one, governments that want to squeeze as many benefits as they can from the global economy are now turning their attention to other impediments to seamless international trade. Synchronizing standards is the next battleground—the last big source of friction between friendly nations seeking to do business with one another.

America has plenty of experience with bringing standards in line, because it's something we had to do—and, in some cases, are still doing—to streamline trade between our own states. In the early days of our republic, each state had its own standards for bread, produce, and other staple items that made selling products across state lines a cumbersome process. Sometimes this was intentional—standards could be used to protect Texas ranchers from competing with Chicago beef, for example—but sometimes the difficulty of interstate commerce was just a by-product of living in a country of patchwork rules. This is why, for many years, baked good packages all across the country were stamped with "Reg. Penn. Dept. Agr."—confirming that they met the standards necessary to be sold in the most stringent state, Pennsylvania.[24] It's also why a New York taxi that drops me off at Newark Airport in New Jersey can't pick up a passenger and cross back over the state line.

Today, though states are constitutionally prohibited from discriminating against each other's businesses, they still occasionally find ways to use standards to gum up the works. States have tried to ban their residents from purchasing all kinds of products over the internet, from contact lenses to caskets to wine, as a way to prop up local manufacturers.[25] On occasion, they couch these protectionist standards as being based on "morality" in order to avoid negative results in court—as when California wineries challenged New York and Michigan laws preventing their citizens from directly importing alcohol. The states weren't really trying to reduce drinking—they had no problem with the sale of out-of-state alcohol by local distributors that they had the opportunity to tax, after all. They just wanted to put a stop to wine-of-the-month clubs and other online sales that they couldn't make money off of,[26] and setting their own standards gave them an opportunity to put a cork in imported wine. In June of 2019, the Supreme Court struck down a version of this practice in a case called *Tennessee Wine and Spirits Retailers Association v. Thomas*—but that's unlikely to stop states from making creative use of standards in other ways to protect their bottom lines.

Though we've largely brought our internal standards into alignment, it's another story when it comes to foreign trade. When the U.S. was negotiating T-TIP—the Transatlantic Trade and Investment Partnership, a prospective trade deal with Europe effectively halted by President Trump—we ran into standards issues that proved rather sticky to resolve. Take chicken, for example. It turns out that, here in America, we wash our chicken with chlorine in order to kill off salmonella; in Europe, however, the use of these chlorine treatments is illegal. The U.S. Department of Agriculture is steadfast in its belief that washing chicken with chlorine is safe and effective—indeed, the incidence of salmonella in uncooked American chicken is only about 2 percent, versus 15 to 20 percent in European chicken.[27] Nevertheless, European regulators argue that allowing chicken to be treated with chlorine makes it easier for farmers to get away with lax health practices, trusting that their failures to guard against contamination will come out in the chemical wash.[28] It's a philosophical disagreement that has yet to be resolved, and it's far from the only one holding up trade with our foreign friends—the battle over GMOs (genetically modified organisms), for example, is yet another game of chicken.

Harmonizing global standards isn't just about making it easier for American chicken farmers to make money overseas, however. It's also about asserting our values in the world—not for the sake of bullying, patronizing, or forcing our beliefs on other countries, but because of one simple reason: if we don't set the standards, somebody else will. Our health standards are based on sound science, so we should feel no qualms whatsoever about promoting those standards among our current trading partners—or about making their adoption a prerequisite for prospective trading partners before they can do business with us. Our Federal Aviation Administration sets the global standards for airline safety—we lose that standard-setting power at our own peril! Labor, environmental, and human rights standards are based more on sound principles than on sound science; nevertheless, we should be doing everything we can to set the global bar on them in accordance with our values before another heavyweight does so in accordance with theirs. That's also true when it comes to services and the rules of the digital road—progress would be severely impeded if we fail to lead and end up with a U.S. standard, a European standard, and a Chinese standard for the 5G era. America is one of very few nations in the world with the economic clout to raise or lower the bar on a grand scale—and we should be frank about the responsibility that our stature carries. We have to acknowledge that *not* imposing our values on the global economy is tantamount to accepting China or another power's values instead, however uncomfortable it may make us to appear so imperious.

The need for America to take the lead on setting global standards is only going to become more pronounced as technology marches on. As artificial intelligence and other groundbreaking innovations become infused into the products we buy, the services we use, and the choices we make every day, we have got to step forward to set responsible standards for ourselves and, ultimately, for the world. America can probably afford to be out of step with the world when it comes to using feet and Fahrenheit versus meters and Celsius. But we can't afford to be out of step when it comes to the prevailing standards of the digital economy. In a world where our phones, our TVs, our fitness trackers, and even our "smart" refrigerators collect personal data about us, who will stand up and set the bar for privacy rights in the 5G era? In a world where our home security systems and baby monitors are connected to the internet, who will lay out worldwide standards for digital security? In a world where climate change is already beginning to devastate communities—exacerbating weather events, distorting agricultural routines, contributing to resource scarcity, and threatening whole industries—who has the moral authority to insist on responsible economic practices?

America has fallen behind: Europe has demonstrated a much stronger commitment to digital privacy rights so far, and, as I mentioned before, we are *literally the only country on earth* that has not indicated a desire to reduce carbon emissions by signing on to the Paris Climate Agreement. Even so, I believe that we are the only nation with the capacity to lift up the standards of the world and bring them into closer alignment—we still have the right combination of global influence and economic might to do the job. If we fail to speak up, there will be no one left with an adequately sized megaphone to make the case for rule of law, privacy, transparency, and security—to say nothing of consumer, labor, environmental, gender, and human rights. We may never impose our inches, miles, or degrees on the world, but, simply put, our values *have* to become the global standard.

CHAPTER 9

Why Winter Came

GOT

In recent years, Americans have been rightly concerned about events transpiring in volatile nations like North Korea, Afghanistan, and Iran. But since 2011, far more of us have had our eyes glued to the erratic, often violent affairs of another location—a place where assassinations, wars, and regime changes are an all-too-common occurrence. I'm speaking, of course, of Westeros: the politically volatile continent that serves as the setting for George R. R. Martin's *A Song of Ice and Fire* book series and its wildly popular TV adaptation, HBO's *Game of Thrones*. If you're one of the twelve Americans who has yet to see *Game of Thrones*, don't worry—it's not required viewing for this chapter. Even if adolescent dragons, wispy White Walkers, and the cunning machinations of about six dozen main characters aren't your cup of mead, you can still appreciate the role that trade plays in bringing us binge-worthy television—whichever series happens to keep you glued to the screen.

Like *Twin Peaks*, *Lost*, and *Saturday Night Live* before it, *Game of Thrones* has entered the pantheon of appointment viewing—what we used to call "water cooler shows," so named because you might gather around the office water cooler with your coworkers to discuss the previous night's episode. Of course, this was more prevalent before the era of on-demand streaming and bottled water at your desk took hold. Though we now have the luxury of watching our favorite shows whenever we'd like, Sunday night television has nevertheless become a huge part of many Americans' weekend routines—when the *Game of Thrones* finale aired in May 2019, at least 7.9 *million* articles were written about it! It's hard to beat that hour of freedom and escape from the impending workweek that a show like *Game of Thrones* can provide. When viewers settle into their couches to watch breathlessly as the latest drama unfolds in Westeros, they probably aren't thinking much about trade—apart from the strict protectionism of the Iron Islands and the consequences of the Seven Kingdoms' bilateral trade deficit with Essos, of course. But perhaps they should! After all, entertainment—like education and tourism—is in many ways one of America's most essential imports *and* exports, and one that supports a large number of U.S. jobs. The TV shows, movies, books, video games, and other sources of entertainment that come to America from other countries help broaden our minds, amuse and fulfill us, and draw us closer to people around the world by exposing us to the creativity of other cultures. And on the flip side of the coin, U.S. entertainment that gets consumed overseas helps portray an image of America to the world that makes us more familiar—and hopefully more appreciated—in the global community. It also happens to make us a boatload of money.

More and more in recent years—and particularly since the advent of worldwide streaming and development services like Netflix—the markets that dictate which TV shows and films get produced are *global* markets. It makes financial sense, of course: the more overseas consumers that gain access to American media, the more Hollywood studios produce movies and shows with global audiences in mind. Of the fifteen worldwide highest-grossing films of all time, only five were released prior to 2015; blockbusters like 2018's *Avengers: Infinity War* and *Jurassic World: Fallen Kingdom* each earned more than two thirds of their box office receipts from foreign audiences.[1] The same trend is taking hold on the small screen, too. HBO, for one, has invested enormous resources in global marketing and licensing to ensure that audiences around the world can watch *Game of Thrones* and other programs. By the time that *Thrones*'s fifth season premiered in 2015, it was simulcast in an astonishing 170 countries.[2]

I'm interested in *Game of Thrones* not simply because it has drawn so many viewers and seeped so thoroughly into our culture, but because it represents a truly global production. In a sense, it is the iPhone of TV shows—that is to say, it's the sort of product that couldn't exist without free-flowing trade across a wide array of nations. The show was created by two American producers, David Benioff and D. B. Weiss, and based on the written works of an American author—George R. R. Martin—who, perhaps because of the middle initials he shares with legendary fantasy writer J.R.R. Tolkien, is often mistaken for British. The whole show is often mistaken for British, in fact; this might have something to do with the characters' accents, which run the gamut from working-class Yorkshire to "posh" Londoner.[3] Why the residents of a fantastical, dragon-infested land seem to speak almost exclusively with various British accents in the first place is a question we'll leave for someone else's book. Of the sixty cast members who have been featured most prominently through the show's eight seasons—and if you watched *Game of Thrones*, you know that sixty is just scratching the surface—forty-six are indeed

British actors. But the core cast is rounded out by five actors from Ireland, two each from Germany, the Netherlands, and America, and one apiece from Denmark, Norway, and Spain.[4] The series is filmed largely on location in Croatia, Spain, Northern Ireland, Iceland, Morocco, and Malta,[5] and is written and produced by a crew made up primarily of Americans. Visual effects are mostly taken care of by a German production company, though additional support has come from Canadian, Irish, British, and American studios as well.[6] The show's music—including its iconic, swaggering main title theme—is created by an Emmy Award–winning German-Iranian composer. All of which is to say that while Westeros may only feature seven kingdoms, bringing *Game of Thrones* to our screens requires substantially more than that.

So what does all of this have to do with trade? Plenty, when we consider that each border-crossing element of the show is, in effect, an export. Every German engineer selling their special effects expertise, every British thespian selling their best brooding stare, and every Maltese tourism official selling their most sun-kissed cliff-side location is exporting a service to America. And, of course, America is turning around and exporting a popular television show to networks around the world. Those exports support a vast ecosystem of jobs both at home and abroad—not just paydays for glamorous stars like Emilia Clarke, but middle-class jobs for American stagehands, set designers, researchers, graphic artists, electricians, caterers, drivers, hair stylists, and editors as well. The global revenue that *Game of Thrones* and other TV and film sensations bring in also allows entertainment companies like HBO to fund other, less lucrative projects from innovative storytellers with large casts and crews of their own.

Needless to say, none of this would be possible in a world of closed borders and nationalist trade policies. If Peter Dinklage couldn't travel freely between countries to pursue job opportunities, there's no way that his character, Tyrion Lannister, could travel from Slaver's Bay to Dragonstone for job opportunities of his own. Just as our products get more innovative when our trade policies allow us to draw on the ingenuity and resources of more nations, our entertainment gets better as we connect more closely with the world. Tariffs and quotas may not impede global entertainment in quite the same way that they can for steel or aluminum, but cultural trade can absolutely be slowed down by those barriers—as well as others. China is experiencing a cinematic boom, with an $8.6 billion film market that more than quadrupled in size between 2011 and 2018.[7] Despite the fact that it imposes a quota on the number of imported movies that can be screened in Chinese theaters—only about thirty-four foreign films make the cut each year, and the producers of those films earn only a one-quarter share of the box office receipts[8]—China has nevertheless become far and away the largest export market for American movies.[9] The number of U.S. films allowed into China is a product of negotiations; the last agreement was struck in 2012 between then-Vice Presidents Joe Biden and Xi Jinping just before tip-off of a basketball game between the Lakers and the Suns in Los Angeles.[10] After a twenty-year period during which China refused to budge, Biden persuaded Xi to raise China's quota from twenty foreign films to thirty-four, and to nearly double the distribution fees paid to American film distributors from 13 percent to 25 percent—let's hope our budding trade war with China doesn't destroy this lucrative market![11]

China's concession may seem like a no-brainer—it has generated more money for everyone involved, including the state-owned China Film Group, the largest distributor in the nation. But for a country that still insists on a high degree of censorship and government oversight of culture, the decision to expose its citizens to a larger number of western movies isn't one that gets taken lightly. In what may be emblematic of a broader trend toward embracing globalization, China has signaled a willingness to raise its quotas even further as part of negotiations with the Trump administration that have begun to materialize in the post-trade-war thaw.[12] With five American blockbusters cracking China's top ten box office rankings in 2018,[13] the vice president of the Beijing Film Academy has acknowledged that allowing more Hollywood movies into China "should be something both parties can agree on."[14] Has China's stance softened because they genuinely want to become more open to the world? Or might it have more to do with the fact that Chinese companies have begun to aggressively invest in Hollywood studios?[15] We can't say for sure, but in either case it represents good news for the American film industry and the many jobs it supports—not to mention an important pathway for greater understanding between the American and Chinese people.

Thanks to the sensational popularity of American media that gets exported around the world, there's very little chance that we'll ever run a trade deficit when it comes to culture—not that trade deficits matter, of course. All told, the U.S. media and entertainment industry is expected to surpass $770 billion in sales for 2019, a number four times higher than China, the second-largest producer of media and entertainment.[16] America accounts for a full third of the global entertainment market, and nearly $200 billion of that impressive total gets exported overseas—once you factor in the associated copyrights, those sales are worth more to the American economy even than major exports like aerospace products and chemicals.[17] Best of all, the U.S. jobs those exports support come with an average salary of just over $93,000—almost 40 percent more than the average American worker makes in a year.[18]

Those numbers are impressive—but in terms of how trade in

entertainment impacts our day-to-day lives, it's really all about the imports. Many of the most beloved TV shows in American history are imported versions of foreign programs, in fact. Those of us who came up watching *All in the Family* probably had no idea that the show and its cantankerous, reactionary lead, Archie Bunker, were adapted directly from the British sitcom *Till Death Us Do Part*. Nor did many of us realize that before there was *Sanford and Son*, there was *Steptoe and Son*—another British import reimagined for American audiences. More recently, we've gone across oceans to procure our own versions of *The Office*, *House of Cards*, and *Queer as Folk* from England, *Homeland* from Israel, and *Ugly Betty* from Colombia. Our most popular reality shows in recent years have largely come from the Netherlands (*Survivor*, *Big Brother*, and *Fear Factor*) and the U.K. (*American Idol*, *Dancing with the Stars*, and *MasterChef*). If you were one of the more than 10 million Americans who has tuned in to see the bizarre spectacle of Fox's 2019 breakout hit, *The Masked Singer*, you have South Korea to thank—or perhaps blame.

Simply put, were it not for a free flow of trade between countries, life in America would be substantially less interesting. Just as our palates have been broadened by imported cuisines from all over the world—many of which we've "Americanized" to our liking—our leisure time has been broadened by imported culture as well. And if a gripping TV drama, sitcom, or guilty pleasure reality show isn't your idea of culture, you can rest easy knowing that you likely have trade to thank for being able to enjoy your favorite foreign authors and playwrights, whose works generally enter the United States as a result of international licensing and publishing deals. Whatever your entertainment preferences happen to be, there's little question that your downtime is made better by trade.

A Throne of Games

There's one particular sector within the entertainment industry that happens to be in the midst of an unprecedented global boom: video games. When the first stand-alone gaming consoles were released in the early 1970s, few could have predicted that they would amount to much more than a fleeting novelty or a teenage diversion—never mind a $140 billion industry.[19] Even as the local arcade became a defining cultural institution for the youth of America by the beginning of the 1980s—draining the nation's allowances, quarter by quarter—the thought of eight-bit aliens, pixelated ping-pong paddles, or a dot-starved, anthropomorphic cheese wheel giving birth to a serious economic powerhouse seemed far-fetched. These games were just frivolous kids' stuff, after all, right?

Wrong. By 1982, though few Americans were aware of it, the arcade video game industry was already generating more money than movie theaters and pop music *combined*.[20] Game cabinets

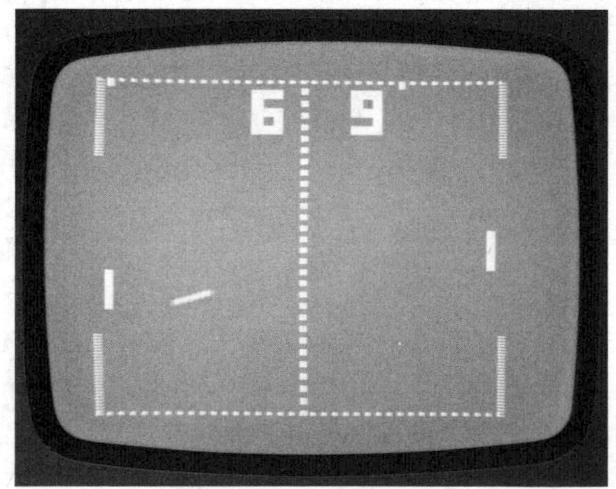

Technology at its finest.

were swallowing quarters faster than Pac-Man could swallow his precious white dots, and as smaller game consoles began making their way into American homes, a new entertainment juggernaut was off to the races. Or at least it might have been, had the bottom not fallen out of the market within just a couple of years. The meteoric rise of the industry had led to a glut of new gaming systems, confusing shoppers and causing a series of conspicuous flops. Some of these commercial disasters would take on the status of urban legends—including, most memorably, Atari's attempt at a video game based on the 1982 smash hit movie *E.T. the Extra-Terrestrial.* Developers were told that they had six weeks to create a game from scratch in order to get it out in time for the holiday sales rush. The result—remembered fondly today as "the worst game ever made"—was a product so strange and unlikable that it led to hundreds of thousands of unsold *E.T.* game cartridges being buried in a New Mexico landfill in the fall of 1983.[21] The mass video game grave was considered by many to be little more than a myth—until the site was excavated thirty years later, turning up thousands upon thousands of unopened cartridges, each now worth huge sums of money as collector's items.[22]

In 1983, video games were a $3.2 billion industry in America. By 1985, that number had shrunk by an astonishing *97 percent* to only $100 million, putting the entire sector on life support.[23] It might have been game over for the whole enterprise, in fact, were it not for—you guessed it—trade. Just as the floundering American auto industry was given a shot in the arm by superior Japanese competition around this time, the U.S. gaming industry was buoyed by a parallel experience. It wasn't a precision-engineered Nissan or Toyota that arrived from Japan to give American gaming an extra life, however—it was a red-capped, mustachioed Italian plumber.

The Nintendo Playing Card Company was already nearly a

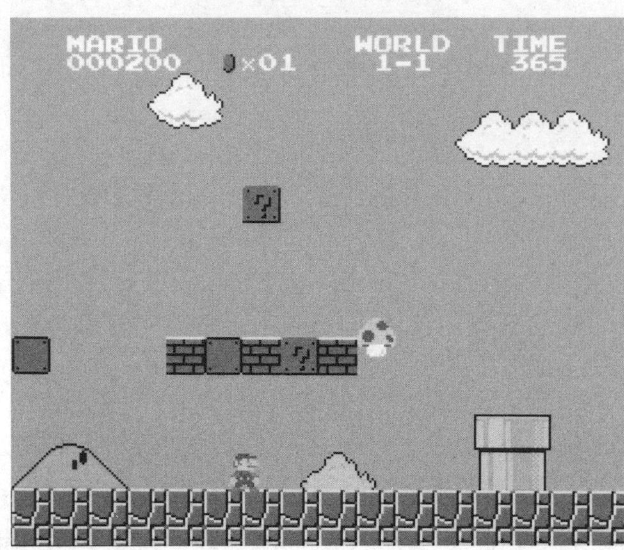

Part racoon—
all tycoon.

century old when it transitioned to video games and ventured across the Pacific. Its signature console—a nondescript gray box launched in America in 1985—and the quality of its game programming set the U.S. industry back on a course of uninterrupted success ever since. The simple protagonist of its earliest games was conceived when Minoru Arakawa, the president of Nintendo's American operation, was loudly and energetically chewed out by the owner of the Seattle warehouse the company was using to develop a game called *Donkey Kong*—a man named Mario Segale—after Nintendo had apparently been late on the rent. The development team was so amused by the animated American hothead and his wild gesticulations that they named their first U.S. video game hero in his honor. And so it was that Mario was born (though no royalties were paid to his namesake).[24]

To this day, Mario endures as one of the most recognizable characters in the whole of American culture. More than 30 million first-generation Nintendo consoles entered U.S. homes, introducing enraptured families to Mario and Luigi, *The Legend of Zelda*, and a spritely menagerie of other breakout sensations.[25] But just as the emergence of Japanese cars had the effect of spurring Ford and GM to improve rather than simply killing them off, the arrival of Nintendo brought about a video game renaissance that dramatically increased the pie for American developers. The years to come would see Nintendo go toe-to-toe with another Japanese company, Sony—makers of the popular PlayStation consoles—as well as a major American competitor in Microsoft, whose Xbox brand became a top seller beginning in the early 2000s. Though Japanese consoles still account for the lion's share of the gaming marketplace, the success of those imports has made it possible for U.S. game designers to flourish. Among the five best-selling video games of 2018 domestically, four were published by American companies and designed primarily or entirely by American developers—the fifth, *Far Cry 5*, was designed in Canada by a French company.[26] Studios like Rockstar of New York, Bethesda Game Studios of Maryland, Activision of California, and Valve of Washington State export popular games all over the world, making it possible for them to support a growing ecosystem of good-paying industry jobs here at home.

As emerging technologies like virtual reality, augmented reality, and artificial intelligence continue to develop, the video game industry is primed to become one of America's most innovative, lucrative exports in the years ahead. Competitive multiplayer gaming—known as "e-sports"—is already a billion-dollar global sector on its own, and is expected to double in size over the next two years on the strength of phenomenons such as *Fortnite* and *Overwatch*.[27] Companies like Coca-Cola, Kraft, Mercedes-Benz, Intel, and Comcast offer sizable sponsorship deals to e-sports tournaments and popular individual players.[28] More viewers now tune into Twitch—an Amazon-owned site where users can spectate as their favorite gamers play—on an average day than CNN or MSNBC.[29] Yes, you heard that right. Video games have evolved from a solitary diversion . . . to a localized social event . . . to a source of global connection . . . to a colossal business on the cutting edge of technological innovation, complete with massive viewership and a corporate advertising presence that will soon rival our major sports leagues. That's quite a transformation for a sector once considered to be child's play—and it was only possible because the best talents, ideas, products, and users were connected to each other by the pathways of global trade.

Coming Up Next . . .

If you wanted to entertain yourself in 1950, you could watch Ed Sullivan or *The Lone Ranger* on your family's black-and-white TV, throw on a Nat King Cole or Patti Page record, or head down to the air-conditioned movie theater to take in a matinee of *Sunset Boulevard* or *All About Eve*. By 1990, it was an entirely different story. TVs came with color and cable—what Bruce Springsteen would memorably describe as "fifty-seven channels and nothin' on." You could bring Madonna and Michael Jackson with you when you left the house with your Walkman or portable CD player, and you didn't even *need* to leave the house to see your favorite movies—*Indiana Jones* and *The Little Mermaid* could come home with you from the video rental store. By 2010, those 57 channels had ballooned to more than 500, while TiVo and other on-demand services gave us the freedom to watch what we wanted when we wanted in sparkling high-definition (and fast-forward through the commercials). CDs were virtually extinct, replaced by iPods and smartphones that stored tens of thousands of songs. And popular services like Netflix allowed us to watch popular 2010 movies like *The King's Speech* or *The Social Network* on our televisions or laptops with the click of a button.

Each of these evolutions was, in truth, a revolution in how we consume media and entertainment. The four decades of innovation after 1950 were as profound a shift as the two decades that followed 1990—which in turn was as big a leap as the ten years that have come since 2010. That is to say: the revolutions are coming faster and faster. This acceleration has consequences for more than just entertainment, of course; it also regularly upends how we gather news and connect with people across the globe. When pro-democracy protesters in the Middle East and North Africa used social media to share their story directly with the world in 2010—setting off a series of events that would come to be known as the Arab Spring—it immediately tilted the playing field of power between governments and people, forever altering the dynamics of civic engagement.

Today, we can live-stream just about anything—including ourselves—around the world without a second thought. Our access to the entertainment, news, and other media of our choosing has basically become both comprehensive and instantaneous. All of this has done wonders for our ability to shower ourselves in choices and tailor the media universe to meet our preferences, of course. But it has also begun to unveil serious questions about the impact that endlessly customizable information will have on our culture and our democracy. We may not be overly concerned when Netflix tabulates our habits and tells us what new show we're likely to enjoy—but we also know that these same methods have been used to much darker effect on platforms like YouTube, where recommendations have been known to funnel vulnerable viewers toward increasingly insidious content such as dangerous conspiracy theories and violent propaganda. This is already having a demonstrable impact on our safety and our civic fabric—

and we'd better hope that we figure out what to do about it before the next wave of innovation crashes over us sometime next week.

The next revolution may not be televised—but it will definitely be streamable over a 5G network on our nearest pair of smart sunglasses. We don't yet know where AI, VR, and who knows what other abbreviations will take us next. The only thing we know for sure is that, within just a few years, today's cutting-edge technologies will seem as antiquated to us as Betamax and car phones. And if you're reading this and thinking, "*great, but don't these revolutions have more to do with technology than trade?*" my response would be: what's the difference? The innovations that will define the way we create and consume media in the future will necessarily be reliant on seamless global exchanges. Like the iPhone, they'll assuredly be far too sophisticated for any one country to produce or sustain in a cost-effective way. Already, Egyptian audiences watch British shows with Irish actors via American streaming services on Japanese devices. Teenagers in Senegal and Australia square off in French video games designed by Canadian developers. When it comes to entertainment, our national borders are all but already gone—and the more advanced the technology grows, the blurrier those lines will become.

As modern trade agreements shift their focus from lowering tariffs and quotas on physical goods to smoothing the exchange of services, policymakers are beginning to think seriously about how media will be produced and experienced in the years to come. The Trans-Pacific Partnership, for example, would have eliminated discriminatory taxes against—or the blocking of—movies, music, videos, games, e-books, and software traveling across borders.[30] It also had clauses designed to bring all twelve countries into closer alignment on digital standards, so that device-building companies wouldn't have to create custom hardware in order for their technology to work in different countries—and consumers wouldn't have to buy special adapters.[31] In addition, TPP also sought to increase high-speed network access, improve digital privacy protections, and smooth the process of international licensing and electronic distribution.[32] None of those provisions have actually come to pass for Americans and U.S. companies, of course—you'll recall that President Trump pulled us out of the deal. But they do provide a blueprint for how future trade agreements can better reflect the reality of modern media and entertainment and our service-based economy.

Carla Hills, who served as U.S. Trade Representative under President George H. W. Bush and was America's lead negotiator of NAFTA, has said that trade agreements are really about the products we don't make yet. She's right—the paths we clear today will allow the technologies of tomorrow to be more affordable, more accessible, more integrated, and ultimately more successful. A hit song or TV show can embed itself in a foreign country in a flash: take the South Korean rapper and producer named Psy, for example. The entertainer was virtually unknown to American audiences when he released his sixth album in July of 2012, but before the year ended the video for his song "Gangnam Style" became the first to surpass one billion views on YouTube—and he would perform live for more than a million people in Times Square that New Year's Eve. Because of that unique speed and power with which culture tends to travel around the world, entertainment is now a critical consideration of our trade policy. We have a special responsibility to ensure that American entertainment can spread freely around the world—and we should do everything we can to make it easier both for foreign entertainment to cross over into the United States and for international collaborations to flourish. The reason for that isn't just because it will lead to more money and more jobs for Americans. Nor is it because global entertainment produces incredible shows like

Game of Thrones that can make our days just a little more fun. It's because, just like we've seen with trade in higher education and tourism, the exchange of culture is critical to fostering greater understanding with the "ROW"—the Rest of the World. They come to know us not just by the things we make, but by the things we love—and we come to know them better in turn. Look beyond GDP, jobs, geopolitics, and everything else, and you'll discover that this is what trade is really all about. For all of its economic benefits, the greatest argument for trade is that—episode by episode, product by product, taco salad by taco salad—it quietly connects us, warms us, and draws us closer to the rest of the human race.

PART THREE

FURTHER BEYOND

CHAPTER 10

Realities

While I've tried my best to offer you an objective look at trade, warts and all, in the preceding pages, the truth is that I'm not really neutral when it comes to this particular subject. Why? Because I know just how powerful a force for good it can be in the world when it is handled humanely and responsibly. I've seen the way that it enriches all of our lives—often in profound, surprising ways. And I've had the privilege of traveling to hundreds of communities, both here at home and abroad, to talk directly to workers and entrepreneurs, and witness firsthand the extraordinary opportunities that trade has made real for them and their families. It's hard not to be excited about the possibilities of trade when you've seen all of the good that it can do.

But this chapter isn't about that. Instead, we're going to talk about trade's most pressing problems: the problems of the past that have never truly been acknowledged; the problems of the present that prevent trade from doing more good for more people; and the problems of the future that we're going to have to solve someday soon. I've seen evidence of many of these problems firsthand, too, in struggling towns that got ignored in our national trade conversation as other industries and other communities seized the fruits of a globalizing economy. Their stories need to be heard, and their futures absolutely must be part of our trade equation moving forward.

The fact is, *everybody* would benefit from our being a lot more honest and candid about trade's unaddressed downsides. Critics of trade have been clamoring to air these grievances for years, of course. But even the staunchest advocates of trade have plenty to gain from grappling openly and transparently with its flaws. If they have a strong argument to make that trade is a net benefit in our lives, as I believe they do, then they should enter this particular conversation with confidence. After all, trade stands to win even broader support and work more effectively for people once we get clear-eyed about its shortcomings and set our minds to remedying them. But it's not the opponents or proponents of trade who would profit the most from a more honest discussion of the issue—it's ordinary citizens everywhere who would see the greatest benefit.

That benefit, by the way, was the reason I wanted to write this very book in the first place. Just like with any other issue, the more unvarnished knowledge we have about trade, the better equipped we'll be to speak, debate, and vote on it. In fact, it's that *lack* of knowledge that has made it possible for trade policy to be so easily used and abused by politicians over the years. So if you leave this book feeling a little more knowledgeable about trade, you'll be doing a service not only to yourself, but to our country: you'll have immunized a tiny portion of the population against being hoodwinked by ideologues who use trade to further their own agendas. Regardless of where you come down on the issues we've covered so far, you're helping to strengthen America's overall trade literacy—and that's a good thing. I solemnly swear that my purpose in writing this book is transparency; it's up to you to decide how we ought to tackle the problems and seize the opportunities of trade . . . as soon as we've developed a shared sense of what, exactly, they are.

The good news is that the central problem presented by trade is pretty simple to grasp. It's so simple, in fact, that our leaders were able to identify it from the very start—long before the NAFTA wars, the World Trade Organization protests, and the globalization of our economy in earnest. You know it. I know it. We've said it a dozen times before. *Trade creates winners and losers*. Now, the number of winners is much higher than the number of losers. And, of course, trade isn't the only thing that creates winners and losers; protectionism—the active decision to *avoid* trade—creates winners and losers, too. But that doesn't change the truth of the matter: trade hurts a number of our fellow citizens, and it is irresponsible, unethical, and ultimately counterproductive for even the most ardent supporters of trade to ignore that fact or attempt to wish it away. Unless we confront that reality and begin to put forward meaningful solutions to alleviate it, we will never build a trade policy that benefits most Americans, offers a hand up to the rest, and creates a consensus that all of us can live with. And until that happens, the door will always remain open for people to fearmonger and take advantage of the resentment of those who get left behind by the forces of the global economy.

To really understand the crux of the "winners and losers" problem—and why it has been so hard for us to solve—it might help for us to take a quick, painless diversion into some basic political economic theory. We know that disruption goes with a capitalist system, frequently forcing our economy and our citizens to adjust to changing times. Increased trade and globalization can hasten that need to adjust—but other events can, too. For example, things like the invention of the cotton gin or the steamship, the dawn of the Industrial Revolution, or the rise of automated manufacturing have all forced us to change the way we operate in order to remain productive and prosperous as a nation. My family's business began as a mail order catalog, which along with

Sears and Montgomery Ward had once disrupted traditional retailers. When online retailers like Amazon came into existence, the new model disrupted us—there are always winners and losers! Anytime our economy changes—whether due to trade or not—some group of workers gets hurt by that change, and some group benefits. We know what that looks like when the change is due to trade, or even just sped up by it: American shoe factories closed when we began buying cheaper shoes from Asia; some number of U.S. autoworkers saw their jobs move to Mexico after NAFTA took effect. But, again, nontrade changes hurt groups of workers, too. Electric light was a big win for our economy, but candlemakers took it on the chin. Suitcases with wheels replaced porters and most baggage handlers at airports and train stations. Travel agents were largely made extinct by online booking services. At some point in the near future, the growing sophistication of vehicles will make the auto repair economy as much about fixing bugs in software as fixing dents in hardware. You get the idea. The point is that these evolutions in our economy are both inevitable and guaranteed to hurt someone, even if they're good for us on the whole.

The question of how we deal with the people who get hurt butts up against two conflicting views of America.[1] The first is the favorite principle of every American capitalist, and one of the most influential forces in U.S. history: the free market economy! Faced with winners and losers in a changing economy, pure free market theory would tell us that the government shouldn't interfere by compensating those who have been hurt by the change—the market has chosen them to fall behind, and those with the skills and resources to find their place in the new economy will do so. The second and far less well-known principle carries the daunting name of the "compensation theory of welfare economics" (phew). It says that when we take any action to improve our economy—say, by adopting automation in order to build better, less expensive cars, or by signing a trade agreement that allows in cheaper toys—that action should never result in one group of people bearing a particularly high cost. The idea, basically, is that because the action has saved a lot of money for Americans on the whole, the government ought to redirect a portion of that money to help those who were displaced by the change so that they don't have to bear the full brunt. As you can imagine, those two strains of thought are in direct conflict . . . but they don't have to be. We can find a middle ground that promotes personal responsibility—but also acknowledges that we're all in this together.

Before you start to worry that all of this political theory talk will get too dense, fear not—we're about to lighten things up with some nineteenth-century British grain laws! In 1939, an English economist named Nicholas Kaldor began to notice that the free market approach wasn't really doing a whole lot for folks who had been left behind by changes in the economy . . . it turns out that many of them weren't so much "advancing to great new jobs" as they were "dying in abject poverty." Kaldor began toying with the idea of compensation by studying how Britain had once dealt with its corn tariffs, which a hundred years earlier had restricted the importing of foreign grains into England in order to prop up domestic farmers. When an unprecedented famine struck the British Isles in 1845—known to most of us today as the Irish Potato Famine—those tariffs had to be repealed to keep the entire population from starving. This change in trade policy created—you guessed it—winners and losers! The onrush of imported grain dramatically lowered the cost of food for British families, while rural farmers already struggling with poor harvests were devastated by the sudden presence of foreign competition. It was Kaldor who, looking back on this event, first raised the idea that no one needed to get hurt by imported goods. The financial gains of British consumers as a result of the tariffs going away were significantly larger than the financial losses of the farmers. So if the government could take just a portion of the money their new policy had delivered to consumers and put it back into the farmers' pockets, everyone would have ended up gaining something. Compensation theory was born, and nobody had to be a loser! Except, of course, for the Irish—who were left behind by the British government, with tragic results.

I'm sharing an abridged version of this history with you because it's the exact thinking that President John F. Kennedy wanted to use to solve the winners and losers problem in American trade. In 1962, the world was less than twenty years removed from a war that had laid bare the existential dangers of nationalism; even normally isolationist powers like the United States had learned the deeper value of entwining our fortunes with those of our friends. We had created global institutions to connect and mutually improve our economies: the World Bank, the International Monetary Fund, the General Agreement on Tariffs and Trade, and the Organisation for Economic Co-operation and Development, to name just a few. And as the specter of an unfriendly—some would say "evil"—empire gained influence in Eastern Europe and Asia, President Kennedy wanted trade to become a weapon that the western powers could wield to overwhelm the Soviets on the economic battlefield. For free trade to save the free world, however, he'd need to convince America and its allies to tear down the tariffs that still divided them. But Kennedy had studied Nicholas Kaldor and those corn laws, too—his father, after all, had been America's ambassador to the United Kingdom years before, and the younger Kennedy had been a student of British history. He knew that a big change in our trade policies would hurt some U.S. workers, and he wanted to make sure that when our economy shifted, nobody got left behind.

On January 25, 1962, Kennedy delivered a message to Congress outlining a bold new trade platform for the country. In a section at the very end—after detailing the many merits of greater economic engagement with the world—he introduced a new idea to America: Trade Adjustment Assistance, which he described succinctly:

> I am also recommending as an essential part of the new trade program that companies, farmers, and workers who suffer damage from increased foreign import competition be assisted in their efforts to adjust to that competition. When considerations of national policy make it desirable to avoid higher tariffs, those injured by that competition should not be required to bear the full brunt of the impact. Rather, the burden of economic adjustment should be borne in part by the Federal Government.[2]

Sounds like a reasonable idea to me. And had we followed through on it, the trade debates of today would probably sound a whole lot different. The idea of Trade Adjustment Assistance (or TAA) was simple: if reducing tariffs led to widespread gains and narrow pains, we could use some of those gains to make up for the pains. Kennedy's plan included three pillars for workers who were hurt by trade, and three for farms and businesses.[3] For workers whose jobs were displaced, TAA would provide direct government payments covering up to about two thirds of their lost wages for a year (or longer, if they were over sixty years old), government-funded vocational training to help them learn new skills, and financial assistance to cover the cost of relocation if they were unable to find work in their community. For companies and farmers, the government would offer free technical support and consultation to help them compete with foreign imports, tax relief rewarding them for modernizing and diversifying their business, and loans and loan guarantees to help them adapt their operations. Perhaps wary of the objections that free market zealots were sure to raise, Kennedy did his best to cut them off at the pass, assuring Congress that TAA "cannot be and will not be a subsidy program of government paternalism. . . . It is instead a program to afford time for American initiative, American adaptability, and American resiliency to assert themselves."[4] And time is an even more critical factor today with the speed of artificial intelligence and automation—where is Kennedy when we need him?

It was a nice turn of phrase, and enough to convince a number of Republicans to publicly cross party lines in support of TAA—including, crucially, former president Dwight Eisenhower, who lobbied members of his party to back the bill.[5] In an effort to convince the holdouts that Trade Adjustment Assistance was more than just a handout, Kennedy quipped that "the accent is on 'adjustment' more than 'assistance.' "[6] Though his plan passed, his effort to distinguish TAA from government interference in the economy fell flat with many free market Republicans.[7] Their objections were more or less predictable, and would be passed down from generation to generation of free market acolytes each time TAA came up for reauthorization every five years or so since. In 2002, for example, Republican senator Don Nickles of Oklahoma referred to TAA as "pretty socialistic," while Republican senator Judd Gregg of New Hampshire branded it a "socialist" idea "which has explosive potential."[8] These were pretty remarkable claims, given the fact that TAA had already been around for forty years at that point and hadn't really made much headway in destroying western capitalism.

On the contrary, TAA actually came in with a whimper, getting off to what can only charitably be described as a slow start. The version that Kennedy was able to get through Congress was so conservative with regard to eligibility requirements, in fact, that in the first seven years of TAA's existence, not a single applicant received benefits—it helped *no one*![9] This would be remedied with a major strengthening of the program in 1974; two years later, TAA was serving a modest 62,000 workers who had lost their livelihoods due to the further loosening of trade restrictions.[10] By the early 1980s, as tariffs continued to fall, TAA covered more than half a million unemployed U.S. workers with direct payments, skills training, and other support.[11] At the urging of Bill Clinton, the program would be updated one more time in 1993 to create specific support services for workers impacted by NAFTA.[12] Clinton had pushed for an even more generous version of TAA at the time, but was met with determined opposition from across the aisle.

By 2014, TAA had been used by a total of 2.2 million Americans to adjust to the losses they suffered as a result of trade.[13] There is an argument to be made—and many have tried—that the program has been fairly effective. In 2014, more than three quarters of displaced workers who made use of TAA found a new job within six months, and 90 percent of that group still had that job six months later.[14] Those numbers are nothing to dismiss, particularly when you consider that more than half of those enrolled have a high school education or less and are, on average, about fifty years old—a demographic that has historically struggled to change careers after being laid off.[15] Ben Hyman of the New York Federal Reserve has conducted a twenty-year study showing that TAA boosts participants' earnings, and in effect pays for itself; he found that workers who take part in the program end up earning about $50,000 more over a ten-year period than those who don't. There is no doubt that, charges of explosive socialism aside, TAA is and always has been a well-intentioned effort to do right by the victims of U.S. trade policy. But even if it has helped some number of workers to land on their feet, it's still hard to call it a successful program given everything we know about the scores of displaced American workers who have never gotten their second chance.

While there remains a vocal faction of free marketers who object to the government stepping in to redirect resources to those who have been hurt by trade, criticism of TAA extends well beyond ideology. For one thing, it doesn't come close to covering the likely number of workers who have been displaced by trade—the program just isn't large or well-funded enough to tackle the scope of the challenge. The workers who *do* successfully land new jobs after using TAA also tend to earn less than they did in their previous jobs—typically, they end up taking a pay cut of about 20 percent.[16] Many displaced workers simply never hear about TAA, and only about a third of those who enroll end up taking advantage of its skills training programs. In addition, those training programs have been chronically underfunded.[17] A popular critique on the right suggests that by doling out money, TAA actually incentivizes laid-off workers *not* to seek out new jobs speedily—and it's worth noting that TAA's allowances tend to be a bit more generous than regular unemployment benefits. Moreover, critics are quick to point out that lots of Americans lose their jobs every year for all sorts of reasons that are beyond their control—why should the victims of trade get special treatment that we don't afford to victims of automation or changing consumer tastes? To that, some would say that because trade-related job losses are a result of policy choices rather than the natural flow of the marketplace, the government bears some responsibility to make things right.

TAA may enjoy some measure of bipartisan support, but that support could easily be characterized as "a mile wide and an inch deep." It hasn't been killed off yet . . . but it also has never been especially well funded. It does seem to offer *some* amount of help to *some* Americans who have been left behind by the global economy, at least. But you'd be hard-pressed to find anyone who truly believes that it's an effective solution to the problem it was designed to solve. And you'd be even harder-pressed to find anyone who gets particularly excited about it—labor leader Richard Trumka has described it to me as "a gold-plated coffin." Perhaps TAA would be better loved if it was better funded, but the tepid support of political leaders over the years suggests that we are unlikely to find out anytime soon. The most telling thing, however, is that TAA is just about the only effort America has made to do right by those who have been hurt by trade. It's been well over half a century since President Kennedy first introduced the idea, and in all that time we have failed as a country to come up with anything better—our tendency instead has been to look the other way.

Looking back from our vantage point today, it's clear that compensating the losers of trade with half measures—or, worse, simply ignoring them—has cost our country dearly. When Donald Trump made the grievances of America's "forgotten men and women" a centerpiece of his 2016 presidential campaign, he tapped into a deep well of pain and resentment that we had allowed to fester for years without sunlight or solutions. In midwestern towns where the hum of the local factory had long since gone quiet, "more funding for Trade Adjustment Assistance" was never going to be a compelling rallying cry. A way of life had changed—something more profound than just the sum of lost jobs—and politicians offering temporary wage allowances and short-lived training courses simply couldn't make up for the dignity and purpose that had been sapped out of whole communities by time, by technology, and, yes, sometimes by trade. Compensation—*true* compensation—required something more. It still does.

Seismic Disruptions

Perhaps the most concerning thing about the "winners and losers" problem is that we're running out of time to get it right. It was never a good idea for America's leaders to minimize the issue of people being left behind by trade and other changes to our economy—but until recently, most of our leaders usually did seem to get away with it without facing serious political consequences. Those days are probably over now, not only due to Donald Trump's harnessing of nationalist resentment, but because the pace of change is about to accelerate beyond anything we've seen before. As automation, technology, and seamless global supply chains pick up speed, we simply won't be able to ignore the scope of the change—or the people it impacts—any longer.

What has made the fallout of globalization particularly thorny in recent years is that, for the most part, its effects have been geographically concentrated. Because such a large proportion of the factories that have closed have been clustered in Midwestern communities, a bit of a paradox has emerged. First, since the vast majority of Americans never felt the negative impact of trade in their own towns, globalization has never taken root as an especially potent political issue among broad swaths of the population. At the same time, though, the fact that the "losers" of trade tend to be packed into key electoral states like Ohio, Michigan, Wisconsin, and Pennsylvania has led to their experiences being disproportionately amplified during presidential campaigns. That paradox has had a profound influence on both our conversations *and* our policies on trade. In fact, I'd go so far as to say that it's one of the chief reasons why we've *talked* about the victims of globalization as much as we have without ever really solving the problem.

The thing is, the next big change in our economy isn't going to look like anything we've seen before. When artificial intelligence becomes a dominant feature of our lives—and our jobs—it won't care whether we're working in Manhattan, New York, or Manhattan, Kansas. The transition we'll make to the next generation of technology and automation won't discriminate against our geography or industry the way the last one did—but it will discriminate against our education level. Americans have already been conditioned to expect that jobs that don't require college degrees might vanish at a moment's notice; we are all too familiar with the image of a robot taking the place of a factory worker or a self-checkout machine replacing a grocery store clerk. But we aren't yet primed for the possibility that white-collar jobs, advanced engineering jobs, and other lines of work that people spend many years after high school training for could fall by the wayside, too. To be sure, the most educated Americans will be better-protected from the next wave of technological progress—but that doesn't mean that every doctor, lawyer, accountant, and programmer will be spared. This anxiety, and the sense of imminence that accompanies it, are part of the reason why our politics have become so razor sharp.

The first step to meeting this challenge will be to change American mind-sets—we have to be completely honest about what learning, working, and making a living will look like in the years ahead. More than a quarter century ago, Bill Clinton bravely told the youth of America that they were going to "change jobs eight times" in their lives. Now, we need young people to understand that most of those eight jobs don't even exist right now—they haven't been imagined yet. Estimates of the percentage of jobs of the future that don't yet exist range as high as 85 percent.[18] What we know for sure is that we can no longer count on a college degree being a lifetime pass that guarantees us security and access to the comforts of the middle class. Of course, plenty of Americans have discovered that already. We also know that there is only one surefire way to prepare for an uncertain future, no matter what it ultimately brings: we have to never, ever, ever stop learning.

In the very near future, college is going to be just a starting point—and we'll finally understand why they call university graduation ceremonies "commencements." Education in America can no longer be seen as something that we get through when we're young and wrap up for good at age eighteen or twenty or twenty-two. That simply isn't going to fly in a world that reinvents itself much more frequently these days than it ever has before. This is a hard truth—and a significant change—that we'll need to lean into. The idea of "lifelong learning" may not be particularly exciting to most people; if you told me that I needed to go back to school, say, to learn a new foreign language, that would sound incredibly daunting to me. But, really, it's less about learning and more about what my friend Ambassador Robert Holleyman, the former deputy U.S. trade representative, calls "lifelong readiness." Bracing for the new economy won't require us to sit in classrooms for the rest of our lives; it will just require us to stay agile and prepared to develop new skills. When a big storm comes, we stock up on supplies in order to stay ready—and when change comes to our economy, we need to stock up on skills. Adapting to that new approach won't always be easy. But it will be nowhere near as hard as the consequences of closing our eyes. If we fail to get continuing job preparation right, we won't just fall behind economically or forfeit our position as a global leader. We'll also be setting the stage for political and social upheaval as our supply of lower-skilled jobs erodes away—leaving millions of Americans stranded and desperate without the income, security, or dignity of other job options. And that's before you account for the rest of the world, where change will likely increase pressure on emerging economies and impact migration and stability abroad.

There will always be voices telling us that we can simply turn off the spigot of the global economy and go back to our regularly scheduled lives. It's a comforting thought—and one that a whole lot of people are no doubt eager to embrace and take refuge in. The problem is, it simply isn't true. Nothing is easier than hearing *you don't have to change a thing—I'll fix it.* But closing ourselves off from the world economy is like deciding to stop receiving treatment for a life-threatening illness: sure, it would make us comfortable and spare us some painful side effects in the near-term. But it would not lead to a robust, thriving life ahead. And globalization isn't a terminal condition! In fact, we're better positioned than just about any other country in the world to come through it stronger than we were before—as long as we're willing to take our medicine, exercise, eat right, and open ourselves up to some healthy change.

For a taste of what that looks like, take a trip to Pikeville, Kentucky, a mountain town of 7,000 people set just along a fork of the Big Sandy River. Just a stone's throw from the Virginia and West Virginia state lines, Pikeville is the heart of Appalachia—to drive the point home, it even hosts a popular festival called, yes, "Hillbilly Days," which attracts more than 100,000 visitors to the town each year to celebrate the music, arts, food, culture, and lifestyle of the proverbial backwoods mountaineer. Pikeville is also where you'll find a fellow named—again, I'm not making this up—Rusty Justice, a local businessman who, like so many men and women of his generation in eastern Kentucky, hauled coal in his youth. Take a look at the bio of Rusty on the website of the company he founded in Pikeville in 2015, and you'll find that he describes himself as "an unapologetic hillbilly [who] loves Jesus, his family, baseball, and all things Appalachia."[19] What surprised me is that the company, nestled deep in the black braids and tawny dust of coal country, is a cutting-edge web development and software start-up called Bit Source.

Just as the auto factories had defined both livelihood and life for generations in the Upper Midwest, coal had always been the birthright of this region. Mining was a paycheck for many—and a rather good one at that—but it was also a source of dignity, identity, community, and connection to the land. What happened to disrupt that? What else—a big change in the economy, of course. Trade wasn't to blame in this particular instance; Americans just got sweet on natural gas, which in addition to being homegrown proved cheaper, cleaner, and more plentiful than coal could ever hope to be. Rusty Justice saw the writing on the wall—maybe coal would get left behind by a changing world, but Pikeville didn't have to get left behind with it. He teamed up with a business partner who had spent four decades in the coal industry, and together they brainstormed ideas for a company that wouldn't just *survive* a sea change in the economy, but would in fact ride the wave.[20]

Pikeville's geography put it at a disadvantage for businesses that relied on moving physical goods; remote and mountainous, it's neither cheap nor easy to transport products back and forth from it to just about anywhere. The town suffered from low education and high unemployment, but Rusty knew firsthand that the local workforce was full of hardworking problem solvers—that was a prerequisite for life in the mines, after all. A visit to a nearby job training conference introduced Rusty and his partner to coding, and the light bulb went off. Here was work that could be done from just about anywhere in the country by trained, hardworking problem solvers, with sky-high demand, zero shipping needs, and little risk of being rendered obsolete anytime soon by shifts in the economy.

Rusty set up shop in a discarded brick Coca-Cola plant on the western edge of town—a faded soft drink sign still perches above the door, blanched by time. When he posted classified ads announcing that a new tech start-up would soon be hiring in Pikeville, nearly 1,000 applicants responded.[21] The Bit Source brass made use of a test designed to measure a person's aptitude for coding, and ultimately settled on eleven ex-miners who, with the help of some basic training, would make up the initial workforce. And just like that, the quintessential hometown of a dying industry took one step closer to embracing a new identity: what the locals now call "Silicon Holler."

Bit Source has gained a fair bit of attention as a regional success story for the way that it was able to do what Trade Adjustment Assistance never really could: seamlessly transition workers from old, low-skill, endangered industries into a high-tech service sector that pays them just as much or more. They represent the ideal solution to the "winners and losers" problem—an organic, entrepreneurial answer that doesn't require the government to step in and redistribute the gains of trade. But however inspiring a story it is to see Rusty Justice and his team of hardscrabble coders breathe new life into their corner of Pikeville, questions remain about the prospects for replicating the Bit Source model.

Some of those questions have to do with the adaptability of the workforce in coal towns, steel towns, and other communities left behind in the new economy. Rusty was able to hire eleven of the most promising potential coders from among the hundreds of under- and unemployed miners in the area, but who knows how many of the remainder are capable of making a similar leap? Other questions concern the capacity of towns like Pikeville to handle high-tech sectors—and those questions do require a little attention and investment on the part of our government. Pikeville itself did not have consistently reliable broadband internet until late 2017, when the commonwealth installed a broadband "hut" in town as part of an initiative to improve rural internet access.[22] That's not uncommon in rural communities across the country, many of which struggle to attract or sustain business and investment in part because they lack the necessary digital infrastructure. We have no way of knowing how many potential businesses like Bit Source have had the ideas, the people, and the will to adapt to the twenty-first-century economy, but haven't been able to get off the ground because they're stuck with twentieth-century technology.

The irony here comes back, as it so often does, to politics and culture. During the summer of 2016, then-presidential candidate Hillary Clinton unveiled the most ambitious internet access plan in history—a "broadband-for-all" proposal that would have equipped every American with reliable internet by 2020.[23] Since 96 percent of people living in urban areas already enjoy that access, this plan probably didn't come across your radar if you, like the media outlets that cover presidential campaigns, happen to live in or around a city. But about 40 percent of Americans living in rural communities like Pikeville don't have broadband—which means they lack the basic ingredients to start and support many tech- and service-based businesses (or, frankly, any business that relies on the internet to reach customers . . . which is to say, all of them). The Clinton plan would have also doubled federal investment in computer science education, freed up capital for tech start-ups, made job benefits portable for workers transitioning to new fields, deferred student loans for people who start tech businesses, and created a program incentivizing towns to build "model digital communities."[24] By contrast, Donald Trump did not offer a plan for rural internet access as a candidate—though he did say at a campaign stop that, "We have to go see Bill Gates and a lot of different people that really understand what's happening. . . . We have to talk to them about, maybe in certain areas, closing that internet up in some way."[25]

So who won the state of Kentucky in 2016? That would be Donald Trump—by 30 points. He beat Clinton in Pike County, the home of Pikeville, by a whopping 80 percent to 17. Few noticed when the budget sent to Congress by the White House for 2018 attempted to do away with the Appalachian Regional Commission, a government body charged with investing hundreds of millions of dollars specifically to help coal communities revitalize their economies.[26] Trump's 2019 budget proposed the complete elimination of the Rural Economic Development Loan & Grant Program[27] as well as the fifty-five-year-old Economic Development Administration, an agency that awards federal matching grants for local initiatives that promote business development in distressed coal and manufacturing communities.[28]

For the moment, identity politics remains the strongest flavor of politics in places like Pikeville—the emotional embrace of coal and the tradition, history, and identity it represents is still more attractive an offer to most folks there than the promise of a bridge to get beyond it. Homegrown solutions paired with state and federal investments could provide a ticket to the future, though. The Eastern Kentucky Concentrated Employment Program is a private initiative that helps retrain workers in twenty-three coal counties; using a grant from the U.S. Department of Labor, it guides laid-off miners through the process of transitioning to new careers, pays for them to go back to school, and subsidizes them during periods of on-the-job training.[29] It was this program that helped Rusty Justice recruit and select the first batch of Bit Source coders, and the organization now works with thousands of Kentuckians seeking a pathway from coal to more reliable jobs in the tech sector.[30] Today, the program is partnering with community colleges in the area to run coding camps, develop online courses that build IT skills, and raise the profile of tech jobs as a realistic, dependable option in Appalachia.[31] In a region that is loath to place its trust in the federal government, success may be as simple as not advertising where the money for all of these new job opportunities comes from.

It remains to be seen whether "Silicon Holler" will succeed in time to rejuvenate this corner of coal country, but at long last a blueprint is in place. Ankur Gopal, a Kentucky native who had launched his own tech start-up called Interapt in 2011, was so taken by the Bit Source story that he created a program called TechHire Eastern Kentucky to re-create the idea.[32] His first "graduating class" of thirty-five coders in 2016 included out-of-work miners, convenience store clerks, and pizza delivery drivers. After a twenty-four-week course and an eight-week apprenticeship, they were app designers and software engineers whose scant hourly wages had been replaced by comfortable annual salaries. Best of all, most didn't have to leave their hometowns for big cities in search of a better life—they brought their skills, their disposable income, and their newfound optimism right back to eastern Kentucky. Another ninety local workers began training in 2018, and Gopal expects that number to continue rising as the program gains momentum.[33] It's an inspiring story, though, again, the politics are complicated. Gopal was only able to launch the program by convincing Kentucky's Republican governor, Matt Bevin, and local Republican congressman, Hal Rogers, to lobby the federal government for funding—which they did. The Appalachian Regional Commission approved $2.7 million to get TechHire Eastern Kentucky up and running . . . and yes, that would be the same Appalachian Regional Commission that President Trump has since sought to eliminate.[34]

What does the future look like for American workers displaced by technology, time, and trade? I'll be frank with you: I don't know. Companies like Bit Source, initiatives like the Eastern Kentucky Concentrated Employment Program, and ideas like TechHire Eastern Kentucky are proving that it's possible to solve the "winners and losers" problem in a positive way—but their long-term success is far from guaranteed. The politics are delicate, culture and identity loom large, our infrastructure is still lagging, and we don't know if these solutions can be scaled up to meet the broader challenge. And yet they do offer hope in a way that Trade Adjustment Assistance never really has.

These apprenticeships, skills education programs, and job retraining models are already making an extraordinary difference for a small number of displaced workers. But the best thing about them is that—even if they ultimately aren't able to tackle the whole problem—they are starting to change the way we think about learning and working. The name of the game in Kentucky is *adaptability*; pretty soon, with AI and automation, that will be the name of the game throughout our country. These new coding jobs will probably change in unrecognizable ways—however, the miners-turned-coders won't be right back where they started. They'll have skills that give them an advantage in all sorts of twenty-first-century industries, and they'll have strengthened the most important muscle of all: the ability to learn new things long after their years in the classroom have ended. In a constantly evolving economy, having that agility and the mind-set that comes with it will be essential—not just for coal miners displaced by the marketplace or factory workers displaced by trade, but for all of us whose careers are going to be disrupted by the next seismic shift of technological progress.

CHAPTER 11

Remedies

"This 'telephone' has too many shortcomings to be seriously considered as a means of communication," wrote William Orton, the president of Western Union, in 1876.[1] "Who the hell wants to hear actors talk?" asked Harry Warner—he of the famous Warner Brothers—the very same year that Al Jolson's *The Jazz Singer* took Hollywood by storm. One of the founders of Twentieth Century-Fox, Darryl Zanuck, predicted in 1946 that television was a passing fad; after all, he reasoned, "people will soon get tired of staring at a plywood box every night." Three years later, *Popular Mechanics* marveled at the thought that "computers in the future may have only 1000 vacuum tubes and perhaps weigh only 1½ tons." Fast-forward to 1995, when internet pioneer and 3Com founder Robert Metcalfe opined that "the internet will soon go spectacularly supernova and in 1996 catastrophically collapse"—at a conference in 1997, he famously stuffed a printout of his doomsaying column into a blender and, to the delight of the assembled audience, quite literally ate his words. More recently, the prominent consulting firm McKinsey & Company predicted in 2007 that the global market for iPhones had the potential to perhaps reach as high as 20 million units (more than a billion have been sold since then), while in 2005 YouTube cofounder Steve

Chen cast doubt on the prospects of his own brainchild, lamenting that "there's just not that many videos I want to watch."

To borrow another quote, usually attributed to Yogi Berra: "It's tough to make predictions, especially about the future." I've been guilty of this as well; when I was at Lillian Vernon in the 1990s and first encountered the idea of ordering products from your TV remote, my initial reaction was, "isn't it nice to actually speak to someone at the other end of a telephone and place your order with a human?" I was so wrong! The point of recounting these spectacularly bad forecasts isn't to mock the rather intelligent folks who made them—it's to remind you, at this critical moment in our story, of just how limited our imagination can be when it's asked to think about what's ahead. The future has always been consistently bolder and more interesting than we give it credit for, and when it comes to the future ahead of us today, that's just about the only prediction I'm willing to make with any confidence. Preparing ourselves for that future—whatever surprises it may bring—is the most important challenge of our time. And that means that we have to do everything in our power to brace ourselves for change: to engage in Robert Holleyman's idea of "lifelong readiness" and become more adaptable, and to embrace new ideas and solutions when we think about the unlikely things that lie ahead.

When I think about the strategies that will serve us best in that effort, I recall what President Obama used to say about America's energy future. While the hearts of Democrats may have been firmly with clean, renewable energy sources, Obama repeatedly embraced what he called an "all-of-the-above" approach; the challenge, he reasoned, was too large and complex to limit our thinking at the time. For energy, that meant pursuing wind, solar, nuclear, fossil fuels, and other avenues all at once. For the future of our economy, it will mean pursuing federal and state programs, municipal experiments, private sector initiatives, and ideas that arise out of our educational institutions and think tanks. Until we know what tomorrow's economy holds, we shouldn't rely on the limits of our ideologies and our current predictions. Instead, we should embrace every idea that makes our workforce more resilient, our economy more durable, and our population better prepared to seize whatever opportunities arise.

Frankly, this sort of approach is exactly what we *should* have been doing all along when it came to global trade. Building lifelong readiness into American workers could have helped stave off so many of the negative consequences we've seen over the years—it would have spread the benefits of trade more widely, made it easier for us to evolve and part ways with old industries, and prevented people from souring on globalization. Unfortunately, as a country, we fell down on the job, failing millions of workers. Rather than get ready for the inevitable changes of the future, we consistently told people that we could push back against the ocean—that nothing in their lives would have to change. And when towns were hollowed out and industries were shattered, leaving behind countless workers who had never been warned that they needed to be ready for something else in life, politicians told them that we could bring the past back . . . that people of color or immigrants were to blame for how their lives had changed . . . and that the *next* round of changes could be stopped. They simply had to buck up and fend for themselves.

The pace of change cannot be stopped. It shouldn't be stopped—not if we're ready to make the most of it. The good news is that we're not starting from scratch—innovative solutions are out there, being road-tested and improved upon in forward-thinking towns, states, and regions across the country. Some are programs built on embracing and harnessing new technologies. Some are policy shifts with an eye toward strengthening the mobility and agility of our workforce. And some are social strategies to help us cope with a future that simply won't require us to perform as much labor as we're used to doing. What they each have in common is that they are all answers to a question that hasn't been put to us yet—a question we will not know the true contours of until it smacks us in the face. How do we prepare ourselves for the economy of the future? How do we account for its global dimensions, its unknown and unknowable variables, and the unintended consequences it will surely impose on the people who will live within it and make it hum? America has spent an enormous amount of time and energy trying to deny or delay the impact of economic changes, technological progress, and global connectivity. We've sat by as our infrastructure and our education system stagnated. We ignore those realities at our peril. If we can embrace solutions that instead allow us to *harness* the inevitable forces of change and use them to our advantage, we can rebuild our middle class for the long haul and set the country on a sustainable path through the uncertain years ahead.

What does it look like to seek solutions with the future in mind? Well, take the case of the Philadelphia City Council, which in February of 2019 decided to confront the widespread issue of stores that refuse to accept cash.[2] For many businesses, moving to a cash-free model seemed like a dependable way to improve efficiency, minimize customers' wait time, and eliminate the threat of robbery. From the city's perspective, however, it presented a fairness issue—a number of low-income locals don't have credit or debit cards to pay with, effectively locking them out from being served by cash-free stores. The City Council voted 12–4 to require retail stores and restaurants to accept paper money; in effect, they looked at this issue that had been created by unmistakable trends in technology and culture . . . and resolved it by forcing businesses to revert to the past. What would a future-facing solution look like? How about a municipal program making it free and easy for every Philadelphian to establish a basic bank account—instead of tackling inequality by making the stores turn back to old methods, they could have done it by helping to lift people up into the cashless future we all know is coming.

We face these sorts of choices all the time as a society, and it's crucial that we train ourselves to make creative decisions that reflect where we're going—not where we've been. That's true when it comes to city retail policies, and it's true when it comes to our national trade policy, where President Trump has time and again chosen to cling to antiquated tariffs: the ultimate backward-facing solution. The future is cashless, sure, but it's also global. And all we'll get for ignoring that reality is a little temporary comfort—the pleasant familiarity of old ways—while the rest of the world moves on to brighter days without us.

Just as we did in the days of the explorers, at the dawn of industry, and in the Age of Information, we must throw away the old maps and venture out further beyond. We've already talked about a few potential solutions for lifting everyone up in a changing world—compensating displaced communities, training coal miners to become coders, and adopting a new view of how we can keep educating ourselves over the course of our lifetimes. But this particular puzzle is as large and complex as any our country has ever faced before; it's going to take a lot of pieces and creative ideas to put it all together and create a picture that works for everybody. We can start by setting our ideologies aside; the left must acknowledge that government programs can't solve this alone, while the right must accept that the market won't simply take care of everything in a way that's acceptable or humane. Nor will our solutions be "one-size-fits-all"—some will work better in rural communities, some will best serve younger populations, and so forth. To borrow a phrase from former defense secretary Donald Rumsfeld, we'll have to face down not only the "known knowns" that we're fully expecting will challenge us, like the continued march of technology and the maturation of rival economies. We'll also have to tackle a host of unknown or only partially known problems, too.

Chief among those unknowns is American politics, which will either be extraordinarily helpful or extraordinarily harmful in terms of preparing the U.S. to face the future responsibly, depending on how things go in the next few years. The truth is that solving the winners and losers problem and insulating our country against the jolts of rapid change would be hard enough even if we knew exactly how to do it. Quite simply, that's because our political system has a nasty habit of stymieing even the most obvious solutions that the vast majority of us agree on. There are plenty of issues where things don't get done in spite of mountains of data and broad consensus suggesting they should: take investing in early education, building climate resilience, rebuilding our infrastructure, and so on down the line. If our country remains bogged down in ideological squabbles and well-funded kneecappings, we'll have zero chance of rising up to meet the enormous wave of economic change looming over us. Could that change? Of course it could. Voters could insist that solutions be taken seriously, and send a flock of like-minded leaders into office. Politicians could recognize the scope of the challenge and forge a consensus. It really could change—and it will have to if we have any hope of staying ahead of changes in the coming economy.

There are plenty of other unknown challenges, too. Because technological breakthroughs are unpredictable, we have no way of anticipating whether the next advancement in artificial intelligence will introduce a technology that displaces half of America's accountants, IT specialists, or graphic designers—or whether a sudden breakthrough will render every optometrist obsolete. The McKinsey Global Institute found that technology will eliminate the need for 30 percent of all human labor worldwide by 2030, forcing up to 375 million people to "switch occupational categories and learn new skills."[3] Perhaps we could make a plan for that—if only we knew which 375 million people will need to change careers first. But we need to be ready. We all need, in our way, to be ready for the future.

As if that weren't daunting enough, it's probably safe to assume that the future will present us with even thornier issues we haven't begun to imagine just yet. These are the questions it never occurs to us to ask—the events that are neither foreseen nor foreseeable, even if we find ways to explain them after the fact. They might take the form of so-called "black swan" events that catch us completely off guard and suddenly change everything: think the outbreak of World War I, the creation of the internet, or the September 11 attacks. By definition, there is just no way to account for them, other than to stay open to the possibility that something might happen at some time that utterly changes the way we see the world. A new technology that instantly allows us to provide clean, cheap, renewable energy to everybody? A catastrophic cybersecurity failure? The discovery of life outside our planet? Who knows what unexpected twists the future might bring—or how those twists will upend the global economy. As we think about how best to prepare ourselves and craft our trade policies for the economy of the future, we have to get comfortable with the fact that even our best-laid plans could be thrown off course or rendered laughable by both predictable and unpredictable developments.

Fortunately, we have something important working in our favor: the resilience and adaptability of people. That's not just empty rhetoric, either. In the 1870s, just prior to the onset of the

Second Industrial Revolution, more than half of working Americans had jobs in agriculture. A century later, that number had dropped below 5 percent[4]—and many of the most popular jobs were in fields like auto repair, switchboard operation, and long-haul trucking that the farmers of the 1870s could not possibly have imagined. The point is, we've done this sort of wholesale adaptation before, and emerged on the other side with more jobs and greater prosperity. The only difference is that we're going to have to do it much more quickly this time around.

It's not just American prosperity that's at stake. This is a matter of national and global stability as well—in addition to national security. A report from the Brookings Institution suggests that if the impending job disruption caused by artificial intelligence and automation ends up being as severe as the average of current forecasts suggests it will be, "Western democracies likely could resort to authoritarianism. . . . The United States would look like Syria or Iraq, with armed bands of young men with few employment prospects other than war, violence or theft."[5] Again, this comes from the Brookings Institution—a think tank not generally known for making melodramatic claims. Whether that grim future is borne out or not, one thing is certain. The country that best prepares its workforce, its policies, its schools, its cities, and its communities to ride these constant waves of change forward—rather than simply let the waves crash into them—will keep its people happy and productive, and put itself in a position to lead the world.

I don't have all the answers; in fact, I don't think *anyone* does. There is no one solution. I believe until we have a better sense of where technologies, trends, and tastes are going to take our economy in the years to come, the best thing we can do for the moment is innovate and experiment with ideas that make us as adaptable as possible. What we can't do is get caught off guard by change—we know it is coming, even if we will invariably misjudge how fast and in what forms it will arrive. While innovations in trade and technology have been vital to America and the world, there have been downsides as well. Some of the impacts of trade and tech evolutions of the past have been like small comets crashing into earth: localized disasters that would never cause most of us outside the impact zone to deviate from our normal lives. It's a safe bet that the next one—in whatever form it takes—will be more like a giant asteroid that knocks us off our axis and forces all of us to recalibrate how we think about our lives and livelihoods.

So what do we need to do? First, we have to start with ourselves. Lifelong readiness means taking responsibility for our own future and preparing ourselves just as we would if we knew that a hurricane was coming—stocking up on a durable supply of skills to have at the ready. Nor should we forget that we are all in this together; yes, we have to ready ourselves, but nobody should be left to make this leap alone. We must move with urgency and honesty to prepare for the future—and, when necessary, prepare ourselves mentally and emotionally to adapt our lifestyles and our culture to changing times. With that in mind, let's explore some of the solutions in the public sector, the private sector, and the arena of global trade that seem to offer the most promising paths forward for all of us.

The Anti-Social Network

While the world waits around for the jobs of the future to be invented, governments don't need to wait to do their part—they can start guarding against us losing the jobs of the present right away. To brace for what's to come, we can start by embracing innovative new approaches to our social safety net. A social safety net, like the safety nets used by high-wire walkers and trapeze acrobats, is essential to maintaining the integrity of our society. That's always true—but never more so than when our economy faces unpredictable headwinds. Addressing our social safety net comes with a big built-in political challenge, however: that one word—*social*—tends to raise the hackles of many Americans and the politicians who represent them. In fact, every social program that has come into our lives—from Social Security in the 1930s to Medicare and Medicaid in the 1960s to the Affordable Care Act in 2010—was initially met with fierce resistance by those who seem to hear a silent "ism" every time they hear the word *social*. It's basically an American tradition at this point that programs designed to protect people from hardship are automatically considered suspect; there must be something in our DNA of rugged individualism and free markets that bristles against the idea that the government will be there to soften our landing if we have the misfortune of getting old, sick, or fired.

Given the scale of the economic upheaval likely headed our way in the years ahead, we're going to have to get over that reaction. In fact, there's reason to believe that we already are. The policy of a universal basic income, or UBI—the idea that the government pays out a baseline salary to every citizen, regardless of their job or lack thereof—was considered little more than a fringe proposal of the far left just a few short years ago. But as the prospect of artificial intelligence replacing workers has become a more visceral and immediate threat, UBI has entered the mainstream at a pretty remarkable speed. A February 2018 Gallup poll found that 48 percent of Americans were supportive of implementing a basic income specifically for workers who get replaced by new technologies; a clear majority of women, college-educated Americans, and those thirty-five and younger said the same.[6] The poll suggested that nearly half of all people were personally willing to pay higher taxes to ensure that workers displaced by artificial intelligence were provided with an income—while 80 percent supported an idea floated by Bill Gates and others to pay for UBI with a "robot tax" on companies that sub in technology for human labor.[7]

That robot tax idea has its roots in Nicholas Kaldor and the British corn laws we talked about in the last chapter, by the way. Just as England's sudden savings on food prices could be used to compensate domestic farmers who were hurt by grain imports, the idea of the robot tax is that if companies can make loads of money by replacing humans with AI, some of that money can be set aside to compensate the people who get replaced. Whether or not UBI proves to be a wise course of action, it's a good sign that Americans are seemingly warming to the idea that we need to do more and spend more to cushion ourselves from the disruption that comes with technological innovation. As a society, we have always been more supportive of Social Security than we've been of, say, food stamps, perhaps in part because it's easier for most of us to imagine ourselves growing old than it is to imagine ourselves becoming destitute. Perhaps those numbers in support of UBI have shot up over the past couple of years because more people can now imagine a world in which *they'll* be replaced by technology—that is to say, a world in which they'll need it. Ultimately, my own hope is that the world ahead of us is one that doesn't require us to rely on ideas like UBI. Humans, by our nature, *want* to be productive—it's part of how we define ourselves. So I'd prefer a future in which the progress we make doesn't render jobs obsolete, but rather allows us to engage in work that brings each of us dignity and purpose. Will we achieve that future? Nobody knows! And that's exactly why UBI is an idea worth keeping in our arsenal in the meantime.

There are other ideas about the social safety net that are

beginning to be explored at all different levels of government. A number of economists, for example, have started advocating for a change to how we pay out unemployment insurance. Typically, if you lose your job, the unemployment benefits you receive will be dispensed in weekly or monthly installments, just like paychecks—but now these economists are beginning to argue that this practice might be holding people back from ever overcoming the need for government help. If unemployment insurance were to be paid out in a single lump sum up front, it would give people who lose their jobs much more freedom to make a big, necessary change in their lives. It also might encourage them to move more quickly in thinking about their alternatives. Instead of collecting just enough to pay rent and afford groceries until the next check arrives while they survey the local job postings, a lump sum payment would give them the instant capacity to invest in their own job training or, if they prefer, spend money moving to an area with greater job opportunities. In short, this alternative would offer them mobility, flexibility, and some control over their future—three things that we know are essential to setting people up well for the long run. It would shift the incentive structure so that more displaced factory workers and retail clerks could actually spend their unemployment checks on readying themselves for new jobs rather than just on staying afloat. Best of all, it's a change that could happen right away with the simple tweaking of a policy. It's worth a trial.

There are plenty of ideas like these out there that we ought to be studying and piloting to see how well they can counteract disruption and brace people and communities for change. Targeted wage subsidies and tax breaks aimed at workers who are likely to be displaced by trade or automation could encourage people to arm themselves with new skills *before* their job disappears. Wage insurance could help workers forced to take on lower-paying replacement jobs make up part of the difference in the wages they've lost—giving them more time and freedom to ready themselves for better opportunities. We could expand the Earned Income Tax Credit, a policy that has been proven to reduce poverty in our hardest-hit communities—and one that has the potential to help the broadest possible swath of Americans in a future where traditional levers, such as raising the minimum wage, won't be sufficient. Not every social program will be big or bold enough to tackle the challenges ahead, and not every new idea will work exactly as intended. But the sum total of these efforts can certainly help gird us for change and put us on a better path as we figure out what the future of work will look like. And, frankly, however averse we sometimes are to "social" programs as a country, we have a moral imperative to cast a strong, wide safety net at this moment in history—the change is coming more quickly than it ever has before, and we simply don't know who or what it's going to bring down.

One social safeguard that deserves a fresh look comes from Harvard economists Robert Lawrence and Akash Deep, who in 2008 sought a creative solution to the problem of whole communities being hollowed out by economic change. The specific challenge they wanted to tackle was the vicious cycle created in towns that get hit abruptly by large-scale job losses—often, this will take the form of a factory closure. If an auto plant shuts down in a town of 25,000 people, the first and most obvious effect is that a quarter of the town is suddenly out of work. But the consequences ripple: struggling families stop patronizing local stores and restaurants, Main Street goes dark, and a diminished tax base means less money for local schools and community programs—dimming the prospects of the next generation, and opening the door to crime, drugs, and civic malaise. The plan proposed by Lawrence and Deep doesn't save the auto plant, but it does end the cycle of depression before it can fully eat into the town. Called "tax-base insurance"—though we should all hold out for a catchier name—it would help communities guard against sudden economic shocks using a mechanism every American knows well.[8]

Flood insurance protects against disasters; car insurance reimburses us for accidents. Tax-base insurance would do exactly the same for widespread job losses. Instead of being left to spiral into blight when a plant closes, local governments could buy into public or private insurance plans. The town would pay premiums just like we do for health insurance, and in return it would receive an influx of money if trade, technology, or some other development decimates its tax base. That payout would make up for some of the lost tax revenue for a period of time, keeping the town afloat long enough to stabilize its budget and invest in new work opportunities for its residents. It wouldn't bring the factory back, but it would remove the secondary threats of volatility and local recession. Some of the funds could be used to train laid-off workers in more durable fields; some could be used to incentivize new businesses. Firefighters and teachers wouldn't have to be let go due to budget shortfalls. This is the type of creative idea that could have made a world of difference in any number of distressed communities over the last decade—for whatever reason, it has not yet gained traction in our national search for solutions.

At times like these, though, we should count ourselves lucky to have a system of federalism—and fifty state laboratories where we can experiment with promising ideas. The smallest of those labs can be found in Rhode Island, where my friend Governor Gina Raimondo has made a big bet on creating new job training programs tailored toward the skills that businesses report as being their biggest needs. That is to say, Rhode Island is explicitly pairing up its education and training programs with jobs that actually exist today or that companies expect to need very soon.

The results so far have been extremely encouraging, too. In 2014, the year that Raimondo was first elected, Rhode Island had the second-highest unemployment rate in the nation.[9] Just four years later, it had climbed all the way up from 49th place to 27th, slicing its joblessness problem essentially in half.[10] Plenty of factors contributed to that rise, to be sure, but the biggest driver of this success story is no secret—strategic job training has been Raimondo's constant refrain since the day she assumed office.

Some of the programs Raimondo has launched as governor could very well prove successful in other regions or on a national level. Demand-driven initiatives like Real Jobs Rhode Island, which the state launched in 2015, engage the private sector to help shape skills education and guide government investment responsibly. In the seaside town of Westerly, the state worked with a century-old submarine manufacturer called General Dynamics Electric Boats to coordinate resources; Rhode Island built a job training center nearby, and worked with the company to develop a curriculum that would meet both the physical needs of General Dynamics—such as pipe-fitting and welding—as well as the advanced IT needs that accompany modern vessels. In less than three years, 1,800 locals have studied at the training center and been hired by General Dynamics.[11] Real Jobs Rhode Island has replicated this story across the state, creating thirty-two employer-led training partnerships that have engaged over 430 local businesses so far—helping ensure that the skills job seekers are learning are those that can translate directly into sustainable careers nearby.

Raimondo has also had her eye on the next generation, and the state has now launched multiple programs designed to prepare children of all ages for the economy of tomorrow. At the beginning of Raimondo's tenure, just one percent of Rhode Island's public school students took courses in computer science. Thanks to an initiative called CS4RI (Computer Science for Rhode Island), by the close of the 2018–2019 academic year, computer science was taught in every public school in the state across all grade levels, with many starting to learn the basics of the field from as early as kindergarten.[12] Another program, PrepareRI (Prepare Rhode Island), matches high school students with internships and apprenticeships in a wide range of industries, including in the tech sector. The program also allows any high school student to take college classes for credit while still in high school without having to pay a dime.[13]

Of course, what works in Rhode Island may not work exactly the same way in Montana, Wisconsin, or New York—but the results so far indicate that creative programs like these that reach across generations and engage the business community can make a noticeable difference in the strength of a local workforce. Former speaker of the house Paul Ryan suggested to me that Democrats want to federalize everything, and Republicans want to localize everything. Perhaps the best solution is a framework that allows for both of those approaches to do what each does best.

As state and local efforts focus on beefing up the skills and resilience of their people, the federal government is seeking ways to complement that progress by channeling investments toward the places that need them most. One such effort is the Opportunity Zone program, which was created in 2017—a bipartisan idea put forward by Republican senator Tim Scott, Democratic senator Cory Booker, former Republican congressman Pat Tiberi, and Democratic congressman Ron Kind.[14] The program asked governors in every state to designate neighborhoods in need of investment, as defined by factors like high poverty rates and low median household incomes. These choices were submitted to the U.S. Treasury Department, which certified nearly 9,000 of these neighborhoods across the country—or about 12 percent of all

American neighborhoods—as Opportunity Zones.[15] From there, the basic idea is that anyone who starts a business, builds new housing, or otherwise invests money in an Opportunity Zone will receive an extremely generous tax benefit—a pretty compelling incentive, if history is any guide. Steve Wilburn, the CEO of a green energy small business called FirmGreen, whom I got to know from my time at the Export-Import Bank, is one entrepreneur who intends to take advantage of the Opportunity Zone initiative. "Without this tax-advantaged investment structure, we typically could not finance projects in low-income areas," he told me. "This is a true win-win situation for us and the communities we serve."

The rationale behind the Opportunity Zone program is hard to argue with: though our economy rebounded strongly from the 2008 financial crisis, half of the new jobs that were created over the first five years of the recovery were located in just seventy-three counties—that's out of about 3,000 counties nationwide.[16] When we talk about "the strength of our economy" today, we're mostly just talking about the strength of our cities, which are accruing almost all the benefits of growth thanks to educated workforces, advanced infrastructures, and free-flowing investments. A completely different story is taking place in rural communities—one that bears little resemblance to national trends on unemployment, GDP, new businesses, or anything else we normally look to when we want to find out how things are going. For tens of millions of Americans, the big jobs boom of the 2010s has been little more than a distant rumor; education rates have stagnated, and no one has been eager to pump money into new homes or businesses.[17] In the absence of opportunity, opiate addiction has grown at a furious speed, exacerbating the tragedy. This is where Opportunity Zones seek to help, though it remains to be seen whether government tax incentives will be enough to encourage meaningful investments that lift these neighborhoods back up. Investors love tax breaks, of course—but as a practical matter, they need educated workers, good local schools, reliable broadband access, and other prerequisites in place before they'll consider putting their money to good use in a community.

At the very least, we've begun to recognize just how out of whack inequality of opportunity has gotten in America—and what an enormous vulnerability it is to our economic and political future. Income inequality is devastating enough, and that's before you factor in the exponential impact of underfunded schools, crumbling physical and digital infrastructure, eroding civic life, skyrocketing drug rates, and so much else. These factors compound each other in brutal ways: most entrepreneurs will avoid struggling school districts, which in turn means fewer jobs to generate revenue to spend on improving schools. The less money available for Little Leagues and community centers, the more young people will turn away from educational or job aspirations and turn toward dangerous habits—endangering their own lives, and further depleting the workforce that funds those vital services. The less stable that life in these neighborhoods becomes, the more willing people are to resort to extreme political beliefs that put practical government solutions at risk. Whether Opportunity Zones or some other program can take the first step toward breaking that cycle, only time can tell.

The Company Line

Let me be clear: I'm a capitalist at heart. I don't believe that governments at the federal or local level can solve these problems entirely on their own. Companies hold extraordinary decision-making power in this arena: they're the ones who develop labor-saving new technologies in the first place, and they choose when and how to hire, fire, or replace workers with those technologies. Of course, they also make plenty of choices about importing and exporting, too. Those decisions aren't made in a vacuum, though—they are generally made with an eye toward maximizing profit, staying competitive in the marketplace, and, on occasion, the reputational risk that comes from putting people out of work. While the government is responsible for setting trade policy—which certainly does have a major impact on the labor landscape—for the most part it falls to decision makers in the private sector to decide just how fast or slow change comes to our economy.

When it comes to our elected leaders, we have the power of the ballot box—we can vote them out of office if we don't like the choices they make. When it comes to the private sector, though, all we really have is *consumer* power: the power to influence companies' behavior by rewarding them with—or denying them—our business. Consumer power is, well . . . powerful. By channeling our combined values and influence, it can compel restaurants like McDonald's and KFC to stop serving chicken and beef treated with antibiotics, start a "fair trade" coffee revolution, and shame media companies into pulling profitable-but-problematic TV hosts like Bill O'Reilly from the air. I believe that, properly channeled, that power is compelling enough to convince corporate leaders to approach the age of artificial intelligence with people's interests in mind. Beyond that, we'll need to rely on laws, regulations, tax incentives, and other levers that the business community is responsive to. I'm optimistic on that front—business leaders are beginning to demonstrate that they understand there is a need to balance profits for shareholders with the needs of other stakeholders. In August of 2019, in fact, leaders at the Business Roundtable explicitly acknowledged that corporations need to have a wider aperture—beyond just creating shareholder value—when it comes to measuring the place of business in our society. That's no small gesture, considering that this is a group made up of the CEOS of Apple, Walmart, JP Morgan Chase, and nearly 200 other major corporations. When properly incentivized and properly held accountable, I believe that companies are capable of doing well for themselves and doing good for the world at the same time.

Every time our economy has undergone transformations in the past, there was always a risk that progress would leave some people behind. Advances in farming spelled the end for America as a mostly agricultural economy—but we developed new industries that offered displaced farmers and their children new, less rigorous work. The computer age could have cost us tens of millions of jobs—but instead, that progress paved the way for a new world of work in digital services. Whenever the marketplace changes, it has a habit of pairing the end of one economic chapter with the opening of a new and better one for our workforce to move on to. Historically, these changes have always left us with more jobs and a better quality of life than we started with. But with the coming era of AI and automation, the challenge is going to be tougher and faster than those we have faced in the past—because of the speed of these changes, we'll have less time to adjust and experiment than ever before.

The thing is, progress doesn't generally look out for people on its own—business leaders have to *choose* to design technologies in a way that opens new opportunities to our workforce even as it may shutter old ones. Uber and Airbnb may have put a damper on the taxi and hotel industries, respectively, but they also created flexible, adaptable work opportunities for hundreds of thousands of amateur drivers and hoteliers in their wake. Will the companies designing driverless vehicles and tomorrow's other industry-busting innovations be sure to do the same? Will their creations carve out new and better roles for people to take on—roles they are uniquely suited to, that require human interaction, communication, and tending skills? Or will they ignore their impact on people altogether? The great American writer Edward Abbey once wrote that "growth for the sake of growth is the ideology of the cancer cell." The private sector cannot live by that ideology in the years to come—it must step up and realign itself around growth for the sake of *people*.

We can help them reach that conclusion with a few legal guardrails and some good old-fashioned public pressure. A prime place to start would be by following the lead of the Business Roundtable and lightening up on the time-honored tradition of "shareholder supremacy"—the corporate philosophy dictating that shareholders are the only constituency a company has to worry about or answer to. We need a little more balance; we need to look beyond the next quarterly earnings report. Not so long ago, the vast majority of businesses were purely domestic; as a result, they had much more of a stake in their home communities. That relationship has largely been severed in an era of globally sourced cars, pencils, taco salads, and software. Combine that decaying connection to American towns with the lingering outlook of shareholder supremacy, and it's no wonder why today's companies are so often held in such low esteem by many Americans on the left and right. We've seen recent instances of the public exercising its power to influence corporate behavior: in February of 2019, for example, New York political leaders crusading against the establishment of an Amazon headquarters in Queens prompted the tech giant to ditch its plans, while in Louisiana the East Baton Rouge Parish school board broke away from years of local tradition by rejecting ExxonMobil's request for an additional $2.9 million in property tax breaks—a stunning stand against the number one manufacturer and taxpayer in the region.[18] In the era of social media, every one of us is in possession of a megaphone capable of reaching just about any company—and plenty of businesses have altered their behavior based on customer service horror stories and other forms of feedback that have gone viral. If corporations really are becoming more responsive—or at least more sensitive—to individuals, perhaps consumers can seize that opportunity to insist on a people-first approach to technological progress.

Another change that the private sector could make involves tearing down some of the barriers currently gumming up mobility and opportunity in our workforce. The American labor market is remarkably opaque; job openings often linger unfilled as qualified candidates are kept at arm's length by our national obsession with credentials and pedigree. In 2017, in fact, there were 6.6 million open jobs—and 6.4 million Americans seeking employment.[19] Part of the backlog is geographical, though technology has allowed businesses across a number of sectors to offer an ever-increasing number of remote working opportunities. Most of it, however, has to do with our deeply ingrained tendency to focus on degrees rather than skills.

The fact is, nearly 70 percent of all American adults don't have a college degree[20]—a credential that, while important, doesn't necessarily say much about their current skills or their capacity to quickly learn new ones. Former White House chief of staff Denis McDonough, who now advises the Markle Foundation's Rework America Task Force on the future of work, sees shifting our emphasis from degrees to skills as essential to helping build more flexibility and opportunity into our workforce. He mentioned to me that about three quarters of job postings for construction managers nationwide now require a bachelor's degree to apply—but that only about a quarter of people already working those jobs actually have one. Businesses' desire to attract what we think of as traditionally well-credentialed candidates is preventing them from taking advantage of a larger pool of potentially adept workers, including those who may have developed critical skills outside of the classroom. This sort of thinking limits the growth of those businesses, and it severely curbs the prospects of 70 percent of our population who very likely would have plenty of skills to offer if given the chance. This isn't just an American problem, either; in Mexico, for example, they require most bank tellers to have a college degree. While it's never a bad thing when people pursue higher education, our country would be much better off if U.S. companies thought a little less about diplomas and a little more about skills. Like General Dynamics, the Rhode Island submarine manufacturer, smart businesses can even work with their local governments to design skills training programs for their hometown workforce designed to meet their specific needs.

Skills-based approaches are at the heart of the idea of "lifelong readiness" that we've explored over the last two chapters. Though degrees will always be valuable, spending year after year in a classroom cannot—and doesn't have to be—the only way for us to stay ahead of a rapidly evolving economy. When I spoke with Gary Cohn, the former top economic advisor to President Trump, he estimated that somewhere between two thirds and three quarters of all job openings in the United States don't require an advanced degree. "The problem we have," he quipped, "is we're sending too many kids to college." In the sectors that are poised for the most growth over the next few years—health care, construction, and IT foremost among them—a six-week training program or apprenticeship could in many cases be just as (or more) helpful than a four-year degree, at a fraction of the cost. The private sector would serve itself and our country well by leading the charge to more closely align hiring with skills—so that workers of all educational levels can better ready themselves to face the future.

So Where Does That Leave Trade?

Now that we've talked about some of the ways we can come together to face the future of work, it's time to return once more to where we began this journey: trade. Our trade strategy in the coming years is going to be an instrumental complement to the domestic solutions we pursue—done right, it will position us to prosper in an economy likely to be driven largely by high-tech global services. In tomorrow's economy, trade will probably be less about direct job creation and more about making ourselves competitive by staying in front of change: instead of, say, knocking down tariffs to sell U.S. products to India and using that money to hire more factory workers, we'll be setting favorable international data security standards that increase the value of U.S. tech. We have no choice but to embrace that evolution, given that more and more goods are being consumed right where they're produced—the better China gets at manufacturing airplanes and health care equipment, for example, the less they'll rely on us to sell them those products. If we use trade as a tool to ensure the free flow of technologies, data, and services—and, critically, if we insist that America write responsible rules of the road for the world to follow—it can be what keeps us on the cutting edge of opportunity as the nature of work continues to evolve.

Where to start? Well, hard as it may be to believe, America has never in its history had a meaningful strategic plan when it comes to trade. Sure, we've had administrations that pursued free trade agreements and those that shunned them; we've had presidents who used trade to exercise influence in the Pacific, and those who saw it as a way to counter Europe. To this day, we embrace protectionism for our dairy farmers in one breath while hailing export opportunities for our energy sector in the next. But we've never tied it all together into one approach, or been explicit about what it all means—what our national goals are, and how every element of our trade policy serves them.

Part of the problem may lie in the fact that our trade policy is spread out across a byzantine web of executive branch departments and agencies. You'll find the International Trade Administration in the Department of Commerce, working to help U.S. industries compete overseas—but the State Department Office of Bilateral Trade Affairs is working on the same mission six blocks away. Trade's impact on workers falls under the Labor Department, while the EPA, Energy, Homeland Security, Treasury, and Agriculture Departments each have dedicated trade responsibilities of their own. Of course, trade negotiations are handled by the U.S. Trade Representative, which isn't part of any of those departments at all. And that's before you even get to the mandate of the U.S. International Trade Commission, the U.S. Trade and Development Agency, the U.S. Export-Import Bank, and the Small Business Administration's Office of International Trade. Bewildering, no?

For generations, we've left our trade policy to be hashed out by an alphabet soup of unconnected departments and offices, each with a mandate of its own—and to make matters worse, sometimes those mandates overlap. I used to sit in meetings of a group established in 1992 called the Trade Promotion Coordinating Committee (with the catchy acronym of TPCC), which often included more than sixty people representing upward of two dozen agencies. We need something much more nimble and much more targeted if we want to pursue a strategic, unified trade policy—perhaps something like a ten-person trade cabinet, for starters. Things aren't any better for workers feeling the effects of trade, who have to figure out which of the *forty-seven* different federal job training programs, scattered across departments ranging from Education to Veterans Affairs, is meant for them. When I was running the Export-Import Bank, I constantly came across entrepreneurs eager to engage in trade who had no idea whether they should be talking to me, the head of the Small Business Administration, or one of the dozen other leaders whose job may or may not have been to help them get their foot in the door.

The answer isn't necessarily to consolidate all of trade into one dedicated agency—but there's no question that what we have now is a recipe for confusion and ineffectiveness. Whether trade ultimately best falls under the bailiwick of one department or five, the larger point is that it needs to all be operating in accordance with a single vision. If we want to be an export powerhouse, and we should, we need to declare it and make a plan. Negotiators need to focus on regions and trade deal terms with that mission in mind. Businesses need to know where to go to get support, and workers need to understand where targeted resources and benefits can be found. Labor, consumer, and environmental interests need seats at the table as the plan takes shape. Resources need to be directed strategically toward skills training and our safety net to ready us for anticipated changes that new deals might bring. And it all needs to be done in concert. This may sound obvious to you—but the fact is, we've never really tried to do it before! The closest we've come was President Obama's National Export Initiative, which set a goal of doubling exports within five years; another program, SelectUSA, led by Commerce Secretary Penny Pritzker, sought to encourage companies to locate in America. Unfortunately, neither effort was properly funded—we need to do much more, and we need to put it all together with a single strategic focus. Exports *do* support good-paying jobs, and we need to encourage American companies to become export-ready. That includes manufacturers as well as entertainment companies and schools of higher education. Too often, we don't think critically enough about service exports—though we certainly have the resources to be a global powerhouse in services. In critical areas like higher education, we have plenty of spare capacity, particularly at small liberal arts and community colleges and state universities that would benefit enormously from more diverse, more global student bodies.

A more coherent trade strategy would also help us learn to talk about trade more frankly and honestly as a nation. For far too long, working people have been completely left out of the process by which we've engaged in trade, and especially the process by which we've forged trade agreements. So it's only natural that when they've been hurt—whether by the impact of those agreements or by some other completely unrelated change in our economy—they've been left to assume that policymakers weren't thinking about them when decisions were made. Naturally, when they've been helped by trade, they've usually been left in the dark about that as well. All people know is what they can see and feel—and when they can't see the process or the rationale, what they feel is a sense of national rootlessness and the erosion of their economic identity. It's no wonder so many assume that trade is responsible for unmooring America from the middle-class dreams and bargains that had always seemed to define it.

Rewriting that story will be difficult, and we don't have time to lose. Our first test, of course, will be China: the country that now commands our and the world's attention. In terms of its size, its growth, and its economic and geopolitical influence, the threat posed by China could be likened to a combination of Japan in the 1970s *and* the Soviet Union in its heyday. They are an economic powerhouse, to be sure, but they also present a serious national security concern—and those two facets are often intermingled. When China exports facial recognition technologies to Middle Eastern governments so that they can track their citizens the same way the Chinese do, what they are really exporting is their own version of authoritarianism. That's the sort of threat that goes beyond simply competing for sales or worrying about the balance of trade.

We've never confronted a competitor like China before—at the very least, we haven't done so since Great Britain in 1812. Just as America once stole technology from England in order to build steel mills, today China routinely plays fast and loose with the rules of global commerce. They may not be a global trade supervillain, but they *have* been a bad actor in many respects: they steal intellectual property, coerce foreign companies into handing over their technological secrets, skirt the rules of the Foreign Corrupt Practices Act, and otherwise do everything they can to tip the global playing field in their favor. The world does business with China because they simply can't afford not to—China is just too big and too important to ignore. But as China continues to push the rules to their limit, doubling down on this strategy under President Xi Jinping, it's critical that we find a way to confront, contain, compete, and coexist with them in the years ahead.

It won't be easy. International bodies like the World Trade Organization simply weren't built to handle forces like China that combine low costs, massive size, and a high degree of government involvement in the economy. Ironically, the smartest way to deal with China would have been to move forward with TPP, which would have created a bloc representing 40 percent of the world economy all playing by the same, American-led system of rules and norms—a coalition strong enough to pressure China into making meaningful changes if they wanted to keep doing business in the Pacific region. Alas, Donald Trump put the kibosh on that solution as soon as he entered office . . . leaving him with a short menu of ineffective options for dealing with China later on. As we've already discussed, TPP wasn't perfect—the concerns raised by some labor, environmental, and consumer groups had merit. But when it comes to China, we can no longer afford to let the perfect be the enemy of the good—if the alternative is doing nothing, or, worse, prolonging a misguided trade war with a competitor who happens to also be one of our top customers, even a flawed regional trade deal looks pretty attractive right about now. Let's not forget: in the world of trade, our choices are often binary.

Our new reality is that Trump's tariff-centric approach to China has hurt American farmers, manufacturers, and consumers without extracting any concessions from China or subjecting them to any sort of lasting accountability. Who knows how long it will take us to put the toothpaste back in the tube following this approach—as we all remember from being little kids, an escalating, tit-for-tat argument can be hard to defuse. But we have to work this out one way or another.

As to the world outside of China, I'd propose a course of action that you probably wouldn't expect from a person who values increased trade as much as I do: let's take a pause on creating any new trade deals until we can forge a better consensus on them here at home. Trade agreements never should have become the lightning rods that they turned into since NAFTA; as long as they remain as politically charged as they are today, good ideas like TPP won't stand a chance, and we'll lose even more ground in the years ahead. We can keep trading without any new agreements in the meantime—heck, we can trade even more than ever. But until the American people are brought into the conversation and become confident that future trade agreements will make their lives better and our country stronger, pursuing them along the razor's edge of a political divide will only lead to more bitterness and a rudderless foreign policy. Fixing that impasse will require serious leadership from the White House and Congress, and, ultimately, concessions from just about everyone who has a stake in trade. Most of all, it will require honesty. Given the current environment on both sides of the aisle, getting there won't be easy—but I'm confident that it can happen if enough of the public comes to understand the threats and opportunities at stake.

In the meantime, it's critical that we work with China to arrive at a set of responsible, enforceable rules for the entire globe to follow—rules that reflect our values, raise the bar on human rights worldwide, and allow every nation to compete on a level playing field. Those rules must work for American workers as well as for our allies around the world. They must create guardrails around intellectual property and technology transfer, as well as the unfair advantages China affords its state-owned enterprises through below-market financing and other below-the-belt tactics. Whether the best path forward for developing those rules will be the path of a multilateral trade agreement with China or a change to the rules of the World Trade Organization remains to be debated and hashed out. But we clearly need some sort of collaborative trade regime that puts pressure on China to reform—the benefits of entry must be great, and the penalties for living outside of the world's rules must be harsh. In any event, America must act quickly—and do so with buy-in from the American people.

We can start to build a better future for trade right now by vowing to bring people into the process. By pulling back the curtain and being open about how, where, and why trade-offs happen, leaders can instill desperately needed credibility and shared purpose into the trade arena. Americans shouldn't have to decide on faith or ideology alone whether or not to take us at our word when we say that trade is good, bad, or somewhere in between. They should be able to truly see and understand why and how agreements are made, what the goals are, and what the full range of consequences may be. When people are given access to that knowledge, they begin to better understand the larger story of trade: how it can be used to influence the world on human rights, labor, equality, and environmental issues . . . how it can counter bad actors and encourage peace in vulnerable regions . . . what a strong, globally connected economy means for our national security . . . and why the economic success of our neighbors pays dividends for us.

There are challenges ahead of us, to be sure. But when I think about the future of trade, I am extraordinarily optimistic about what it's going to bring to your life and mine, and to the fortunes of communities across our country and around the world. At the risk of repeating myself: trade is *not* a four-letter word; it's a force that binds us together. It helps us learn from each other, experience new tastes and trends and technologies, and broaden our understanding of what it means to be alive in the twenty-first century. America remains uniquely equipped to move the world in that direction, guided by our values and standards—though that essential leadership is lacking right now. And that's where you come in. Yes, you! America and the world are eager for a candid, progressive (as opposed to partisan), better-informed view of trade—and you can make a difference. If we go into that future together, speaking honestly and acting in good faith, clear-eyed about what stands to be lost and gained, we'll build an economy that benefits all of us and gives us greater purpose. There will always be a need for work that relies upon our human judgment, empathy, intelligence, creativity, and care—work that values us uniquely. We'll venture out, Plus Ultra, further beyond anything we've ever known or imagined into the thrill of the future. I felt that thrill when those rickety runway lights snapped on and briefly lit the dark during my first trip to China decades ago. And I can imagine my mother and her family felt it when they first reached Ellis Island and laid eyes on an America far better than any dream.

Epilogue

True or false?

> Free trade with foreign countries is good for America because it opens up new markets and we cannot avoid the fact that it is a global economy.

In the summer of 2019, an NBC News/*Wall Street Journal* poll found that almost two-thirds of Americans agreed with that statement—a double-digit jump in less than four years, and the highest mark ever recorded by that particular survey.[1] And that includes majorities of both Republicans and Democrats. On the one hand, this shouldn't be terribly surprising; the vast majority of Americans are now living through the first real trade war of their lives, and the results haven't been pretty. President Trump's tariffs on Chinese goods are estimated to hurt the average American family to the tune of more than $2,000 per year,[2] a figure that would certainly spike if the president were to follow through on his repeatedly tweeted threats to tax U.S. consumers with even more tariffs.[3] The head of the American Farm Bureau Federation, Zippy Duvall, has called the trade war a "body blow" to domestic farmers, as the loss of China as a top customer for U.S. corn and soybeans has obliterated profits and precipitated a tragic rash of farmer bankruptcies and even suicides.[4] And American businesses whose fortunes rely on Chinese goods are already reeling from the chaos—one study conducted by the Federal Reserve Bank of San Francisco found that for every dollar spent on a product labeled "Made in China," 55 cents go to U.S. companies.[5] In other words, a whole lot of Chinese companies supply components that go into U.S.-made goods, and vice versa.

On the other hand, you wouldn't know that there was a trade war at all from the 2020 presidential race. In another era, high stakes economic brinkmanship with China and the self-inflicted wounds of a shortsighted tariff frenzy would be the dominant political stories of the day. Today, however, amid the horse-race election coverage, the daily flurry of Oval Office tweets, and—as of this writing—the swirling winds of impeachment, there isn't much oxygen left over for trade. But even in a saturated news environment, the time is ripe for Americans to tune in and think anew about an issue that is quietly becoming more urgent than ever before.

When they *have* spared a moment for trade, the Democratic presidential candidates have, for the most part, correctly assessed much of what's wrong with the policies pursued by President Trump. On the primary debate stage, they've pointed out that his tweet-fueled negotiations with China are haphazard, that his tariffs have already cost us more than 300,000 jobs, and that American crops meant for export are instead now rotting in storage bins across the heartland.[6] They all seem to agree on the diagnosis—but for the most part, they haven't offered an alternative to Donald Trump's prescription. More specifically, they haven't made the case for why trade is *good*, and because of that failure, millions of voters have likely been hard-pressed to tell the difference between Trump and his potential successors when it comes to trade. To listen to the Democratic candidates, trade is, at best, an issue to be ignored. At worst, it's a threat to American workers—the same story Trump has told us, just with different villains.

You know that walking away from the promises of expanded trade is a critical mistake; you read this book, after all! And, frankly, it doesn't matter if we're snubbing trade for Trumpian nationalistic reasons on the right or because, to paraphrase President Obama, we are "letting the perfect be the enemy of the good" on the left.

I'm not naive—the politics in a presidential primary are always going to be rocky in this regard. The primary voters and local activists candidates often court to become the nominee of either party tend to be far less moderate than the general voting population. In the case of trade, that means heightened opposition to NAFTA and skepticism about trade deals generally. Most candidates probably feel as though they have little to gain from loudly and proudly speaking up for the undeniable benefits of trade—and they may be right about that. But if America is ever going to reclaim its place of global leadership in the years ahead—and claim the jobs, the prosperity, the vital influence, and the cultural profits that come along with trade—somebody has to put forward an honest and optimistic vision.

That honesty won't come from President Trump, who showed us the fatal flaw of his worldview almost immediately in his inauguration address, which will long be remembered for its horrifying depiction of "American carnage." Trump sees and speaks about Americans as though we are victims in a defensive crouch, desperate for his protection—and his tariffs further that view by functioning as defensive economic walls, insulating us from the threats outside. The problem is, Americans rightly just don't see ourselves that way. Nothing in our history or our nature suggests that we're inclined to shield ourselves from competition.

On the contrary, we have always been seizers of opportunity, spoiling to compete—children of *Plus Ultra*.

Almost two-thirds of Americans are ready to venture further beyond. They are eager to hear how we might prepare ourselves to compete and win in a future marked by stunning innovation, permanent uncertainty, and rapid-fire change. They know that the world will grow ever more interconnected and that our products and our fortunes will too. I believe that most Americans are ready to stop blaming immigrants and people of color when economic evolutions strike and to start thinking smartly about how to take advantage of those evolutions. They are willing to learn how to face automation and to make it work for them. They are ready to let go of the past if it means embracing a better future.

The facts will be on the side of any leader who summons the courage to pick up that mantle and tell the truth about trade. And now it seems that public sentiment could be, too.

Acknowledging that trade creates winners and losers, as I've sought to do in this book, is a critical first step in creating pro-trade policies. The second step is ensuring that more of us win when we trade—and, to borrow a line from President Trump, Americans will *no*t get tired of winning if we can make the gains of trade more widespread and do right by those whose lives are disrupted by economic changes. Americans are ready for an honest, holistic, progressive vision of trade—one that lifts up our values around the world and doesn't leave people behind. We already know what that case might sound like, and we already know where some of the pitfalls will lie. But the path to 2020 has not filled me with hope that anyone will choose to lead on this issue. And that's why you are needed.

This book was meant to show how you, your family, your neighbor, and everyone else has benefited from trade—and how we could again if we set things right. But it also comes with a plea: if our leaders aren't taking up this issue, it's up to us to make them. And now you have some tools to do so. Do you enjoy bananas? Blueberries? Hondas or Chevys or Fords? Your iPhone? Your favorite TV shows? More important, do you care about the opportunities you'll leave to future generations and the values that will shape their economy? If you do, I implore you to think and talk and vote with trade in mind. The rest of the world has already embraced trade in a full-throated way, and *we* need more voices in this chorus if we're going to keep time with our partners and our competitors on the global stage. I hope you'll join me.

Who knows how much we've already lost by our recent penchant for "canceling" good ideas around trade—not only did we cancel our place in TPP, but we've practically canceled the very notion of trade deals in our culture. We have to reverse that impulse in the years ahead. So bug your neighbor; bug your senator; bug anybody who will listen. Because if we don't begin to care about trade, we will lose its fruits before we know it, and the world will leave us behind. So go out there and spread the word—and let's propel our country further beyond!

Acknowledgments

I never in my wildest dreams thought I would write a book—certainly not one about trade. So a special acknowledgment to my partner, Tom Healy, a brilliant writer who has made me a better one and who inspired and harassed me throughout the process. In addition, I would like to acknowledge the following:

First and foremost, the hundreds of exporters and thousands of American workers I had the chance to meet with and learn from both during my time in government as well as in the private sector. Many of them served on the advisory committee of EXIM during my term. This book in many ways is a tribute to them, as they know how trade works and how vital it is to our future.

To Bill Clinton, who first had faith in me coming from the private sector and named me to the Small Business Administration in 1998. To Hillary Rodham Clinton, who was my senator for eight years, provided valuable insight to this book, and has been a friend for many years. And to Rahm Emanuel, who has been my political rabbi for twenty-five years—I've always thought that if you're going to have a rabbi, they should be Jewish!

To Barack Obama, for naming me as president and chairman of the Export-Import Bank, where I gained the experience in trade and global exports that formed the basis of the book. And to the many members of Congress who are supportive of companies that are "looking further beyond"—exporting their goods and services to the rest of the world (ROW).

To the extraordinary team I had the pleasure of working with at the Export-Import Bank, all 400-plus strong who had the patience to teach me about export finance and were generous in their time and experience. In particular I want to thank Dan Cluchey, I could not have completed this book without him at my side, helping articulate my views and significantly augmenting and expanding upon them. Also to Matt Bevens, Chris Semenas, Scott Schloegel, and Claudia Slacik, who worked with me at EXIM and provided key input on this book. Additionally, my colleagues across the Obama administration, as well as local officials who work tirelessly to support small businesses and exporters, and make trade a reality in community after community across our country.

To Matt Latimer, Matt Carlini, Robin Sproul and the team at Javelin, Ben Loehnen, Carolyn Kelly, and Alexandra Primiani at Simon & Schuster, as well as my assistant, Tom Strong-Grinsell, for their work to ensure this book is a success.

To my sixth-grade teacher, Mary Ann Dexter, at Hackley, who encouraged me to read the editorial page of *The New York Times* each day to improve my writing skills.

To the late Alan Krueger, who passed recently. Alan generously introduced me to many scholars and academics who made this book better by bringing a rigor to this work.

To Doug Irwin, author of Clashing over Commerce, whom I met and whose class I audited at the University of Chicago. He, in part, inspired me to look further beyond and write this book.

To a number of friends and colleagues who took time out of their busy lives to read and provide feedback on the book while it was in progress. Your thoughts, your candor, and your inspiration have helped make this a better book, and I cannot thank you enough: Kirk Adams, Marland Bruckner, Ambassador

Peter Burleigh, Seth Cameron, Ryan Clancy, Linda Douglass, TJ Ducklo, Michael Grunwald, Mark Halperin, Omar Hendrix, Liz Hochberg, Steve Holloway, Alex Jutkowitz, Secretary Ray LaHood, Evan Leatherwood, Robby Mook, Matt O'Conner, Ana Navarro, Susan Ochs, Robert Raben, Sally Susman, Julia Sweig, Secretary Tom Vilsack, and Howard Wolfson.

To David Axelrod, Representative Bill Delahunt, Mark Gearan, Nicco Mele, Amy Howell, Alicia Sams, Abbie James, Samuel Huang, and the many students and staff at the Institutes of Politics at the University of Chicago and Harvard University; my fellowships at both led to turning a seminar into this book. And in particular my fellow fellows—Jeff Roe, Scott Jennings, Ed Gillespie, and Symone Sanders—who helped me understand trade from a different perspective.

To Mary Andringa and Daryl Boukamp for their help in organizing conversations in Des Moines and Pella, Iowa, where I was able to get a first-hand look at the political and economic impact of trade policy.

A special thanks to John Norris for his efforts in organizing an agricultural roundtable in Iowa, and to all of those who took their time to share their experience on trade and agriculture and for opening up your lives to this endeavour, including Mark Bishara, Jay Byers, Ryan Carroll, Mark Core, Gordon Duff, Billi Hunt, George Meineke, Kevin Middlesworth, Senator Zach Nunn, David Rawsom, Tom Rial, Senator Ken Rozenboom, Matt Rustlecolt, and Senator Dan Zumbach.

To the more than 100 individuals who gave their time to talk trade and four-letter words with me over the last eighteen months, including: Ted Alden, Ambassador Gerard Araud, David Autor, Ambassador Martha Barcena, Ambassador Charlene Barshevsky, Fred Bergsten, Jared Bernstein, Karan Bhatia, Josh Bolten, Senator Sherrod Brown, Representative Eric Cantor,

Tim Carney, Kevin Cirilli, Charlie Cook, Gary Cohn, Dave Cote, Nelson Cunningham, Secretary Bill Daley, Paul Delaney, Representative John Delaney, Representative Rosa DeLauro, Jamie Dimon, Representative Debbie Dingell, Shawn Donnan, Tom Donohue, Frank DuBois, Debbi Durham, Liz Economy, Tony Fratto, Ambassador Michael Froman, Jason Furman, Senator Kirsten Gillibrand, Gary Ginsberg, Allan Goodman, Austan Goolsbee, Governor Christine Gregoire, Secretary Carlos Gutierrez, Richard Haass, Marcia Hale, Jim Harmon, Melanie Hart, Representative Denny Heck, Senator Heidi Heitkamp, Ambassador Bruce Heyman, Governor John Hickenlooper, Ambassador Carla Hills, Ambassador Robert Holleyman, Ambassador Stuart Holliday, Doug Holtz-Eakin, Mary Howe, Bob Iger, Greg Ip, Barry Jackson, Ambassador Roberta Jacobson, Secretary Mickey Kantor, Bruce Katz, Tim Keating, Niamah King, Ambassador Ron Kirk, Ron Klain, Steve Lamar, Madame Christine Lagarde, Robert Lawrence, Thea Lee, Deborah Lehr, Ed Luce, Susan Lund, Curt Magelby, James Maniyka, Manny Manriquez, Governor Terry McAuliffe, Denis McDonough, Mack McLarty, Jim McNerney, Representative Gwen Moore, Brent Neiman, Indra Nooyi, Shannon O'Neil, Ambassador David O'Sullivan, Doug Oberhelman, Secretary Tom Perez, Secretary Penny Pritzker, Governor Gina Raimondo, Bill Reinsch, Ambassador Susan Rice, Governor Bill Richardson, Dani Rodrik, Dan Rosen, David Rothkopf, David Rubenstein, Representative Paul Ryan, Lydia Saad, Ambassador Arturo Sarukhan, Senator Chuck Schumer, Jerry Seib, John Sexton, Representative Donna Shalala, David Simas, Fred Smith, Arne Sorenson, George Stephanopoulos, Bruce Stokes, Secretary Larry Summers, Cass Sunstein, Neera Tanden, Gillian Tett, David Thomas, Jay Timmons, Richard Trumka, Kevin Varney, Leslie Vinjamuri, Senator Mark Warner, Representative Maxine

Waters, Vin Weber, Dave Wasserman, Steve Wilburn, Ann Wilson, Senator Ron Wyden, Fareed Zakaria, and Ambassador Bob Zoellick. (And if I did speak to you and left you out of this list, my sincere apologies!)

To the Wilson Center where I was a resident fellow conducting research and interviews, and in particular to Representative Jane Harman, Robert Litvak, Sean Morrow, and the staff at the Center.

And to President Donald Trump, perhaps an unlikely source, who moved the conversation around tariffs and trade from the back pages of the business section to page A1 of our newspapers.

And to the late Ross Perot, whose comments on NAFTA at the October 15, 1992, presidential debate have permanently kept NAFTA at the center of our conversations about trade.

Notes

Chapter 1: The Rockies, the *Rocky*s, and 300 Years of American Trade

1 http://www.worldstopexports.com/united-states-top-10-exports/.
2 https://books.google.com/books?id=hX01AQAAIAAJ&pg=PP5&hl=en#v=onepage&q&f=false.

Chapter 2: The Giant Sucking Sound

1 https://www.congress.gov/bill/98th-congress/house-bill/3398/actions.
2 https://news.gallup.com/opinion/gallup/234971/george-bush-retrospective.aspx.
3 https://news.gallup.com/poll/110548/gallup-presidential-election-trial heat-trends-19362004.aspx#4.
4 https://www.nytimes.com/1992/10/26/us/1992-campaign-overview-perot-says-he-quit-july-thwart-gop-dirty-tricks.html?pagewanted=all&src=pm.
5 Jeffrey E. Cohen, *Presidential Responsiveness and Public Policy-Making: The Publics and the Policies That Presidents Choose* (Ann Arbor: University of Michigan Press, 1997), doi:10.3998/mpub.14952. ISBN 9780472108121. JSTOR 10.3998/mpub.14952.
6 https://www.govtrack.us/congress/votes/103-1993/h575.
7 https://www.govtrack.us/congress/votes/103-1993/s395.
8 http://www.sice.oas.org/trade/nafta/chap-01.asp.
9 https://www.history.com/news/the-birth-of-illegal-immigration.
10 https://www.debates.org/index.php?page=october-21-1984-debate-transcript.
11 Heyer, https://piie.com/sites/default/files/publications/pb/pb14-13.pdf.
12 https://ustr.gov/about-us/policy-offices/press-office/fact-sheets/archives/2003/november/nafta-10-myth-nafta-was-failure-united-stat.
13 https://www.fas.usda.gov/data/percentage-us-agricultural-products-exported.
14 http://www.pewhispanic.org/2012/04/23/net-migration-from-mexico-falls-to-zero-and-perhaps-less/.
15 https://archive.nytimes.com/www.nytimes.com/specials/issues/world/

wordepth/0916perot-infomercial.html OR https://piie.com/sites/default/files/publications/pb/pb14-13.pdf.

16 https://www.politifact.com/truth-o-meter/statements/2016/mar/07/bernie-s/sanders-overshoots-nafta-job-losses/.

17 https://www.politifact.com/truth-o-meter/statements/2018/sep/24/donald-trump/did-nafta-kill-millions-jobs-donald-trump/.

18 http://www.cnn.com/2008/POLITICS/02/25/clinton.obama/index.html.

19 http://www.pewresearch.org/fact-tank/2017/11/13/americans-generally-positive-about-nafta-but-most-republicans-say-it-benefits-mexico-more-than-u-s/.

20 https://www.seattletimes.com/seattle-news/politics/nafta-bashing-popular-but-is-it-justified/.

21 https://www.politifact.com/truth-o-meter/statements/2018/sep/24/donald-trump/donald-trump-has-point-NAFTA-shuttered/.

22 https://ustr.gov/about-us/policy-offices/press-office/fact-sheets/archives/2003/november/nafta-10-myth-nafta-was-failure-united-stat.

23 https://ustr.gov/about-us/policy-offices/press-office/fact-sheets/archives/2003/november/nafta-10-myth-nafta-was-failure-united-stat.

24 Kletzer, https://www.jstor.org/stable/2646942.

25 Gary C. Hufbauer and Jeffrey J. Scott, *NAFTA Revisited: Achievements and Challenges* (Washington, D.C.: Institute for International Economics, 2005).

26 https://fas.org/sgp/crs/row/R42965.pdf.

27 BLS stats from https://data.bls.gov/PDQWeb/ap.

28 https://www.investopedia.com/articles/economics/08/north-american-free-trade-agreement.asp.

29 https://www.politifact.com/truth-o-meter/article/2017/jul/21/how-big-coal-mining-compared-other-occupations/.

30 https://www.marketwatch.com/story/trumps-tariffs-will-hurt-the-65-million-us-workers-at-steel-consuming-manufacturers-2018-03-02.

31 https://www.theguardian.com/business/2018/jan/13/us-retail-sector-job-losses-hitting-women-hardest-data.

32 https://www.wsj.com/articles/SB867621554649917500.

33 https://www.washingtonpost.com/news/fact-checker/wp/2017/08/18/the-trump-administrations-claim-that-the-u-s-government-certified-700000-jobs-lost-by-nafta/?noredirect=on&utm_term=.a25b17f12580.

34 https://millercenter.org/the-presidency/presidential-speeches/december-3-1900-fourth-annual-message.

Chapter 3: A Myth-Busting Interlude

1 https://www.scmp.com/news/china/diplomacy-defence/article/2139809/united-states-waking-chinese-abuses-us-senator.

2 https://www.facebook.com/senatorsanders/posts/10156965768897908; and https://www.businessinsider.com/americans-paint-china-globalization-villain-2018-8.

3 https://thehill.com/policy/international/392636-schumer-on-china-tariffs-china-needs-us-more-than-we-need-them.
4 https://www.finance.senate.gov/hearings/the-presidents-2018-trade-policy-agenda.
5 https://www.ft.com/content/2003d460-94bf-11e8-b747-fb1e803ee64e.
6 https://www.cnn.com/2016/05/01/politics/donald-trump-china-rape/index.html.
7 http://www.trumptwitterarchive.com/archive (excluding retweets).
8 https://twitter.com/realdonaldtrump/status/195207050261823493.
9 https://www.washingtonpost.com/news/fact-checker/wp/2018/03/06/fact-checking-president-trumps-trade-rhetoric/.
10 https://www.nytimes.com/2018/03/05/us/politics/trade-deficit-tariffs-economists-trump.html.
11 Ibid.
12 Hhttps://www.census.gov/foreign-trade/balance/c5700.html.
13 Hhttps://www.politifact.com/truth-o-meter/statements/2018/mar/28/donald-trump/did-us-have-500-billion-deficit-china-2017/.
14 https://ustr.gov/countries-regions/china-mongolia-taiwan/peoples-republic-china.
15 https://www.cato.org/blog/growing-us-trade-surplus-services-part-two.
16 https://www.nbcnews.com/politics/donald-trump/trump-aide-kudlow-acknowledges-u-s-consumers-pay-tariffs-not-n1004756.
17 https://footwearnews.com/2019/business/opinion-analysis/shoe-manufacturing-production-us-1202727879/.
18 https://tradevistas.org/whos-footing-the-tariff-bill/.
19 Ibid.
20 https://www.washingtonpost.com/news/monkey-cage/wp/2016/08/02/yes-the-tpp-agreement-is-over-5000-pages-long-heres-why-thats-a-good-thing/?noredirect=on&utm_term=.a90d6d6a1688.
21 https://ustr.gov/trade-agreements/free-trade-agreements/trans-pacific-partnership/tpp-full-text.
22 https://www.nytimes.com/2018/07/05/business/china-us-trade-war-trump-tariffs.html.
23 Ibid.
24 https://www.produceretailer.com/article/news-article/imported-blueberries-numbers.
25 https://obamawhitehouse.archives.gov/the-press-office/2010/12/04/remarks-president-announcement-a-us-korea-free-trade-agreement.
26 https://www.reuters.com/article/us-japan-russia-economy-idUSKBN13P0QA.
27 https://www.reuters.com/article/us-trade-nafta-mexico-president/mexico-president-calls-trade-agreement-a-win-win-win-deal-idUSKCN1MB2QN.
28 https://wtop.com/business-finance/2018/10/canada-us-reach-deal-to-stay-in-trade-pact-with-mexico/.
29 http://www.worldbank.org/en/topic/trade/publication/the-role-of-trade-in-ending-poverty and https://www.wto.org/english/tratop_e/devel_e/w15.htm.

30 https://thehill.com/policy/national-security/277879-trump-warns-against-false-song-of-globalism.
31 https://talkingpointsmemo.com/edblog/trump-rolls-out-anti-semitic-closing-ad.
32 https://www.politico.com/story/2016/06/full-transcript-trump-job-plan-speech-224891.

Chapter 4: The Spice of Life

1 http://www.scrumptiouschef.com/2011/05/31/consumed-by-fritos-the-life-of-charles-elmer-doolin/ and https://ocweekly.com/so-did-mexicans-invent-the-taco-salad-and-how-does-it-tie-back-to-disneyland-7172466/.
2 Food Marketing Institute data at https://www.consumerreports.org/cro/magazine/2014/03/too-many-product-choices-in-supermarkets/index.htm.
3 Ted Ownby, *American Dreams in Mississippi: Consumers, Poverty, and Culture, 1830–1998* (Chapel Hill: University of North Carolina Press, 1999), pp. 1–2.
4 Timothy J. Colton, *Yeltsin: A Life* (New York: Basic Books, 2008), pp. 161–62.
5 Leon Aron, *Yeltsin: A Revolutionary Life* (New York: St. Martin's Press, 2000), pp. 328–29.
6 Colton, *Yeltsin*, p. 162.
7 Ibid., p. 163.
8 https://twitter.com/realdonaldtrump/status/728297587418247168?lang=en.
9 https://www.ers.usda.gov/webdocs/publications/83344/ap-075.pdf?v=42853.
10 https://gcrec.ifas.ufl.edu/media/gcrecifasufledu/images/zhengfei/FE—-US-tomato.pdf.
11 Ibid.
12 "Lettuce (with Chicory) Production in 2015; Countries/Regions/Production Quantity from Pick Lists," U.N. Food & Agriculture Organization, Statistics Division (FAOSTAT), 2015, http://www.fao.org/faostat/en/#data/QC.
13 https://atlas.media.mit.edu/en/profile/hs92/0705/.
14 https://www.agmrc.org/commodities-products/vegetables/lettuce.
15 https://www.bloomberg.com/news/articles/2013-02-04/freezing-california-lettuce-boosts-salad-costs-chart-of-the-day.
16 http://thestockexchangenews.com/beef-imports-and-exports-what-is-the-impact/.
17 http://beef2live.com/story-beef-imports-ranking-countries-0-116237.
18 https://data.ers.usda.gov/reports.aspx?programArea=veg&stat_year=2017&top=5&HardCopy=True&RowsPerPage=25&groupName=Dry%20Beans&commodityName=Black%20beans&ID=17858#P6bcc4b367d38483890552656f2b2c8ce_3_292.
19 https://www.onions-usa.org/all-about-onions/where-how-onions-are-grown.
20 https://munchies.vice.com/en_us/article/jpa9j8/the-us-is-the-worlds-largest-producer-of-corn-so-why-are-we-importing-more.

21 https://www.motherjones.com/kevin-drum/2018/06/us-trade-policy-on-dairy-is-simple-we-basically-allow-no-imports-at-all/.
22 Ibid.
23 https://www.washingtonpost.com/news/wonk/wp/2015/01/22/the-sudden-rise-of-the-avocado-americas-new-favorite-fruit/?noredirect=on&utm_term=.d19eda06a6c9.
24 http://ucavo.ucr.edu/General/EarlyHistory.html; and https://www.californiaavocado.com/avocado101/the-california-difference/avocado-history.
25 https://www.californiaavocado.com/avocado101/the-california-difference/avocado-history.
26 https://www.washingtonpost.com/news/wonk/wp/2015/01/22/the-sudden-rise-of-the-avocado-americas-new-favorite-fruit/?noredirect=on&utm_term=.d19eda06a6c9.
27 Data at http://www.fao.org/faostat/en/#data/QC/visualize.
28 Ibid.
29 https://www.washingtonpost.com/news/wonk/wp/2015/01/22/the-sudden-rise-of-the-avocado-americas-new-favorite-fruit/?noredirect=on&utm_term=.d19eda06a6c9.
30 https://www.washingtonpost.com/news/wonk/wp/2015/01/22/the-sudden-rise-of-the-avocado-americas-new-favorite-fruit/?noredirect=on&utm_term=.d19eda06a6c9.
31 https://www.wfla.com/news/we-eat-how-much-super-bowl-food-by-the-numbers_20180312042532911/1030557478.
32 https://www.washingtonpost.com/news/food/wp/2017/05/15/dont-mess-with-millennials-avocado-toast-the-internet-fires-back-at-a-millionaire/?noredirect=on&utm_term=.c0787cde0926.
33 https://www.smithsonianmag.com/science-nature/holy-guacamole-how-hass-avocado-conquered-world-180964250/.
34 https://www.agmrc.org/commodities-products/fruits/avocados.
35 https://www.pma.com/content/articles/2017/05/top-20-fruits-and-vegetables-sold-in-the-us.
36 https://www.theguardian.com/fashion/2015/oct/05/the-avocado-is-overcado-how-culture-caught-up-with-fashion.
37 https://www.telegraph.co.uk/culture/books/3671962/John-McCain-Extraordinary-foresight-made-Winston-Churchill-great.html.

Chapter 5: The Most American Car on the Road

1 https://www.wardsauto.com/news-analysis/foreign-invasion-imports-transplants-change-auto-industry-forever.
2 Ibid.
3 Ibid; and https://www.google.com/url?q=https://auto.howstuffworks.com/1945-1959-volkswagen-beetle4.htm&sa=D&ust=1548700540670000&usg=AFQjCNFNkDcIMldZ79MCdUeQHDE2DvjWyg.

4 https://www.epi.org/publication/the-decline-and-resurgence-of-the-u-s-auto-industry/.
5 https://www.nhtsa.gov/sites/nhtsa.dot.gov/files/documents/2018_aala_percent_09102018.pdf.
6 Ibid.
7 https://www.bizjournals.com/wichita/news/2017/04/14/boeing-s-2016-supplier-awards-list-includes-no.html.
8 http://www.airframer.com/aircraft_detail.html?model=B737.
9 https://www.theglobalist.com/a-brief-history-of-supply-chains/.
10 http://www.airframer.com/aircraft_detail.html?model=B737.
11 https://www.sccommerce.com/news/jn-fibers-inc-locating-facility-chester-county.
12 https://www.industryweek.com/expansion-management/indian-textile-manufacturer-opens-plant-georgia.
13 https://www.forbes.com/sites/jwebb/2016/03/30/trumps-war-on-the-american-supply-chain/#4cd138c1d7fd.
14 https://www.nhtsa.gov/sites/nhtsa.dot.gov/files/documents/2018_aala_percent_09102018.pdf.
15 Ibid.
16 https://www.greenvilleonline.com/story/money/2018/02/13/bmw-manufacturing-remains-leading-u-s-auto-exporter-despite-pros-2017-exports-decline-amid-overall-s/333490002/.
17 http://knowhow.napaonline.com/domestic-foreign-cars-whats-difference/.
18 https://www.consumerreports.org/cro/magazine/2013/02/made-in-america/index.htm.
19 https://www.chicagotribune.com/business/ct-americans-prices-vs-made-in-usa-20160414-story.html.
20 Ibid.
21 https://www.nhtsa.gov/sites/nhtsa.dot.gov/files/documents/2018_aala_percent_09102018.pdf.
22 https://abcnews.go.com/US/made-america-us-made-car-creates-jobs/story?id=13813091.
23 https://www.usatoday.com/story/money/cars/2017/07/11/foreign-automakers-american/467049001/.
24 Trump at Gettysburg, Pennsylvania, https://www.youtube.com/watch?v=qShSxG-Jm3w.
25 https://twitter.com/realDonaldTrump/status/1067812811068383232?ref_src=twsrc%5Etfw%7Ctwcamp%5Etweetembed%7Ctwterm%5E1067812811068383232&ref_url=http%3A%2F%2Ffortune.com%2F2018%2F11%2F28%2Ftrump-steel-tariffs-gm%2F.
26 https://www.marketwatch.com/story/gm-slammed-by-tariffs-as-steel-and-aluminum-costs-soar-2018-07-25.
27 http://fortune.com/2018/06/29/gm-warns-trump-administration-tariffs-lead-lost-jobs-lower-wages/.
28 https://www.bloomberg.com/news/articles/2018-06-29/gm-warns-trump-tariffs-could-lead-the-carmaker-to-shrink-in-u-s.

29 http://fortune.com/2018/11/26/gm-slashes-jobs-cuts-production-car-models/.
30 http://fortune.com/2018/11/28/gm-plants-closing-trump-subsidies-threat/.
31 http://fortune.com/2018/06/25/harley-davidson-trump-trade-war-eu/.
32 https://www.msnbc.com/stephanie-ruhle/watch/trump-tariffs-the-threat-to-new-jobs-at-volvo-factory-1260848707976 or https://www.fastcompany.com/90180122/the-u-s-job-losses-from-trumps-tariffs-are-starting-to-pile-up.
33 https://www.washingtonpost.com/business/2018/07/30/after-trumps-farmer-bailout-manufacturers-ask-what-about-us/?utm_term=.65ed5ac92362.
34 https://www.businessinsider.com/trump-tariffs-trade-war-layoffs-business-losses-2018-8.
35 https://www.usatoday.com/story/news/politics/2018/08/08/trump-tariffs-companies-might-close-lay-off-american-workers-trade-war/929019002/; and https://www.wsj.com/articles/we-are-at-the-limit-trumps-tariffs-turn-small-businesses-upside-down-1533660467?redirect=amp and https://www.cnbc.com/2018/08/03/the-associated-press-florida-lobster-fishermen-fear-trade-war-amid-irma-recovery.html.
36 https://www.uschamber.com/tariffs.
37 https://www.businessinsider.com/trump-steel-aluminum-tariffs-on-canada-europe-mexico-will-hurt-us-jobs-2018-6.
38 https://www.epi.org/publication/estimates-of-jobs-lost-and-economic-harm-done-by-steel-and-aluminum-tariffs-are-wildly-exaggerated/.

Chapter 6: The $10 Banana

1 http://www.unitedfruit.org/keith.htm.
2 https://www.vox.com/2016/3/29/11320900/banana-rise.
3 Dan Koeppel, *Banana: The Fate of the Fruit That Changed the World* (New York: Hudson Street Press, 2007).
4 http://abm-enterprises.net/unitedfruit.html.
5 https://www.bls.gov/opub/mlr/2014/article/one-hundred-years-of-price-change-the-consumer-price-index-and-the-american-inflation-experience.htm.
6 https://www.statista.com/statistics/236880/retail-price-of-bananas-in-the-united-states/#0.
7 https://www.delish.com/food-news/a20139077/trader-joes-bananas-price/.
8 https://www.vox.com/2016/3/29/11320900/banana-rise.
9 https://www.nass.usda.gov/Statistics_by_State/Florida/Publications/Citrus/Citrus_Statistics/2016-17/fcs1617.pdf.
10 https://www.cnbc.com/2018/08/23/brazil-florida-orange-juice-tariff-trade-war.html.
11 http://citrusindustry.net/2017/09/11/what-is-happening-to-the-orange-juice-market/ and https://www.zerohedge.com/news/2017-09-26/floridas-orange-growers-may-never-recover-hurricane-irma.
12 http://articles.orlandosentinel.com/1996-10-08/news/9610070991_1_coca-cola-juice-plant-citrus-products.

13 https://qz.com/1438762/us-orange-juice-companies-are-selling-juice-in-smaller-bottles-for-the-same-prices/.
14 https://www.statista.com/statistics/297317/us-fruit-juice-exports/.
15 https://www.cheatsheet.com/money-career/made-america-iconic-american-products-arent-actually-made-us.html/ or https://www.businessinsider.com/basic-products-america-doesnt-make-2010-10#gerber-baby-food-2.
16 https://www.theatlantic.com/business/archive/2012/04/how-america-spends-money-100-years-in-the-life-of-the-family-budget/255475/.

Chapter 7: How Do You Like Them Apples?

1 https://www.statista.com/statistics/236550/percentage-of-us-population-that-own-a-iphone-smartphone/.
2 https://www.theverge.com/2017/6/13/15782200/one-device-secret-history-iphone-brian-merchant-book-excerpt.
3 Ibid.
4 https://appleinsider.com/articles/13/02/15/supply-chain-visualization-shows-how-apple-spans-and-impacts-the-globe.
5 https://financesonline.com/how-iphone-is-made/.
6 Ibid.
7 https://www.cultofmac.com/304120/corning-gorilla-glass-4/.
8 https://www.dailymail.co.uk/news/article-3280872/iPhone-mineral-miners-Africa-use-bare-hands-coltan.html.
9 https://www.lifewire.com/where-is-the-iphone-made-1999503.
10 Thomas L. Friedman, "Foreign Affairs Big Mac I," *New York Times*, December 8, 1996.
11 Thomas L. Friedman, *The World Is Flat*, p. 421.
12 https://www.reuters.com/article/us-usa-trade-china-apple/designed-in-california-made-in-china-how-the-iphone-skews-u-s-trade-deficit-idUSKBN1GX1GZ; and https://www.statista.com/chart/5952/iphone-manufacturing-costs/.
13 https://twitter.com/realdonaldtrump/status/195207050261823493.
14 https://financesonline.com/how-iphone-is-made/.
15 https://www.businessinsider.com/apple-iphone-sales-region-china-chart-2017-3.
16 https://www.reuters.com/article/us-usa-trade-china-apple/designed-in-california-made-in-china-how-the-iphone-skews-u-s-trade-deficit-idUSKBN1GX1GZ.
17 Ibid.
18 http://theconversation.com/we-estimate-china-only-makes-8-46-from-an-iphone-and-thats-why-trumps-trade-war-is-futile-99258.
19 https://mashable.com/article/trump-to-apple-iphone-us-china/#n3dpIXpziqq6.
20 https://www.nytimes.com/2018/10/24/us/politics/trump-phone-security.html.

21 https://www.businessinsider.com/trump-iphone-tapped-report-china-russia-huawei-phones-2018-10.
22 https://www.nytimes.com/2019/01/28/technology/iphones-apple-china-made.html.
23 https://www.businessinsider.com/you-simply-must-read-this-article-that-explains-why-apple-makes-iphones-in-china-and-why-the-us-is-screwed-2012-1.
24 https://www.washingtonpost.com/news/wonk/wp/2017/09/18/scott-walker-signs-3-billion-foxconn-deal-in-wisconsin/?noredirect=on&utm_term=.62263b16dd33.
25 https://www.theguardian.com/cities/2018/jul/02/ its-a-huge-subsidy-the-48bn-gamble-to-lure-foxconn-to-america.
26 https://twitter.com/scottwalker/status/890328411863994371.
27 https://subsidytracker.goodjobsfirst.org/prog.php?parent=foxconn-technology-group-hon-hai-precisi.
28 https://www.jsonline.com/story/news/politics/2017/07/28/foxconn-could-get-up-200-million-cash-year-state-residents-up-15-years/519687001/.
29 https://www.washingtonpost.com/news/wonk/wp/2017/09/18/scott-walker-signs-3-billion-foxconn-deal-in-wisconsin/?noredirect=on&utm_term=.62263b16dd33.
30 https://twitter.com/DPAQreport/status/895389440838946817.
31 http://www.milwaukeeindependent.com/syndicated/eminent-domain-state-interests-helped-foxconn-seize-land-private-gain/.
32 https://beltmag.com/blighted-by-foxconn/.
33 https://www.chicagotribune.com/news/local/breaking/ct-met-foxconn-lake-michigan-water-20180305-story.html.
34 https://www.theguardian.com/cities/2018/jul/02/its-a-huge-subsidy-the-48bn-gamble-to-lure-foxconn-to-america.
35 https://www.washingtonpost.com/business/economy/how-foxconns-broken-pledges-in-pennsylvania-cast-doubt-on-trumps-jobs-plan/2017/03/03/0189f3de-ee3a-11e6-9973-c5efb7ccfb0d_story.html?noredirect=on&utm_term=.358dddf00dec.
36 http://www.milwaukeeindependent.com/curated/unable-reach-job-creation-goals-foxconn-fails-qualify-first-round-tax-credits/.
37 Ibid.
38 https://www.reuters.com/article/us-foxconn-wisconsin-exclusive-idUSKCN1PO0FV.
39 Ibid.
40 https://www.businessinsider.com/you-simply-must-read-this-article-that-explains-why-apple-makes-iphones-in-china-and-why-the-us-is-screwed-2012-1.

Chapter 8: A Matter of Degrees

1 https://www.washingtontimes.com/news/2012/aug/19/armed-with-us-education-many-leaders-take-on-world/.
2 https://www.reuters.com/article/us-south-sudan-midwives/special-report-the-wonks-who-sold-washington-on-south-sudan-idUSBRE86A0GC20120711.
3 Ibid.
4 https://www.theatlantic.com/international/archive/2011/07/us-played-key-role-in-southern-sudans-long-journey-to-independence/241660/.
5 https://www.brookings.edu/blog/brown-center-chalkboard/2017/01/31/sealing-the-border-could-block-one-of-americas-crucial-exports-education/; 2018 numbers from Allan Goodman.
6 https://www.washingtontimes.com/news/2012/aug/19/armed-with-us-education-many-leaders-take-on-world/.
7 https://www.npr.org/2018/12/21/679291823/north-korea-promotes-basketball-as-an-important-project.
8 https://www.nytimes.com/1978/11/30/archives/east-germans-line-up-to-buy-a-pair-of-levis-local-venture.html.
9 https://www.voanews.com/a/us-international-students/4656132.html.
10 Ibid.
11 Ibid.
12 https://www.reuters.com/article/us-usa-immigration-students/fewer-foreign-students-coming-to-united-states-for-second-year-in-row-survey-idUSKCN1NI0EN.
13 Ibid.
14 Ibid.
15 https://www.voanews.com/a/us-international-students/4656132.html.
16 Ibid.
17 https://www.wttc.org/-/media/files/reports/economic-impact-research/countries-2018/unitedstates2018.pdf.
18 https://www.worldatlas.com/articles/10-most-visited-countries-in-the-world.html.
19 https://www.e-unwto.org/doi/pdf/10.18111/9789284419876.
20 https://www.bls.gov/news.release/metro.t01.htm.
21 https://www.prnewswire.com/news-releases/a-new-record-for-us-travel-orlando-first-to-surpass-70-million-annual-visitors-300646729.html.
22 https://www.forbes.com/sites/lealane/2018/08/07/share-of-u-s-international-travel-drops-sharply-the-trump-slump/#746e5884d303.
23 https://www.thedailybeast.com/the-trump-slump-hits-us-tourism; and https://www.forbes.com/sites/lealane/2018/08/07/share-of-u-s-international-travel-drops-sharply-the-trump-slump/#746e5884d303.
24 https://www.agriculture.pa.gov/pages/default.aspx.
25 Larry Downes, *The Laws of Disruption: Harnessing the New Forces That Govern Life and Business in the Digital Age*, pp. 57–58

26 Ibid.
27 https://www.thegrocer.co.uk/buying-and-supplying/food-safety/chlorinated-chicken-explained-why-do-the-americans-treat-their-poultry-with-chlorine/555618.article.
28 Ibid.

Chapter 9: Why Winter Came

1 https://www.boxofficemojo.com/alltime/world/.
2 https://www.telegraph.co.uk/culture/tvandradio/game-of-thrones/11464580/Game-of-Thrones-simultaneous-world-broadcast-why-is-the-UK-missing-out.html.
3 https://mashable.com/2017/11/29/game-of-thrones-accents-guide-british/#hgbwfcw4imqS.
4 IMDB.com.
5 https://www.boredpanda.com/game-of-thrones-real-life-locations/?utm_source=google&utm_medium=organic&utm_campaign=organic; and https://www.skyscanner.net/news/38-amazing-game-thrones-locations-pictures.
6 http://www.emmys.com/shows/game-thrones; and https://web.archive.org/web/20140820004621/http://mackevision.com/123live-user-data/user_data/6084/public/DOWNLOADS_DE/HOME/20140710_GOT_Nominierung_de.pdf.
7 https://www.reuters.com/article/us-usa-trade-china-movies/hollywoods-china-dreams-get-tangled-in-trade-talks-idUSKCN1IK0W0; and https://variety.com/2017/biz/asia/u-s-and-china-struggle-over-film-quotas-1201979720/.
8 https://www.reuters.com/article/us-usa-trade-china-movies/hollywoods-china-dreams-get-tangled-in-trade-talks-idUSKCN1IK0W0.
9 https://variety.com/2017/biz/asia/u-s-and-china-struggle-over-film-quotas-1201979720/.
10 https://variety.com/2017/biz/asia/u-s-and-china-struggle-over-film-quotas-1201979720/ and https://www.reuters.com/article/idUS22096264620120220.
11 https://www.reuters.com/article/idUS22096264620120220.
12 https://www.reuters.com/article/us-usa-trade-china-movies/hollywoods-china-dreams-get-tangled-in-trade-talks-idUSKCN1IK0W0.
13 https://www.boxofficemojo.com/intl/china/yearly/?yr=2018&p=.htm.
14 https://www.reuters.com/article/us-usa-trade-china-movies/hollywoods-china-dreams-get-tangled-in-trade-talks-idUSKCN1IK0W0.
15 https://variety.com/2017/biz/asia/u-s-and-china-struggle-over-film-quotas-1201979720/.
16 https://www.trade.gov/press/press-releases/2017/new-international-trade-administration-report-indicates-steady-growth-for-the-us-media-and-entertainment-industry-along-with-barriers-to-international-exports-licensing-062917.asp.

17 Ibid.
18 Ibid.
19 https://www.bloomberg.com/news/articles/2019-01-23/peak-video-game-top-analyst-sees-industry-slumping-in-2019.
20 Everett M. Rogers and Judith K. Larsen, *Silicon Valley Fever: Growth of High-Technology Culture* (New York: Basic Books, 1984), p. 263, https://books.google.com/books?id=frYrAAAAYAAJ.
21 https://www.cbc.ca/news/world/atari-games-buried-in-landfill-net-37k-on-ebay-1.2837083; and https://www.bugsplat.com/articles/video-games/great-video-game-crash-1983.
22 https://web.archive.org/web/20140426232656/http://www.npr.org/templates/story/story.php?storyId=307031037.
23 https://www.bugsplat.com/articles/video-games/great-video-game-crash-1983.
24 http://community.seattletimes.nwsource.com/archive/?date=19930617&slug=1706910; and https://www.nytimes.com/2018/11/02/obituaries/mario-segale-dies-super-mario.html.
25 https://www.webcitation.org/5nXieXX2B?url=http://www.nintendo.co.jp/ir/library/historical_data/pdf/consolidated_sales_e0912.pdf.
26 https://www.fool.com/investing/2018/12/30/the-10-best-selling-video-games-of-2018.aspx.
27 https://www.axios.com/business-of-sports-sunday-night-live-1548439232-c18393d4-8b82-4124-9f47-fc2e84992190.html?utm_source=newsletter&utm_medium=email&utm_campaign=newsletter_axiosdeepdives&stream=top.
28 https://www.egencyglobal.com/2018/04/13/the-lucrative-esports-business-is-attracting-big-name-sponsors/.
29 https://www.businessinsider.com/twitch-is-bigger-than-cnn-msnbc-2018-2.
30 https://blog.trade.gov/2016/11/02/tpps-impact-on-the-media-and-entertainment-industry/.
31 Ibid.
32 Ibid.

Chapter 10: Realities

1 See, generally, https://repository.law.umich.edu/cgi/viewcontent.cgi?article=1818&context=mjil.
2 *Public Papers of the Presidents of the United States: John F. Kennedy, 1962*, p. 76, https://books.google.com/books?id=L7raAwAAQBAJ.
3 Ibid.
4 Ibid.
5 https://library.cqpress.com/cqalmanac/document.php?id=cqal62-1326212.
6 *Public Papers of the Presidents of the United States: John F. Kennedy, 1962*, p. 76, https://books.google.com/books?id=L7raAwAAQBAJ.
7 https://library.cqpress.com/cqalmanac/document.php?id=cqal62-1326212.

8 https://www.govinfo.gov/content/pkg/CREC-2002-05-16/pdf/CREC-2002-05-16-senate.pdf.
9 Katherine Baicker and M. Marit Rehavi, "Policy Watch: Trade Adjustment Assistance," *The Journal of Economic Perspectives* 18, no. 2 (Spring 2004): 239–55.
10 Ibid.
11 Ibid.
12 Ibid.
13 https://obamawhitehouse.archives.gov/blog/2015/06/11/trade-adjustment-assistance-what-you-need-know.
14 Ibid.
15 https://www.usatoday.com/story/opinion/2015/06/24/trade-adjustment-assistance-labor-editorials-debates/29246193/.
16 https://www.demos.org/sites/default/files/publications/Broken_Buffer_FINAL.pdf.
17 Ibid.
18 https://360.here.com/preparing-for-the-jobs-that-dont-exist-yet.
19 http://v2.bitsourceky.com/node/108.html.
20 See, generally, https://www.theguardian.com/us-news/2017/apr/21/tech-industry-coding-kentucky-hillbillies and https://www.reuters.com/article/usa-broadband-coal-idUSL1N0YI24P20150608.
21 https://www.theguardian.com/us-news/2017/apr/21/tech-industry-coding-kentucky-hillbillies.
22 https://www.lanereport.com/84126/2017/11/kentuckywired-installs-broadband-hut-in-pikeville/.
23 https://thehill.com/policy/technology/285132-clinton-pledges-broadband-access-for-all-households-by-2020.
24 https://www.telehouse.com/2016/07/hillary-clintons-tech-plan/.
25 https://money.cnn.com/2015/12/08/technology/donald-trump-internet/.
26 https://www.theguardian.com/us-news/2017/apr/21/tech-industry-coding-kentucky-hillbillies.
27 https://www.washingtonpost.com/graphics/2018/politics/trump-budget-2019/?utm_term=.11dd3298071d.
28 https://www.vox.com/2018/2/13/17004590/trump-budget-cuts-manufacturing-michigan-west-virginia.
29 https://www.ekcep.org/about-us.
30 https://www.reuters.com/article/usa-broadband-coal-idUSL1N0YI24P20150608.
31 Ibid.
32 https://www.nytimes.com/2018/09/21/opinion/sunday/silicon-valley-tech.html.
33 Ibid.
34 Ibid.

Chapter 11: Remedies

1 https://books.google.com/books?id=Hg4rDwAAQBAJ&pg=PA78&lpg=PA78&dq=%2B%22william+orton%22+%2B%22has+too+many+shortcomings%22&source=bl&ots=s0xSodbbrW&sig=ACfU3U2lwaQh9Ce5CG0EuL7OhxbNslWd1g&hl=en&sa=X&ved=2ahUKEwiOrZKy5b7hAhVEtlkKHdugBvwQ6AEwDHoECAgQAQ#v=onepage&q=%2B%22william%20orton%22%20%2B%22has%20too%20many%20shortcomings%22&f=false.

2 See, generally, https://www.phillytrib.com/news/local_news/city-council-bans-cash-free-businesses-sends-bill-to-kenney/article_f42ef41f-2cdf-5ffd-b6a6-b8e77a2329b8.html.

3 https://www.mckinsey.com/featured-insights/future-of-work/jobs-lost-jobs-gained-what-the-future-of-work-will-mean-for-jobs-skills-and-wages.

4 https://www.bls.gov/opub/mlr/1981/11/art2full.pdf.

5 https://www.brookings.edu/blog/techtank/2018/04/18/will-robots-and-ai-take-your-job-the-economic-and-political-consequences-of-automation/.

6 https://news.gallup.com/poll/228194/public-split-basic-income-workers-replaced-robots.aspx.

7 Ibid; and https://qz.com/911968/bill-gates-the-robot-that-takes-your-job-should-pay-taxes/.

8 See, generally, http://www.hamiltonproject.org/assets/legacy/files/downloads_and_links/Stabilizing_State_and_Local_Budgets-_A_Proposal_for_Tax-Base_Insurance.pdf.

9 https://www.bls.gov/lau/lastrk14.htm.

10 https://workingnation.com/rhode-island-economic-recovery/.

11 Ibid.

12 Ibid.

13 Ibid.

14 https://www.the74million.org/article/the-investing-in-opportunity-act-hidden-in-the-tax-bill-a-new-program-that-could-help-charter-schools-secure-the-funds-they-need-to-expand-in-high-needs-areas/.

15 https://fundrise.com/education/blog-posts/what-are-opportunity-zones-and-how-do-they-work.

16 https://www.the74million.org/article/the-investing-in-opportunity-act-hidden-in-the-tax-bill-a-new-program-that-could-help-charter-schools-secure-the-funds-they-need-to-expand-in-high-needs-areas/.

17 See, generally, https://eig.org/dci.

18 https://www.nytimes.com/2019/02/05/us/louisiana-itep-exxon-mobil.html.

19 BLS data at https://www.markle.org/rework-america/.

20 Ibid.

NOTES

Epilogue

1 See https://www.documentcloud.org/documents/6297116-NBCWSJ-August-2019-Poll.html.

2 See, e.g., https://www.forbes.com/sites/stuartanderson/2019/09/09/trump-tariffs-will-soon-cost-us-families-thousands-of-dollars-a-year/#5cc2ae515b4b.

3 See, e.g., https://www.cnbc.com/2019/08/23/trump-will-raise-tariff-rates-on-chinese-goods-in-response-to-trade-war-retaliation.html.

4 See https://www.forbes.com/sites/chuckjones/2019/08/30/amid-trump-tariffs-farm-bankruptcies-and-suicides-rise/#15d7d43c2bc8.

5 https://www.frbsf.org/economic-research/publications/economic-letter/2011/august/us-made-in-china/.

6 See https://finance.yahoo.com/news/trumps-trade-war-has-killed-300000-jobs-194717808.html.

Illustration Credits

Page x: No Credit
Page xii: No Credit
Page xiv: Seth Cameron
Page 12: Library of Congress
Page 14: Library of Congress
Page 21: MGM/UA/Kobal/Shutterstock
Page 27: Dataset produced by World Bank
Page 35: Mick Stevens
Page 37: Bob Daemmrich/Alamy Live News
Page 46: U.S. Bureau of Labor Statistics/Federal Reserve Bank of St. Louis
Page 47: U.S. Bureau of Labor Statistics/Federal Reserve Bank of St. Louis
Page 66: *The World Factbook 2019*. Washington, DC: Central Intellegence Agency, 2019.
Page 68: No Credit
Page 77: No Credit
Page 92: Fritos marks used with permission of Frito-Lay North America
Page 95: *Houston Chronicle*
page 97: No Credit
Page 112: U.S. Department of Transportation
Page 130: Neil Baylis / Alamy Stock Photo
Page 131: Niday Picture Library / Alamy Stock Photo
Page 132: mooziic / Alamy Stock Photo
Page 136: Patti McConville / Alamy Stock Photo
Page 146: The Advertising Archives / Alamy Stock Photo
Page 156: No Credit
Page 159: Storms Media Group / Alamy Stock Photo
Page 173: Pictorial Press Ltd / Alamy Stock Photo
Page 175: No Credit
Page 190: INTERFOTO / Alamy Stock Photo
Page 192: pumkinpie / Alamy Stock Photo

Index

Page numbers in *italics* refer to illustrations.

INDEX

INDEX

INDEX

INDEX

INDEX

INDEX

INDEX

INDEX

INDEX

About the Author

FRED P. HOCHBERG served as the chairman and president of the Export-Import Bank of the United States under President Obama from 2009 to 2017, becoming the longest-serving chairman in the agency's history. Hochberg also served for five years as dean at the New School in New York City and has been a fellow at the Institutes of Politics at both the Harvard Kennedy School and the University of Chicago. Previously he served as acting administrator of the Small Business Administration under President Clinton. Hochberg began his career at the Lillian Vernon Company, where, as president, he oversaw a forty-fold increase in sales.